THE PRODIGAL PILOT

The End of the Hughes Empire

Robert F. (Bob) Wearley

Published by FastPencil

Published by FastPencil
307 Orchard City Drive
Suite 210
Campbell CA 95008 USA
info@fastpencil.com
(408) 540-7571
(408) 540-7572 (Fax)
http://www.fastpencil.com

Printed in the United States of America.

First Edition

I dedicate this book to everyone who shares my passion for life,
my passion for flight and my appreciation of a God
who uses both to draw all of us closer to Himself,
and to those... "who have slipped the surly bonds of earth
and danced the skies on laughter-silvered wings..."

As you read this book, please bear in mind
that it is my account of my life and that I
have included what I believe is important
to an accurate statement, the wonderful,
the not so wonderful and the regrettable.
It was not my intent to shock or upset anyone,
especially those I love most. If I have offended
you in any way, I am sorry.
— Bob Wearley

Contents

Foreword: Endorsements

"For aviation buffs this is a personal account that includes aviation history, intrigue, enough excitement to keep you riveted to the book and most of all the opportunity to view the inner world of aviation through the eyes of one who lived it."
—Clyde F. Autio, Maj. General, USAF (Ret.)
Past President, National Aviation Hall of Fame

"Bob Wearley has had an almost unbelievable varied and interesting career in aviation, the military, business and politics – and he describes it vividly in this book."
—James Fallows
National Correspondent, The Atlantic Monthly

"Often reading like a spy novel, Wearley recounts the intrigue of 14,000+ hours of flights around the world in a fast paced style."
—Jack Schultz
CEO Boomtown Institute / Author, <u>Boomtown USA</u>

"Bob was one of the early business aviation pioneers. He met and flew very important people during his 50-year career."
—Bruce N. Whitman
President and CEO / Flight Safety International

Acknowledgements

MY WIFE SHARON
For her patience and support without which this book could not have been written.

CLIFF CARLE
Cliff has been "on-board" with me since June, 2007. His expertise and ongoing advice have been invaluable. I ventured into the unknown world of book publishing only to be confronted with obstacles I was not prepared to resolve. Cliff was always there with comforting advice that consoled and encouraged me to finish what I started.

ATTORNEY MAX A. MYERS
My attorney and good friend for over 30 years, for his inestimable advice and encouragement that kept me focused when I "drifted off course" due to unforeseen distractions.

PETE McHUGH
For his relentless encouragement to tell my story and his leadership as FAA Program Manager for NASA's SATS Program.

JASON DAENENS & JEREMY REDDING
For their countless hours of chronologically organizing all of the newspapers, magazines, photos, etc., I've collected over the years so my story could be woven.

JACK REAL
For his leadership as my boss at Hughes and for inspiration through his book "The Asylum of Howard Hughes".

KEVIN FORTRIED

My "Bonus" son-in-law for his relentless efforts to find my Watergate transcripts in an Indianapolis Library.

FRITZ BUSCH

A fellow USAF pilot and owner of Envision Graphics who used his creative talents to design the cover and layout "hard copies" for the editor and offered encouragement and excellent advice. Having Fritz in my "corner" was a source of strength.

TED SAVAS

Thanks to Theodore P. Savas, the Managing Director of Savas Beatie LLC, for his assistance. Ted, who has been in the literary field for more than two decades, helped me with the manuscript with suggestions large and small to make this a better book and acceptable for publication.

FLIGHTS OF FANCY

"AFTER THIS FLIGHT, BOB, I'm going to tell everyone I slept with Robert Goulet," teased my wife, and she hung up the phone. Though she was a small-town girl at heart, Ruth just loved rubbing shoulders with the rich and famous. Of course, everyone on board (except me and my co-pilot) would be able to say we were "sleeping" with Mr. Goulet that night. We would, after all, be flying across the country with him through the early morning hours.

It was just past midnight on Sunday, March 17, 1974. Mr. Goulet had finished his second show at the Sands that night, and my instructions were to fly the singer from Las Vegas to an engagement in Philadelphia. For this Saint Patrick's Day flight, we'd be using a Lockheed JetStar, so a refueling stop would be necessary—the early Jet-Stars did not always have coast-to-coast capabilities with adequate IFR (instrument flight rules) reserves. I'd already called Goulet to ask how many passengers he'd be bringing on board and whether he had any special requests for food and refreshments. When I mentioned the plan to refuel in Fort Wayne, Indiana, he agreed; so long as there was plenty of vodka and orange juice on board.

I was always looking for a way to get closer to "home" – Woodburn, Indiana, the little town where my wife and I grew up – on these coast-to-coast flights. Woodburn is just 20 miles east of Fort Wayne Municipal Airport, which many of us still know as Baer Field, after Lieutenant Paul Baer, a Fort Wayne native and WWI ace who flew for the French. Since the JetStar had nine-passenger seating and Goulet's group numbered only four, I brought up the idea of my wife and our teenage daughters, Robin and Roxanne (Roxie), joining us for the first leg of the flight. Goulet was all for it.

After I'd called Ruth to let her know – and she'd quipped about her new "claim to fame" – she gathered our daughters and a few belongings. Soon they were boarding the JetStar along with Goulet and his entourage. At Baer Field, Ruth's mother and dad and my mother could pick up my family and take them home for a very short visit. This was not unusual. Hungry for a little taste of home after living in "Sin City" we'd often made such quick arrangements. Especially in the several years since I'd been employed as the chief pilot for reclusive billionaire Howard Hughes' personal fleet of aircraft.

Two days prior I had received instructions from Walter Kane, the entertainment director for Hughes' hotels in Las Vegas, to arrange the trip at Goulet's convenience. At that time, Mr. Hughes owned the lion's share of lucrative property along the Strip in Las Vegas, including the Sands, Frontier, Landmark, Desert Inn, Silver Slipper, and Castaways hotels and casinos. In addition, he owned the fixed base of operations (FBO) at Vegas's McCarran Field and the North Las Vegas Airport. Howard Hughes knew a lot of powerful people, and he was especially enamored of the Hollywood glitz, so it was nothing unusual for me to be flying glamorous movie stars John Wayne, Dean Martin, Sammy Davis Jr. and other performers to and from Las Vegas on his dime.

During the years I worked for Hughes, my passengers included not only Robert Goulet but also such celebrities as, Dinah Shore, Joe DiMaggio, Alan King, Danny Thomas, Bob Hope, Don Rickles, and Wayne Newton. (The only reason I never flew Sinatra was that he had his own Gulfstream II.) I also transported various elected officials, including Governor (and later Senator) Paul Laxalt; Judy Agnew, wife of Vice President Spiro Agnew; various astronauts, including Gene Cernan and Tom Stafford; and, of course, members of Howard Hughes' elite board of directors. In some cases I never knew whom I was flying – passengers would board the aircraft and remain anonymous throughout the entire flight, even to myself and the flight crew. I'd learned early in my tenure to always be at the ready and to expect the unexpected when it came to the Hughes organization. And to ask no questions.

This Las Vegas–Philadelphia flight would be a swift trip in one of the nine Lockheed JetStars owned or leased by Mr. Hughes. The JetStar – designated L-1329 by the Federal Aviation Administration (FAA) – was one of the early corporate jets designed for the United States Air Force and was used as a VIP aircraft in the Special Air Mission (SAM) Squadron at Andrews Air Force Base near Washington, DC. Lockheed had tried to sell the aircraft as a two-engine jet, but the USAF insisted on four engines, so it came to be sold also as a business jet. The nine-passenger plane, fitted with Pratt & Whitney JT 12-6 or -8 engines, weighed approximately 40,000 pounds and had a range of about 1,800 nautical miles.

Mr. Hughes had bought four JetStars directly off the assembly line at Marietta, Georgia. At his request, his trusted aid, Norm Larson, had been sent down to Marietta to facilitate storage of the four aircraft. (Larson believed he would only stay a few months, but he ended up staying indefinitely and eventually married a "Georgia peach.") Two of the planes were kept in a dehumidified, air-conditioned hangar, with a guard posted on duty 24/7, while the other two sat on the tarmac, totally unprotected from the elements. They were "green" (unpainted), and both eventually sustained flat tires from sitting there so long. This was typical of Hughes' bizarre way of doing things.

Naturally, those two neglected airplanes in Georgia stirred up much curiosity, and rumors began to fly among the pilots taxiing by. Those of us within the Hughes organization may not have understood his inconsistent behavior either, nor his (sometimes) ultra-detailed instructions on how to maintain his airplanes. But we knew it didn't need to make sense. We just did what we were told to do.

For example Hughes had five other Lockheed JetStars, one of which was stored at Red Bird Airport near Dallas, Texas. That particular aircraft was brand-new, with only six hours' total time in the air – yet upon Mr. Hughes' request it had been painted and new interior and avionics had been installed.

The other four were stored in various places – one in Burbank, California, two in Van Nuys, and one in Las Vegas. This last one was the airplane available for Goulet's flight: N1622D, previously owned by Texaco.

As we neared Baer Field in the predawn hours, my co-captain, Warren Bachelor, called the approach tower, which cleared us for landing. Then came an odd query: "Is this Bob Hope's airplane?"

Warren and I looked at each other, bewildered. "What in the world prompted that question?" I asked and then I said, "Tell them it's Howard Hughes' plane. That will blow their minds!" (Kidding, of course).

Then it hit me: There'd been a situation a few years back, involving Bob Hope and one of Mr. Hughes' planes – in fact, this very plane.

Walter Kane had directed us to fly Bob Hope and some of his personnel to Notre Dame University for an appearance at a special event, and then back to California. I assigned that flight to Warren and Charlie Wilson, another captain. They had arrived in South Bend, Indiana, early in the evening and, as instructed, parked on the ramp with the cabin lights on and the auxiliary power running, to await the return of the entertainer and his group. After the last scheduled airline flight, however, the South Bend tower had turned off the airport ramp lights. When Hope and his group had arrived at the airport in their limo, they couldn't locate the JetStar because it was too dark.

At that point I received a frantic call at my home in Las Vegas. It was Walter Kane, who always panicked at the slightest problem. "Bob, where's the JetStar?" he asked me breathlessly. We had two telephone lines in our home, one for the family, teenage girls you know (this was before the age of cell phones) and one for the Hughes organization; So I immediately picked up the family phone and called the South Bend tower. I asked if there was a Lockheed JetStar, tail number 1622D, on the ramp. They said yes. Then I asked them to turn on the ramp lights so Hope and his entourage could find the airplane. A short while later they informed me that they could see the limousine heading toward the airplane. Back on the other phone, I assured Kane that Bob Hope's group had found the plane and would be airborne in 20 minutes. Crisis averted.

Well, the very same air traffic controller who'd witnessed the South Bend event must have taken a job at the Fort Wayne approach control tower. He probably remembered the tail number of that aircraft and assumed that Bob Hope's airplane was about to land. Laughing, I disabused him of that assumption.

Once on the ground at Baer Field, Ruth and our daughters were whisked off to Woodburn by her parents and my mother. With Goulet and his passengers still on board, Warren and I continued our flight to Philadelphia. After they deplaned, we quickly refueled again and took off once more. I was eager to return to Indiana.

Around 10:00 that Sunday morning, the Baer Field approach tower positioned us for landing, and we dropped down to 2,000 feet just south of Woodburn. As we descended, Warren and I did a little sightseeing. I pointed out my Uncle Noah's farm and the spot where my father, who'd been a mail carrier, used to tie up the horse with a feedbag in the barnyard while he ate his own lunch. Typically, Dad would have a vehicle to deliver the mail – after all, this was in the 1920s. But in many cases back then, after heavy rains or winter blizzards, the back roads were impassible by car, so the horse and buggy worked out well.

As I continued to point out familiar sites – my Uncle Harry's farm, a large grain elevator towering above the trees – my mind drifted back 30 years. And suddenly I told Warren, "I can't stand it any longer. Call approach and cancel our IFR flight plan. Tell them we'll be operating on VFR."

We were going visual.

A Trip to the Past

It was still early on a lazy summer Saturday morning in 1943 when a distant sound tugged me out of my dream-state oblivion. To a sleepy 10-year-old, it could have been any of the familiar and comfortable sounds you get used to when growing up in a small town in the Midwest: Grandpa starting his 1927 Chevy. One of my sisters, Doris or Jean, clanging around in the kitchen or firing up the noisy vacuum cleaner. Maybe even my buddy, John Moser, across the street, working on his contraption of a go-cart, banging away as he tried to get the Briggs & Stratton motor running.

But as the sound moved closer and I began to rouse, I realized it was definitely not one of those familiar noises I was used to hearing in Woodburn, a quiet little community tucked away in the far northeast corner of Indiana, surrounded by cornfields and just a hop from the Ohio state line. Suddenly, I knew exactly what it was.

In mere seconds, I had pulled on my jeans and T-shirt. I sprinted barefoot out the front door of my family's Center Street home, which my father had built in 1912. I ran as fast as my young legs could carry me – in my fantasy world, I ran with the speed of the big red Zephyr horse mounted on a pole at Paul "Auggie" Augspurger's corner gas station and Ford dealership, leaping blindly through the air in a quest for flight.

The faint sound grew louder and louder as it quickly approached Center Street and Main. It wasn't careening through the middle of town as a freight train would, but coming from somewhere up above my head – somewhere high in the sky!

In order to get a better look, I ran down Center and right up to Main Street, where I spied Auggie and several other men perched on the roof of the dealership. Auggie held a huge checkered flag as high as he could and was waving it madly. I raised my eyes to the heavens ... and stared into the face of Woodburn native Lieutenant Willard Roemke, piloting a B-17 Flying Fortress so low over the town, I felt I could reach out and touch his plane.

Willard was buzzing the town!

At this time, America was in the midst of World War II, and lots of Woodburn's young men were heading off to war. Willard and his crew were jam-packed in that B-17, heading to England to fight for our country. Gunners were hanging out of the aircraft, waving down at us. And Willard himself was grinning from ear to ear as he swooped even lower, waggling his hand madly in farewell.

Just the day before, Willard had faked engine trouble and landed at Baer Field, a newly developed U.S. Army base in Fort Wayne (later to become Fort Wayne Municipal Airport, and today called Fort Wayne International Airport). His intent had been to spend one last night at the family farm, located one mile north of Woodburn on Highway 101, before heading off to war. That next day, as the plane and crew flew low over our little community, the cheers and enthusiastic shouts of the people watching from below rose through the crisp morning air, bringing delight to those men in the plane.

Woodburn, Indiana, looking east

As Willard Roemke gave what turn out to be his final salute to his hometown and the plane flew out of sight, I marveled at the emotion conjured by our young hero. That outpouring of love and respect, though occupying such a brief moment in time, greatly influenced my life. Someday, I vowed, I, too, would be respected and admired for my accomplishments. And to reach that goal, aviation would be my stepping-stone*.

Second Time Around

Shaking myself back to the present, I overheard Warren cancel the IFR, and we went to visual flight rules. I pulled the throttles back to idle, lowered the speed brakes, and negotiated a 90-degree turn north toward Woodburn. Already going way too fast to make the first circle over the town, I slowed to the maximum flap placard speed, then lowered the flaps to decelerate even more. Soon we were heading out over Ohio (only two miles away) and over the home of my half brother, Homer, just one mile east of the state line.

See Appendix A for Willard's story, El Paso And Beyond, by Wilbur E. Meyer

Then I lined up due east with Woodburn Road, an extension of Main Street. I dropped down to about 500 feet, raised the flaps and speed brakes, and pushed the throttles open. With those JT 12-6 engines, the plane was a noisy one, and at an altitude that low, the sound was deafening! I am sure it woke up more than a few sleeping Woodburn residents and disrupted a few sermons in this town of fewer than 1,000 people and four churches.

There I was, buzzing my hometown the same way Willard Roemke had done 30 years before! I flew right along Main Street and over the Lutheran church where Ruth and I had been married. As luck would have it, Ruth and our families and friends were just leaving the Sunday morning service when my good friend John Hetrick and his wife, Donna, heard the buzz and looked up to see the JetStar.

As I learned later, John joked, "That has *got* to be Bobby (as I was affectionately referred to) Wearley." It wasn't until he turned around and saw Ruth and our daughters coming out of church that he realized it really was me.

Mission accomplished! A little surprise for the community I grew up in, one that the townspeople would end up talking about for decades. And Ruth's only comment? "There goes Bobby Wearley, riding his bicycle down Main Street without touching the handle bars – showing off as usual."

Craving Aviation

My fascination with airplanes and aviation didn't just start the day I looked Willard in the eye as he zoomed down on Woodburn. Even before the tender age of 10, I knew all the World War II fighters and bombers. I had dozens of airplane photos in my dresser drawer at home, which I stockpiled as some collect baseball cards, and I studied them with intense interest.

When I was a kid, Woodburn had just one small, grass airfield where I hung out until one of the local pilots caved in and gave me a ride. My uncle, Ott Scheppleman, owned the blacksmith shop next to the Ford dealership and knew Auggie well. So my first airplane ride, as I vividly recall, was with Auggie, who owned an Arrow Sport – a 1930s airplane with an automobile engine.

Originally, the Arrow Sport was built by Arrow Aircraft Corporation in Lincoln, Nebraska. It was ordered by the development section of the Bureau of Air Commerce (the forerunner of the Federal Aviation Administration) to explore the possibilities of using low-cost, mass-produced automobile engines for aeronautical purposes. The Arrow Sport was powered by a 1937 Ford V-8 engine with standard bohnalite heads. Conversion of the engine to aviation use was accomplished by the installation of a reduction gear to reduce the propeller speed from 3,000 rpm to 1,500 rpm. This engine was the only 1937 automobile engine granted an unqualified approved type certificate by the United States Department of Commerce.

In later years, Auggie would "soup up" that Arrow Sport with a '39 Mercury engine. And one day, in the far distant future, I'd have an opportunity to repay Auggie for his patience and acts of kindness toward a little kid who was just nuts about airplanes.

The Arrow Sport hanging in the Terminal at the San Francisco Airport (exactly like "Auggie's" except his was red)

News Spreads Quickly

When you grow up in a small town, there isn't a whole lot to do. Woodburn was a close-knit community, a typical little town with no secrets. Everybody knew everybody. If something tragic happened, everyone knew about it almost instantly. All sorts of information – only relatively accurate, of course – was relayed through the antiquated telephone system. Party lines were the staple, and ringing up the operator – whom we all knew by name – to place calls by numbers like 86, 94, and 72 was the norm. Rural telephones were equipped with a crank, and because we were on party lines, you might crank one long and two shorts to reach a particular neighbor. Whether it was just gossip or an emergency call, all you had to do is pick up the receiver and talk to Lila, the operator.

For example, my mother regularly got up early on a Monday morning to do the laundry before heading to work at the post office. The mail arrived the night before on the Wabash Cannonball train, which ran from Toledo, Ohio, to Fort Wayne. My mother put up the mail in the individual boxes, as was normal for delivery in a small, rural town, then returned home and hung out the laundry to dry on the outdoor clothesline. That's exactly what she was doing one day when she noticed that the neighbors' house was on fire. She ran into the house, picked up the phone, and said to the operator without dialing, "Lila, Hank and Hilda Roemke's house is on fire!" The fire siren sounded immediately. Ironically, Hank was one of our volunteer firemen. He certainly didn't have to go far on this particular emergency run. Fortunately, Mom had notified them before much damage was done.

Party-line telephoning allowed any news, good or bad, to get around at the speed of light. That's probably how I heard about the tragic incident that claimed the life of my hero, Willard Roemke, who was shot down over Germany during the war.

At the time, it was completely reasonable that I would consider a local aviator like Willard to be my hero. Most little boys look to their fathers as their hero figures. Unfortunately, my dad died when I was just three years old. I remember the funeral and sitting restlessly on the lap of my mother's brother. I looked up at Uncle Asa Ehresman and said, "My daddy is dead. Can you be my daddy now?" As I recall, he gave me a stick of chewing gum to open during the service, which took me a long time to unwrap. Something to keep me occupied.

Times were tough. We were in the midst of the Great Depression, and my mother was now a widow with three children to care for. That may have been the reason I spent some time living with my Uncle Asa, Aunt Anna, and three of their older children, Melvin, Willowdean, and Betty, on their farm after my father passed away. My bedroom was on the second floor of the house, and in the morning I woke up to the sweet smell of bacon and eggs, toast, and coffee. To this day, Willowdean reminds me of how I called down to the family in the morning through the register in the floor, in a language only a three-year-old would understand. "Oming or Moyon, come and get me," I said. One of them climbed the stairs and carried me down to breakfast.

I stayed with Uncle Asa and Aunt Anna for several months. Then my mother's unmarried sister, Aunt Leona Ehresman, moved into our house and took care of me while my mother continued to work at the post office. We called her "No'nee," and she stayed with us until I turned six years old and started school.

First Impressions

After all these years, I remain good friends with John Moser, who lived directly across the street. John also lost his father when he was very young, just two and a half years old. His grandfather, Dr. Edward Moser, literally walked across the street to deliver me. Dr. Moser and his wife, Mary, raised John and his younger brother, Mike, while their mother worked in Fort Wayne, returning to Woodburn on weekends. John and Mike lived in their grandparents' house from 1936 until 1962. During that time John Moser and I became friends and attended the same school.

Our little neighborhood was filled with kids. While John's interest was cars, mine was airplanes and sports. I probably had a lot more in common with my other good friend, Leon Gerig – better known as Lee. Lee's father was the pastor of the Woodburn Missionary Church. The Gerigs lived right next to the church, in the parsonage, across the street from me and next to John Moser.

When I was 11 years old, Lee and his family moved to Detroit. I was devastated. But I did have an opportunity to visit him there and take in a Tigers baseball game at Briggs Stadium. A parishioner from Lee's church worked at the stadium and was able to finagle us box seats on the first-base line. I was especially awed at Lee's dedication. He knew all the big-name baseball players on the team: Rudy York, Hank Greenberg, Hal Newhouser. That was a big deal to me. Detroit won the World Series the year after I visited: 1945.

Lee Gerig was the older brother I never had. If someone started picking on me, he was the first to step in. During that trip to Detroit, Lee treated me like a little brother, making sure to show this small-town boy the big city. I vividly recall one incident when we were swimming at a public pool and another boy started harassing me. Lee intervened, and he wound up taking a punch meant for me. I came away unscathed, while he ended up with a bloody nose.

While Lee made an impression on me during those early years of growing up, the Boy Scouts were at least as influential. I really never realized what Scouting was all about until I observed a Scout troop at some sort of event in a Detroit park. They were all lined up and repeating the Scout Oath. I couldn't wait to get home and find out how I could join. Before long, I knew every one of the 12 Scout Laws verbatim. I can quote many of them still to this day.

Games Children Play

John Moser, Lee Gerig, and I could always generate some excitement with the other neighborhood kids. During those tough times, money was scarce. Hand-me-down clothes came from the wealthier families on the other side of town, and entertainment was whatever we children could think up.

One particular event we staged from time to time was a made-up game called Town. We collected bottle caps and use them as money. Pepsi was worth so much, and Coke was worth so much, and we used these "coins" at carnival-style booths on the lawn. The girls set up a hair styling salon, and the boys invented carny games. The Roemkes' yard was always a good place for this. The alley next to their house was also the perfect spot to play Kick-the-can.

Those early lessons in childhood economics played into the future of at least one of the Woodburn kids. Don Lipsett, who played those same neighborhood games with us, went on to make a name for himself at Hillsdale College in Michigan, becoming a player in an economic think tank. When we were kids, Don was an amateur photographer who started from scratch. I had a little camera with 127 film and a "Coke bottle" lens, and I took tiny pictures that we developed in Don's basement with glass bowls full of chemicals. Don later built his own darkroom and took pictures for the first high school yearbook in 1947. He also worked as a page at the *News-Sentinel* in Fort Wayne. He had a knack for conning guys, like me into subcontracting work from him, like delivering his newspapers so he have time for jobs with greater financial potential.

Don was an inventive person, and he knew how to make money. He created and sold Barry Goldwater sweatshirts at Indiana University, and later became friends with Edward Meese. As a child, he made molds of soldiers and filled them with melted lead. He would sell these lead soldiers to the neighborhood kids. He sold some to me, in fact, and when his father found out about it, he gave the money I'd paid Don back to my mother. He knew how precious every penny was to us.

In fact, Don's parents used to give my mother Don's hand-me-down clothes for me to wear. I remember one particularly embarrassing incident at school one day, when Don loudly said in home room, "Hey, that's my old shirt you're wearing." Poor or not, I never wore that shirt again. What Don lacked in social graces, however, he made up for in ambition, and that I admired. I later heard that he was involved in a conservative movement and was a fundraiser for Hillsdale College. Unfortunately, he died of leukemia at a relatively young age.

Don and another boyhood acquaintance, Steve Keller, earned the distinction of First Class Scout in Boy Scouts. At the time, that was the highest rank anyone had earned in Woodburn's Troop 57. I was so enamored of the Boy Scouts and worked so hard at it that I eventually earned the rank of Star Scout and went on to Assistant Scoutmaster at the age of 19. Having achieved and surpassed Don's and Steve's rank, I didn't even feel driven to pursue the rank of Eagle Scout – an indication of how high in the pecking order I placed these two young men. Because of a lack of good

Scoutmasters, I was encouraged to take over as Assistant Scoutmaster after one of the dads agreed to sign on as Scoutmaster only if I ran the troop.

I absolutely loved being Assistant Scoutmaster. From time to time I even load up my troop in my 1950 Chevy Club Coupe and headed off for a swim at the YMCA in Fort Wayne. Afterward, we went to Gardner's Drive-In Restaurant to see if I could catch a glimpse of my "girlfriend," (that is what I called her) who was a waitress there. Of course, she wasn't really my girlfriend, but I fantasized that we were going steady. The Scouts all ordered food then give me their money, but it never added up to enough. Inevitably, it cost me a buck or two extra to cover their debt – but to me, it was worth it, just to see my "girlfriend" once again.

Earning a Few Pennies

John Moser and I discovered how to make a little money at a young age: We collected the corncobs left at the grain elevator after the farmers had their corn shelled, and sold them for 50 cents per gunnysack. People used the cobs to in their cook stoves for heating, cooking, and baking, and for the hot water in the range reservoir. This was a way to cut expenses as we were just coming out of the Great Depression. John and I always had other friends, too, but we remained close throughout our teenage years. After roller-skating on the weekend, our ritual was to go to Gardner's Drive-In for one of their famous hamburgers and a frosty chocolate malt. We wanted to "see and be seen" a particularly fine thing to do to show you had a car, since few teenagers owned a car. My car was a '40 Chevy I bought with the $400 that I saved working at Norms Supermarket in Woodburn. We would cruise around Gardner's until the local police officer made us park. One of my favorite carhops (my fantasy Girlfriend) used to call me "Curly," and I would just melt. As we drove around, she would stand in a newly vacated space and save it for us until we could claim it. We tipped pretty generously. Back then, 50 cents was a good tip, but John and I would pull together 75 cents or even a dollar. You can bet she held us a good parking spot every time.

Although I was never really motivated by money, I knew that making it would help both me and my family. When I was around 10 years old, Leroy Stucky – who owned the local hardware store, which also sold furniture and John Deere farm implements – gave me my first job. I swept the floors and emptied the trash for 50 cents a day. Leroy sold out and moved to Florida and today Stucky Brothers is an appliances and electronics outfit in Fort Wayne.

Then in 1945, when I was just 12 years old, Norm Brenneke hired me to count World War II ration stamps at the his family grocery store, originally called Brenneke's and later renamed Norm's Grocery. My sister, Doris, and my cousin, Max Ehresman, also worked at Norm's.

As young as I was, I took my job quite seriously, and at the age of 19, I essentially functioned as an assistant manager of the store. Prior to enlisting in the USAF, I was making $1 an hour. My half brother, Homer, who was an electrical engineer at General Electric in Fort Wayne, thought it would be a good idea for me to get a job where he worked. So I started working mornings at Norm's and the second eight hour shift at GE, starting at 4:00 PM.

After two months at GE, I got a wake-up call. I'd walked to the end of the assembly line, where the workers were packing and shipping the transformers that I tested. I asked them how long they had been doing their jobs. "Twenty years" was their answer! I suddenly realized I didn't want to work at GE for the next 20 years, only to wind up packing transformers at the end of the assembly line. Nor did I have the inclination to become an electrical engineer like Homer. Sure, I was making $1.55 an hour at GE – which my mother thought was great – but I enjoyed being around the local people at Norm's and working for him much more. Besides, if you deducted the gas I consumed in getting to GE and the thirty minutes it took me to travel there and back from Woodburn, I really wasn't making any more money. In fact, I was making about the same amount, because I was putting in 60 hours a week at Norm's versus 40 hours a week at GE. I do recall hitting up Norm for overtime pay, to which he replied, "Bob, if I paid you overtime, you'd be making more money then me!"

Always the Prankster

When Norm married his wife, Lorraine, I played what I thought was a particularly funny joke on them. My friend John Hetrick found a cowbell in his father's barn, and I wired it underneath the frame of Norm and Lorraine's car. The incessant ringing drove them nuts as they headed off on their honeymoon. They later had it bronzed, and it's on display in their home to this day.

We always were the pranksters of Woodburn, but somehow we managed to avoid getting into any kind of "serious" trouble. One of our favorite pastimes was harassing the town constable, Dick Radtke. One particular Halloween – it was a Monday evening – a few of us had worked late, putting out the following week's groceries on the shelves at Norm's. We always worked as quickly as possible so we could still go out and have some fun. As my buddies and I walked past the town hall, I was fiddling with a piece of baling wire I'd picked up along the way. And there, parked right in front of the building, was Dick's Model A Ford – sitting in the dark, right next to a telephone pole.

The setup was perfect. We had no choice. What could we do but tie his rear bumper to the telephone pole with the baling wire? It was, after all, Halloween.

Suddenly, Dick came out of the town hall. We scattered. Of course, he demanded that we stop, and of course, none of us did! I don't recall whether he shot his pistol in the air or not – he was known to do that – but we ran like crazy anyway. I diverted, doubled back, and headed for home, where I leaped straight into bed – a far cry from my usual evening ritual, especially on Halloween night. I don't know if

Dick saw the wire and removed it or not, he did however pay my mother a visit at the post office the very next morning. He questioned her about my whereabouts the evening before. When my mother asked me about it later that day, naturally I knew nothing about the incident. Still, she was especially suspicious: Hadn't I gone to bed rather early and all of a sudden? But I never confessed.

Even at a young age, I liked living on the edge.

Small Town, Big Hopes

Back then, the population of Woodburn was 472. I read that population sign every time we walked down Main Street to Woodburn Grade School and later, Woodburn High School, where Glen "Goody" Henderson was the principal. Of those 472 townspeople, only 100 attended our high school, which meant there were only 20 students in my graduating class of 1951.

One year the local mayoral election was between my future father-in-law, Fred Meyer, and Eddie Keller, Steve's older brother. The result was a tie, and the winner was eventually determined by the flip of a coin – what could be more "small town" than that? In the end, Eddie Keller was our new mayor. Later Eddie purchased a Mooney single-engine aircraft, and we went flying when I was back in Washburn on vacation.

Few people know that for a time Woodburn was called Shirley City, after Robert "Bob" Shirley, an Indiana state senator. In fact, I was named after Robert Shirley, though my middle name, Franklin, came from Franklin D. Roosevelt – I was born in 1933, the year of FDR's first inauguration. As you might have guessed, my dad was a staunch Democrat.

"Bob Shirley lived right out here in rural Woodburn," Norm Brenneke told me one day. This was in 2004, and my former employer and good friend – now deceased – was still sharp as a tack. "All the land along the river, just two miles north of town, was called Shirley Park. But it never took off for building, because the ground was too low. It's really in a flood plain. When Bob Shirley was in the state senate, he had 'Woodburn' changed to 'Shirley City' without the residents knowing it. I guess he realized that his park idea along the river was not taking off, and he wanted to leave some sort of a legacy. Ultimately, he didn't get his way, because Shirley City never caught on. So back in the '50s the name was officially changed back to Woodburn." This was news to me; I'd never heard anyone call it Shirley City. Senator Shirley went to great lengths in his attempt to create a legacy, and to some degree he finally succeeded. A new bridge built on Highway 101 was initially called Butt Bridge, because Jim Butt had been a longtime resident and owned the adjacent land. I guess that name didn't go over too well, because the state legislature soon changed it to the Robert B. Shirley Bridge, which is still its name today.

Stepping back even further, Norm actually remembered how the town of Wood-burn got its original name. "Way, way back when they started draining the Marsh

Ditch," he explained, "they had to get rid of all of the brush and trees they took down in order to clear the land, so people could farm it. They did a whole lot of burning to get rid of the wood, and people came out from Fort Wayne and the surrounding areas to see the giant piles of flaming logs. So that's how the town came to be named Woodburn!"

Midwestern Values

How does growing up in a small Midwestern community like Woodburn, Indiana, influence your life? For me, it taught accountability, humility, honesty, and trust in my faith in God – qualities I may not have realized had I lived in a bigger city. Money was scarce, so I learned at an early age that if I worked hard and saved, I could probably make some of my dreams come true.

To support us, my mother worked long hours at the post office. She also was a strong influence in getting me to church on Sundays. One of the lessons she taught me was how to tithe my earnings. She did so faithfully, putting one-tenth of her weekly paycheck – which she referred to as her "tenth" – into a small change purse in the top drawer of her bedroom dresser. When Sunday came around, however, she didn't give all the contents of that little purse to God. She held some back, just in case she needed to borrow from her "tenth" if she ran short during the week. This little gesture of hers taught me that money was God's, not mine – though it paid to be frugal about our needs here on Earth, too. It also taught me to trust Him and have faith that He will provide for those needs – not our *wants*, but our *needs*. I can unequivocally say that every time I have faithfully tithed during my life, God did provide. And abundantly, I might add.

There are other things you learn, when you grow up in a small community, about making life-long acquaintances and friendships and holding to what's truly important. I have been around the world numerous times as an aviator; achieved rank and status as an Air Force pilot; flown Boeing 747s for two international airlines; and worked for one of the wealthiest and most reclusive men in the world. I felt I always valued my small-town values. Tom Fuelling, a fellow Boy Scout and Woodburn High School classmate in later years we reminisced about being raised is a small town, and how it shaped our lives. Tom, after graduating from College went to work for Lawry's Foods in Los Angeles and worked his way up to became president.

Life lessons are those experiences that remain with you forever. No man is oblivious to temptation, especially when the taking is so easy – and believe me, there were many times when I faltered. But something inherent in my upbringing would always keep me focused and grounded, even while my eyes were on the skies.

POOR VISIBILITY

A **HIGH-PITCHED SOUND TORE** me from the depths of slumber, like a coverlet stolen by a thrashing bed partner. *Rrrrrring!* I jolted up in my hotel bed. It was just after midnight. The sharp ringing was no emergency – only the crew call. The Singapore Airlines operation at the Dubai airport was calling to brief me on the weather (both locally and at today's destination), the en route time, and the fuel load.

I rousted myself out of my hotel bed and prepared to start my day.

One glance outside, and I knew the weather would be a factor on that trip. Though safe inside my heavily air-conditioned room, I could feel the intense humidity pressing against the windowpanes, looking for a way to seep in. As a Boeing 747 captain, I was accustomed to various routes, destinations, and arrival times that exposed me to such conditions: Low-visibility approaches. Early-morning fog. It all had to do with temperature and dew point convergence. Here in Dubai, on the spit of sand owned by the United Arab Emirates and jutting into the Persian Gulf, this sort of climate was to be expected.

It was 1983, and I was 50 years old, with 30 years of pilot experience under my belt. I knew the peril that could confront an aircraft – and its crew – in this kind of weather. But by the time the crew had checked out of the hotel and gathered at the bus stop just outside, there was some serious fog rolling in, and the knowing glances and conjecture about canceled flights had begun.

We were scheduled to work flight number SQ12 from Dubai to Athens, then on to London. As our bus pulled up to the terminal, however, we heard a loud roar and saw that an aircraft had missed an approach. We realized right away that Singapore Airlines flight number SQ12, the 747 that we were supposed to fly out of Dubai, had pulled up and was heading back into the skies. It would be diverting now to an alternate airport, probably the one in neighboring Sharjah.

I suddenly saw the scene as if from the outside looking in, through another person's eyes. The weather conditions, the sand dunes, the palm trees, the camels howling in the distance – the memories flooded back so quickly, I reached out a hand to steady myself, not wanting to appear out of sorts in front of my crew. But the sights and sounds continued to flash in my head. It was impossible not to recall the scene of more than 25 years ago, on another night when the fog had dropped from the sky like a heavy, velvet curtain. Exactly like this.

The author Captain Bob Wearley (far right) with his Singapore Air Lines Boeing 747-200 crew. (Taken on the ramp after landing in Frankfurt, Germany circa 1980)

Heading for Disaster

I was a 23-year old first officer in the United States Air Force, one of two co-pilots in the USAF Military Air Transport Service (MATS) crew of a Charleston-based C-121C Super Constellation (Lockheed 1049G). The date was December 30, 1956 – just shy of the New Year and all the celebrations I hoped it would bring – and we were en route to Dhahran Airfield in Saudi Arabia. Our mission: to transport U.S. military personnel from Charleston Air Force Base in South Carolina to Dhahran.

One of many important links in the global chain of American strategic bases, Dhahran was located just two miles inland from the waters of the Persian Gulf. Built on dusty tracts of sand leased from the oil-rich King Saud as part of a 1940s deal with the Roosevelt administration, it offered such modern and ample resources as 10,000-foot runways and facilities for 1,500 airmen.

Our aircraft was one of just three expected in Dhahran that night. But, I found out later, due to inclement weather, the other two planes had already diverted to the alternate airport in Bahrain.

Piloting the plane along with me were Major Clyde W. Ellis, a designated aircraft commander, and second pilot Lieutenant LaVerne W. Alitz. The Lockheed Constellation, nicknamed "Connie" was a wonderfully designed aircraft with a body sculpted into an *S* shape. It was built for the long haul, which made it perfect for our particular military mission on this trip. The Connie was a dual-purpose aircraft: It could be configured for passengers or cargo, and was also prepared for any airvac situation – it could become a flying hospital of sorts, capable of handling the ill or injured. Its basic crew consisted of an aircraft commander, a co-pilot, one engineer, and one navigator. Crew duty time was restricted to 12 hours.

But this time around, because after departing Charleston our flight had collected passengers at McGuire Air Force Base in New Jersey – headquarters for MATS' 21st Air Force – and would make additional stops at Lajes Air Base in Portugal's Azore Islands and Wheelus Field in Tripoli, Libya, we were carrying an augmented crew: an aircraft commander, two co-pilots, two flight engineers, two navigators, and the regular complement of flight attendants. Being designated as an augmented crew allowed for 16 hours of crew duty time, including two hours for preflight briefings and such, prior to take off.

Major Ellis was an administrative officer, a designation meaning he was assigned to the 41st ATS (Air Transport Squadron) to maintain his pilot currency. In other words, his full-time job was as an ADMN officer, not a pilot. So the Air Force required a first *and* a second pilot to accompany him in lieu of two second pilots, to provide the added experience of an individual (the first pilot) who was actually in line for an upgrade to the rank of aircraft commander. That was why I was on board this particular flight. I was the first pilot.

Lieutenant Alitz and I had decided to take turns in the co-pilot's chair for take-offs and landings, swapping seats every other leg of the trip. The extra man would find a spot elsewhere in the cramped cockpit, usually behind the aircraft commander's seat, and would assist when necessary throughout the flight. This put Lieutenant Alitz in the co-pilot seat when we set out from Charleston, and I would assume the position as we departed McGuire and headed to the Azores. Yet for some reason forever lost to the passing of time, Lieutenant Alitz remained up front during the flight from McGuire to the Azores. Thus our sequence changed, and – fatefully – he was in the co-pilot position once again when we departed Tripoli late in the afternoon on the day before New Year's Eve, headed for Dhahran.

Politics in the late 1950s were such that we had to change course slightly south to fly over Khartoum in Sudan; the Egyptians were at odds with our administration at the time and persistently refused flight clearance for American aircraft. After leveling off at around 16,000 feet, Major Ellis put the airplane on autopilot and left his seat, heading back to relax in the crew rest area, between the cockpit and the passenger compartment. I climbed forward to replace him, and Lieutenant Alitz and I proceeded to fly the aircraft.

Ten hours went by uneventfully. I received the weather report, which revealed nothing but a forecast of beautiful conditions. Even though the temperature and the dew point were close together – a situation often conducive to fog – the winds were very calm and the skies were clear. Visibility on the ground reportedly went for miles.

During the eleventh hour, Major Ellis returned to the cockpit, refreshed. I squeezed out of the left-hand seat, allowing him to slip in and grab the yoke. I briefed him on the weather conditions. Foreseeing no problems, I left the cockpit, passed through the navigator's station, and sat down upon one of the crew bunks near the large cargo door. Lieutenant Pete Goch, seated sideways at the navigator's panel, twisted around to talk to me for a moment, and then turned again to face forward. I half listened as he spoke into his headset, informing Major Ellis about the approach.

The four crew relief seats faced one another, two abreast. Lieutenant Robert Saylors was sitting in one of them. Another man, slightly built – a student navigator – was seated next to the cargo door. Lieutenant Colonel Ali A. Rafat, on board as an ACM (additional crew member), was seated in the passenger compartment next to one of the emergency exits; he was a transportation observer from the Iran Air Force and had just attended the U.S. Air Force Command and Staff School.

I was tired. I had flown the plane for ten hours straight. So I lay down on the bunk with my feet pointed toward the front of the aircraft. To get more comfortable, I decided not to fasten my seatbelt. When I heard the landing gear go down, I would simply jump up and buckle myself in.

After saying a little prayer, thanking God for the safe trip thus far, I closed my eyes and soon drifted off to sleep.

Exactly what happened next, I do not know even to this day. But the aftermath still haunts the darkened corners of my soul.

Crisis Training

When I awoke, I was no longer lying in the bunk but standing at the edge of the open cargo door, my eyes peeled wide in shock and my entire body bruised with an unidentifiable pain that was both sharp and blurry. The Connie had crashed – that much was clear. We had broken apart upon impact. The fuselage was engulfed in flames from top to bottom, and the nose was no longer there. It had simply ... evaporated.

Somewhere in the distance, I heard nightmarish screams. All was confusion ... and then, a familiar voice. It was Staff Sergeant Robert J. Sanders, calling to me: "Lieutenant! Lieutenant Wearley!" The cargo door had been wedged all the way open, and I could just barely make out the shape of a man outside the gaping, six-foot-wide maw – it was Sanders. He must have seen me standing there among the flames. Out of the smoke and chaos, he reached for me and – by the grace of God – managed to lead me out of the flaming aircraft, laying me down on solid ground. Saving my life.

And then ... blackness.

I soon regained consciousness, but still I was in a daze, and badly hurt. Blood and sand filled my eyes, oozed down my face, and dripped away from my chin. A lightning bolt of excruciating pain tore through my back. Then I felt nothing. I thought I was probably going to die. Sanders' valiant effort would be in vain after all.

Slowly, as my body began to recover from the shock and as the blood started flowing back to my brain, I became conscious of my surroundings. Fire trucks were pulling up all around us, and I did my best to roll over and get out of their way. Without thinking, I put my hand to my forehead; it was ripped open, a jagged, leaking gash. I imagined myself lying beneath the upper bunk, hitting the webbing as we struck the unforgiving land. But I didn't remember a single moment of it.

I asked Sanders if Major Ellis had survived. He answered me with a sharp turn of his head, right to left. "All the crew has been accounted for ... dead or alive," he said in a voice that was lifeless, hollow, desolate.

The fire had spread so rapidly, the flight attendants were unable to fight their way back into the plane to help those still trapped inside. An Army major on board had managed to twist the crude handle of a sliding passenger entrance and slide the door open, helping several people out of the death trap of metal and fire. One was a woman cradling a baby in her arms, who just stood at the rear door, suspended in disbelief. Then she dove back into the blazing wreckage to rescue her other two children ... and never returned. The husband waiting at the terminal never saw his wife or children again.

Sanders kept reassuring me and telling me to lie still. So I just lay there in the sand, doing my best to bear the pain. Thinking back to my Boy Scout training in the '40s, I assessed my injuries: My back was broken – I was fairly certain of that. There was no doubt that I had head injuries.

Thanks to our teacher, Harry Henney – who would later follow Goody Henderson as high school principal – Woodburn's Boy Scout Troop 57 always came through with flying colors when we competed in the Anthony Wayne Council's First Aid Competition over in Fort Wayne. During an interview with Mr. Hanney for this book he recalled, "those were pretty serious classes," "The competition included giving the Scouts, in writing, a tragic situation that a person might face. They read it, then some of the Scouts role-played the victims while others were the caregivers. The judges watched what they were doing and judged them on how they were handling the first-aid situation. Our troop always did well in that exercise."

I struggled through the murky stupor of my pain, and made a promise to myself: I would send Principal Henney a heart-warming letter, letting him know of his influence on my life. Being able to take stock of my injuries in the heat of crisis allowed me to gain some sort of control over the pandemonium and invite a semblance of calm into these initial post-disaster moments. Harry and his wife Jeanette have since passed away in their 90's.

Sergeant Sanders stayed close by me until emergency personnel arrived. The first physician on the scene was quite nervous. He talked rapidly and seemed intent on getting me to a stretcher quickly so he could whisk me away from the scene of the crash. "I'm a doctor, I'm a doctor," he kept saying. He was young and, I suppose, new to the business.

"Doc, calm down," I croaked in response.

He grabbed a pair of scissors and cut open my shirt, then stuck a needle in my arm. He called to the medics and told them to put me on the stretcher. But as they started grabbing my head and feet, Sergeant Sanders yelled, "Be careful! His back is injured!"

Again, I thought of the Boy Scouts and learning how to transport a person with a spinal injury. Bob Sanders' quick response, ordering the medics to load me onto the stretcher with care, surely prevented further injury to my back, and may even have prevented lifelong debilitation. To this day, Sanders and I remain friends. In 2003, at our USAF 41st ATS reunion at Charleston Air Force Base, I was finally able to thank him properly for saving my life.

If there is one thing I will never forget about that flight and the accident that ended it so tragically, it's the prayer I said just before falling asleep. God was watching over me, and for whatever reason, my life was spared.

The Fate of the Connie

The $2.2 million Connie was totally destroyed. According to a final report by MATS headquarters, 41 individuals – 30 passengers and 11 crewmen – were on board when it crashed. Air Force informants told the Associated Press that 15 people were killed outright or fatally burned, while the rest scrambled to safety.

These dreadful losses were blamed on the fog. When the aircraft hit the sandy ground, the cockpit broke off and folded underneath the plane. The fuselage continued its journey for some distance, sliding over the nose and finally crashing and exploding in flames. The left wing broke off and sliced through the fuselage, spreading the fire and separating the flight attendants from the passengers.

Was there some clue that we missed, some indication that the weather would change so dramatically in a matter of hours or even minutes? It's impossible to know. What we do know is that in the military at that time, most landings in inclement weather were made using a ground-controlled approach (GCA). The Dhahran Airfield was equipped with a GCA system, but apparently the equipment was not up and operating when the Connie began its descent.

"26 Survive Crash in Saudi Arabia" was the headline in Charleston's paper, the *News and Courier*, on December 31, 1956. Here is what staff reporter Coyte White had to say:

Twenty-six of the 41 persons aboard survived the crash of a Charleston-based C121-C Super Constellation at Dhahran, Saudi Arabia, just past midnight. Capt. Irving H. Breslauer, Charleston Air Force Base public information officer, said word has been received here that seven of the 26 survivors are crew members.

Four crew members have been listed by the USAF as missing. They are Maj. Clyde W. Ellis, aircraft commander, of North Charleston; 1st Lt. LaVerne W. Alitz, co-pilot, of North Charleston; Master Sgt. F. A. Lorch, engineer, of North Charleston; and Sgt. F. A. Rodgers, engineer, of North Charleston. Seven others known to have been aboard also have been declared missing by the USAF.

The Air Force listed eight survivors as Charleston-based crewmen and a foreign observer. They are Airman 2nd Class (WAF) Florence A. Hogan, of Stamford, Conn.; **1st Lt. Robert F. Wearley, co-pilot, of Charleston Heights;** *1st Lt. Peter Goch, navigator, of Jersey City, N.J.; 1st Lt. Thomas W. Heenan, navigator, of Glen Ellyn, Ill.; 2nd Lt. Robert L. Saylors, navigator, of Ninety Six, S.C.; Staff Sgt. Robert D. Proctor, flight attendant, of Charleston; Staff Sgt. Robert S. Sanders, flight attendant, of Charleston; and Lt. Col. Ali A. Rafit, a transportation observer from Iran.*

The latest report from Dhahran said that some of the 26 patients were injured seriously.

Who or what was to blame for the devastating crash of the Connie, for the injured, for all the lives that were lost? Two things went terribly wrong on our descent that day. First of all, the fog rolled in around Dhahran thicker than thieves. Second, unlike the instrument landing systems (ILS) we have today, which are automatically on, 24/7, the GCA unit was comprised of radar tubes, much like an old television set. To ensure a safe landing in spite of the fog, we would have had to wait about 30 minutes for the antiquated technology to warm up so we could be "talked down" by the GCA controller via an instrument landing.

Normally, on an instrument flight, the pilots plan on having enough fuel to get to their destination; hold for 15 to 20 minutes, in case they must wait for conditions to change; and then, if necessary, proceed to an alternate airport. We should have had adequate reserves to fly to the alternate airport in Bahrain, twenty miles across the Persian Gulf. Because I was asleep during our descent, I can't be sure what the weather was like when Major Ellis attempted his approach, but he must have decided that attempting to land in Dhahran was preferable to proceeding to the alternate airport. Fog banks come in very rapidly. Perhaps the visibility had been above the designated landing minimum when the major elected to make what's called a "range approach" –then it had quickly deteriorated.

When a pilot comes over the "low range station" 500 feet above the ground, he can't land straight in because of the aircraft's close proximity to the end of the runway. The premise of a range approach – which today is a very antiquated procedure – is this: If you proceed from 500 feet and you can physically see the airport, you keep visual contact, circle, and land. A pilot must follow a definite procedure under those conditions; there are certain ways to maneuver the airplane in order to keep within the obstruction clearance requirements of the landing runway and safely land the plane. But the approach has to be made under strict visual conditions. If you lose sight of the runway, you are required to follow the published "missed approach" procedures.

Major Ellis may have decided not to wait for the GCA, attempting instead to execute a range approach. Coming off of the null, a low station at 500 feet AGL (above ground level), he apparently elected to proceed with a visual pattern configuration while still in IFR mode, shifting 45 degrees right to proceed on a downwind leg, then returning parallel to the runway. He must have anticipated that the visibility would be better at the other end of the runway.

In calm winds, if he broke out of the fog, he would be free to execute a visual approach and land safely. The altitude for a visual pattern is 1,000 feet AGL. The aircraft was not traveling at a tremendously high rate of speed. The aircraft's flaps, RPM, etc., were perfectly configured for a downwind leg. The major may have misread the altimeter, thinking he was at 1,500 feet when in actuality he was at 500 feet. He must have been thinking in terms of a visual approach executed at 1,000 feet AGL during the downwind leg. Assuming he was at 1,500 feet, he let down to 1,000 feet AGL, and that's when we crashed, 1,000 yards opposite the runway touchdown point, in the sand.

That oppressively humid morning in 1983, Singapore Airlines flight SQ12 from Dubai to London via Athens never lifted off. While modern instruments and the fog-burning rays of the sun probably would have allowed us to keep our scheduled departure time, the incoming aircraft had diverted to Sharjah. We simply had no plane to fly. We had to wait until the fog lifted so our aircraft could return from the alternate airport and be readied for our flight to London.

Nearly 30 years earlier, however, a flight under similar conditions, just a short distance from Dubai, had ended in horrific tragedy. Many lives were lost – those of vital young men who were both my friends and my fellow officers. It doesn't escape me that, had we stuck with the original plan of alternating co-pilot duties, *I* would have been seated in the cockpit instead of Lieutenant Alitz. Would I have been able to prevent the accident? Why was I saved? Only God knows. Life is a mystery. Along the way, there are certain milestones that inevitably change you. For me, this was one of those milestones – perhaps the most profound one of all.

Recuperation and Recovery

I was transported first to the Dhahran Airfield hospital, and the next morning to the Arabian American Oil Company's Aramco Hospital near the USAF base, where I was to spend the next week. A surgeon sutured my forehead and fitted me with a body cast so I would be mobile – to some degree, at least. Then came the endless days of laying in that hospital, unspeakably sore from head to foot, and still quite unable to move. But alive – thankfully, undeniably alive.

Back home in Woodburn, Principal Henney said, "Folks were pretty upset when they heard about the accident." There were a lot of prayers said on my behalf during the time it took me to recover.

When my mother received an encouraging Western Union telegram that told of my return to the United States, she and my mother-in-law took the train from Fort Wayne to Charleston to spend some time with us.

Department of the Air Force
Woodburn, Indiana
Jan. 9, 1957 – 4:16 PM

Mrs. Alice Wearley – Report Delivery fone 23594, Woodburn, Ind.
Unclassified from 1606 ATRWPOS 9-A27. I am happy to inform you that your son Lieutenant Robert F. Wearley has departed from Dhahran Airfield, Saudi Arabia, for the United States via military aircraft. He is expected to arrive at the U.S. Naval Hospital, Charleston, South Carolina, on or about 11 January 1957. I feel sure that your son will contact you upon his arrival.
Clinton C. Wasem, Colonel, USAF Commander

The Air Force may have informed my mother about my repatriation and recuperation, but my wife, Ruth, at home in Charleston, had been the first to be notified of the crash. My squadron commander, Major Jack Bickford, along with the base chaplain, paid a visit to our house in Charleston. It's a scene every military wife dreads: a squadron commander and an Air Force chaplain side by side, slowly walking up the sidewalk to the front door. That's never good news.

Communications between Dhahran and the United States were less than adequate, and every time the list of injured or dead was read aloud, the broadcast became garbled. So the news at the base was that I had been killed in the crash, but fortunately, Ruth never heard the false reports. The authorities withheld that information from her, as she was already en route to Dhahran anyway.

Because of her condition – she was seven months pregnant with our first daughter, Robin – Ruth was accompanied by Nell, a nurse from the base clinic, and our good friend Lieutenant Doug Smith, a fellow Connie pilot. I was very concerned about my wife traveling while she was this far along in her pregnancy. When she and her companions landed at Wheelus Field, the World War II air base in Tripoli, Colonel Wasem – the wing commander from Charleston Air Force Base, and author of the telegram to my mother – met the aircraft. He had just returned from his fact-finding mission at Dhahran. He reassured Ruth that he had visited me, that I was alive but critically injured, that I would survive and recuperate. Few wives could have handled this kind of news with such ease. As ever, she was stoic. Ruth was always so calm about everything that befell us in our life together, accepting it all as the unavoidable result of Divine Will. Later, Major Bickford observed, "Bob, you have a very strong wife."

I just thanked him. It sure wasn't news to me.

The first C-121 "Super Connie" delivered to the 41st ATS at Charleston AFB, S.C. in 1956

INTO THE WILD BLUE YONDER

In March 1952, several years before Ruth and I were married, my buddy John Moser and I decided to enlist in the United States Air Force. With the Korean War going on, the country was in the middle of a draft, and both John and I knew our numbers would soon be called. By enlisting, we could beat the military to the punch and select which branch we wanted to serve in. So, at the recruiter's encouragement, off we went to Indianapolis to take the physical exam.

Initially, I didn't think that I would even pass. When I was 12 years old, my mother had taken me to a doctor in New Haven – a town somewhat larger than Woodburn, on the east side of Fort Wayne – for a physical, so I could play grade-school basketball. This doctor told my mother that I had a heart murmur. He read us the riot act, saying that I couldn't do this, I shouldn't do that … And I most certainly "couldn't" play basketball! He made it sound as though I would collapse to the floor and die if we didn't follow his rules precisely.

Yet to my surprise, I passed the military physical. Perhaps I'd been misdiagnosed by that earlier doctor and didn't have a heart murmur after all, or perhaps I'd simply overcome it. Whatever the cause, I was free to do as I pleased without fear of heart problems.

I immediately signed up for the Air Force.

John and I stayed in a seedy hospice in Indianapolis for the night, and the next day we were on a train headed for Lackland Air Force Base in San Antonio. We were giddy with anticipation. En route to Texas, we saw some parts of this gigantic country we had never seen before. I particularly remember stopping in Arkansas – and my first exposure to segregation in the South. I saw firsthand the way black people were treated, and it was a shock. The bathrooms and drinking fountains were individually marked "*Whites* and *Colored*" For a kid from Woodburn, Indiana, this was appalling. I felt very out of my element. But for the most part, we had a ball on that train. We weren't taking anything too seriously. After all; we were only nineteen.

Our rude awakening came when we arrived at boot camp and started basic training. Before we knew it, our heads were shaved and we were dressed head to toe in the standard-issue uniform. Even more shocking to me was the vocabulary I was hearing all around me. The drill instructors had a knack for using four-letter words in a way that gave a whole new meaning to the English language!

Once the initial shock wore off, basic training was pretty easy for me. The only thing I really hated was getting up at the break of dawn. Other than that, I just tried to stay as low-key as possible. When it came to assigning tasks like kitchen patrol, they always started at the beginning of the alphabet. So, with a last name starting with *W*, I never had to pull KP – they had plenty of guys picked long before they got to me. Basic training wasn't a walk in the park for some of the other recruits, though. One fellow in the bunk next to me, from Kentucky, just about broke down crying due to the stress. I tried to console him by joking, "This is like Boy Scout camp. If you were in the Marines, I think you'd have something to complain about."

John and I made the most of our weekend passes to explore San Antonio. We went into the city one Sunday morning, and as soon as we got off the bus, a man from the local Baptist church was standing there. He invited us to services, and we went. We were already in the habit of attending church regularly, and it sounded like a good opportunity to check out a different kind of church. It was huge, what we would call today a "megachurch". These folks reached out to the servicemen in the area, providing a home-cooked meal afterward for all the airmen who showed up to worship. The young ladies in the congregation mingled with us during the meal—a nice change from the "chow hall". Then John and I toured the Alamo and other sights before meeting the bus to return to the base.

At first, I didn't excel in boot camp. In fact, nobody really knew who I was – until aptitude testing started. That's when my credibility shot through the roof. My grades were high enough that I could choose any enlisted school I wanted. My first choice was Air Traffic Controller; Medic was second. But as I told my counselor, that wasn't what I really wanted to do. I was fascinated by pilot training.

Of the 50 men in my unit, only 10 took the pilot training tests. And after all the psychomotor testing was completed, only two airmen qualified for pilot and navigator. One of those men was me.

Instantly, I became a "somebody." The assistant drill instructor, a Sargent, even called me into his room, because he was considering applying for the Aviation Cadet Pilot Training as well since he was young enough to apply, to ask me all about the tests. This was all quite humorous to me. Wasn't I the same guy who had been there all along, the one nobody had noticed? I was even taunted by a recruit who said, "Wearley, you'll never make it. You don't have what it takes to be an officer."

My retort was "Well, we won't know that until I try, will we?"

To fast forward and perhaps shed a little light on this type of remark, when stationed at Charleston AFB, SC and after landing on a flight to Ramey AFB in Puerto Rico, I ran into an airman I knew from our time in boot camp back at Lackland AFB. We had just parked and boarded the crew bus to go to our quarters when, passing through the guard gate, I recognized the air policemen who came out to check our bus. I asked the bus driver to stop, and I got out to introduce myself. Instead of a salute which is required by Military Protocol when an enlisted man meets or passes an Officer, the Air Policeman's (AP's) remark was, "Where in the hell did you get those bars?"

Here he was an airman/enlisted man and I was an officer. His behavior was a totally inappropriate statement for an enlisted man to make! (Does the Bible verse in Luke 4:24 apply here? "..no prophet is accepted in his hometown…".) I could have reprimanded him. Instead, I just tried to understand where he was coming from, and this I learned, in time, makes me a better man for it.

But in 1952, at boot camp back in Lackland, I had just started on the path to becoming an officer, and the other airmen had definitely noticed.

Fate Leaves a Calling Card

At that time, the Pentagon planners decided they needed to build up their pilot numbers to fight "brushfire wars" – what they deemed small-scale skirmishes going on in Korea. The World War II pilots were aging, and the USAF was in need of "fresh" pilots. They started a gigantic aviation cadet program, similar to the one initiated during WWII, and soon there was a backlog. So the plan was to send all airmen who qualified for the aviation cadet program to various Air Force pilot training bases, where we would wait – doing odd jobs around the flight line – while they were gearing up to start our pilot training.

At this point, John and I parted ways and I headed off to my new destination: Enid Air Force Base in Oklahoma. I vividly remember the trip from Lackland to Enid. Our route was to fly from the San Antonio Airport to Tulsa and then on to Enid. We were flying high to Tulsa in a DC-4, and the flight was uneventful. But in Tulsa we were transferred to a twin-engine, unpressurized DC-3. It was a very hot day, and the plane had no air-conditioning. We flew at a low altitude, which resulted in a lot of turbulence due to the thermals rising from the heated Oklahoma ground surface. This made the trip quite bumpy and … well, I got sicker than a dog. I couldn't believe it. There I was, on my way to becoming a pilot, and I was airsick!

At that time, the USAF ran advanced training bases for either fighters or multi-engine planes. Enid was an advanced, multiengine training base with T-6s and B-25s. The 40 of us incoming cadets would be assigned to either a T-6 or a B-25 maintenance squadron. As it turned out, I was among those assigned to the T-6.

Our job was to get up in the wee hours of the morning and work the flight line. We would preflight the T-6's by starting the engine and advancing the throttle to a predetermined propeller RPM (revolutions per minute), then check the oil pressure and such, and take the aircraft form 1 (the maintenance record) into the maintenance NCO.(Non Commissioned Officer) who signed the form, indicating that the airplane was fit for flying. We also refueled the planes and helped the cadets or student officers "buckle in" when they came out for their solo or instructional flight. Another one of our duties was to stand fireguard. Armed with big fire extinguishers, we would be at the ready in case there was a fire when the pilots started up their engines. It was also our duty to pull the chocks from under the wheels (where they were positioned to keep the aircraft from moving in case the brakes didn't hold) when the pilot gave the signal and to wing-walk them out to the taxiway, ensuring that while taxiing, the wing tips had clearance vis-à-vis other parked aircraft. Once the plane departed, we were left with plenty of time to eat breakfast, make our beds, or just goof off for an hour or so. Then we headed back to the flight line when the student officers returned.

While I waited to be transferred to a flight training base, I talked to those student pilots every chance I got, trying to gain as much information as I could. Another airman and I even went to the graduation ceremonies held at the base theater. After the ceremonies concluded, we walked over and saluted one of the new officers. There is a long-standing ritual in the U.S. Air Force: When a cadet graduates and becomes an officer, the first enlisted man to salute him is handed a business card with a dollar bill to declare his new status. On this day, the new officer fulfilled the ritual by handing his business card and dollar bill to me. I thought nothing of it at the time, not knowing that this particular new officer would become very influential in my aviation future.

Keeping the Faith

When I was stationed at Enid, the very first break we got was the long Fourth of July weekend in 1952. I hitched a ride home with a buddy heading to Michigan through Fort Wayne. We had dropped off my friend Don Glockner in Indianapolis, and then proceeded to Fort Wayne, where my mother met me at the YMCA downtown. I went home to spend the next 24 hours in Woodburn, and then started the return journey in my 1950 Chevy Club Coupe. Along the way, I stopped in Indianapolis to pick up Don, and together we drove back to Enid, eating a lunch of fried chicken and sandwiches my mother had prepared for us.

We didn't always follow the rules at Enid. For example, we didn't bother putting on our A3C stripes that showed our rank: airman third class. Our thinking was that, when we eventually did put on our second lieutenant bars, we didn't want anyone to see where the airman stripes had left marks. Looking back, I realize that would be sort of tacky for a new second lieutenant. What we were doing was acting as if we were student officers, which wasn't likely to gain us much respect.

I did make a lot of friends at Enid, one of whom I will never forget: Keith Hall. Everybody loved Keith. He was a super guy. But somehow the first sergeant forgot about him when assigning duties. Keith was on the roster, but he didn't have a specific job. Nobody knew he was there. He got up in the morning (usually after the rest of us left), made his bed, and went to the day room to watch television or to the pool for a swim. Eventually Keith got tired of doing nothing, and he went to the first sergeant and asked him for a job. He got one, painting the day room where we lounged and watched television. After he finished there wasn't another job, so he went back to his old ways.

Our squadron probably best remembers his shenanigans at the swimming pool. Keith was a clown who'd put on a show for anyone who was willing to watch. He situated himself on the high dive with a crazy hat on and a cigarette hanging out of his mouth. He then dove off the board, striking some silly pose, and splash into the water, leaving his hat floating on the surface. For his grand finale, he'd come up from the depths, right under his hat, and flip the cigarette back out of his mouth, smoking it as he swam to the edge of the pool. He had flipped it over so the lit end was in his mouth until he surfaced again! At one point I asked Keith to teach me to dive, but I should have known better. I didn't have the necessary coordination.. I took a belly loud, painful flop my first time off the high board. That ended my excitement about being a show-off. Keith and I spent a lot of time together during the next four years, until he left the Air Force, married a gal from South Carolina, and became a born-again Christian. That didn't surprise me – he always did have a heart of gold and a mind for charity. He collected used clothing, took it along on his flights to the USAF Air Base in the Azores, where we landed the C-54 (civilian DC 4) on a refueling stop crossing the Atlantic on flights to Europe or North Africa. He then went off the base and give the clothes to the less-fortunate Portuguese people living there. After our stint together in the Air Force, Keith and his wife moved to Arizona, where he started an organization called Wings for Christ (www.wings-for-christ.org). He and his brother flew into the desert, in small airplanes, to hold Sunday School and Church Services, at remote Indian reservations. Eventually he moved the whole operation to Waco, Texas. Word has it that he once prayed over a young girl who had diabetes. He supposedly asked God to spare her life and said he would take on her sickness instead. The girl lived. Keith later died at a relatively early age – of complications from diabetes.

In my entire life, I've never met anyone who epitomized the Christian faith more closely than he did. He was a living, breathing man who did more than just talk the talk – he walked the path that Christ walked. Keith was a phenomenal person.

While on leave for Christmas 1952, I found out that we'd been accepted for pilot training. On Christmas Eve, back in Woodburn, my family went to the church program then retrurned home to open our gifts. When the phone rang, I expected it to be someone wishing us a Merry Christmas. Instead, it was a call from the telegraph office, relaying a telegram from my squadron commander, Captain Snow:

Congratulations. You will start aviation cadet training at Lackland Air Force Base in January.

I let out a war whoop so loud, my family must have thought the roof was going to come off. My future brother-in-law, Army First Lieutenant Verne Lausen, was there to congratulate me – soon I would be a fellow officer. Verne was visiting my sister Doris at the time, but soon after that he left to serve in Korea.

As for me, I was eager (to say the least!) to get back to Lackland. I was going to be a USAF Pilot and according to Congress an Officer and Gentleman.

Officer Training

Keith and I and another fellow, Gorm Paulsen (a U.S. citizen from Denmark), drove from Enid back to Lackland Air Force Base in January 1953. The next three months were committed to officer training. Which consisted of a commitment to following a lot rules and regulations that didn't seem to make much sense, but obviously designed to discipline us to obey orders.

During the first month, as underclassman, we had to "square the corners" – run every place we went. When we came to an intersection, we had to shout, "Clear to the left, clear to the right, clear up above, clear down below, clear to go!" We had hundreds of inspections, at all times of the day and night, and the middle-class and upper-class members were our mentors – and our tormentors. The real revenge for their own time as underclassmen came from the upperclassman, who would "gig" you if you didn't do something right.

We had to carry a "gig slip" in our pocket with our name on it, and if we were caught disobeying procedures, the upperclassman wrote down our infraction on the slip. This was what it meant to be "gigged". Examples were; if our shoes were not shined to their licking, or our military bearing wasn't military enough, uniforms lacked tidiness ETC. At the end of the week, the gigs were posted. If our we had more than ten gigs, we had to walk the parade grounds that weekend – in full dress uniform, one hour for each gig in excess of ten. It was supposed to be demeaning punishment. We marched back and forth, and it sure was hot in the Texas sun. But I still knew we suffered nothing like a Marine on a 50-mile hike with a heavy back-pack.

Things went worse for you if you didn't take it seriously and keep a straight face. It was an unwritten rule: *Never smile or laugh when you're being chewed out by an upperclassman.* To wipe the smiles and giggles off our faces, we were ordered to march the giggles into the latrine and flush them down the toilet. We had to say, "Smiles, ten hut! Forward … march! One, two, three, four!" – literally pretending that we were wiping the smiles off our face and into the toilet. This silly little game was supposed to be part of our character training, teaching us discipline. To me it was such kid stuff, but some people actually broke down over this.

In the barracks with us at Lackland AFB were two French cadets training in the United States to be pilots in the French air force. One of them didn't understand English very well, so he had a tough time with the discipline. One of the upperclassman was really giving him a hard time, and finally one evening he just cracked. The French military issued shoes that were very dull and difficult to shine. Sitting on his bunk trying to shine his dull shoes, the cadet burst out into tears. Obviously the pressures of the training, the language barrier, and the culture shock were getting the better of him. (I doubt it was truly about the shoes.) Before we knew it, he was crying uncontrollably. A lot of us witnessed this, but it was compassionate Keith who came to the rescue. He sat on the bunk next to the French cadet, put his arm around him, and said, "Here, let me help you." Then he took the cadet's shoes and started spit shining them. That was classic Keith.

After three months, we finished our cadet training at Lackland and were assigned to various bases. I was stationed for the next six months at Marana Air Base in Arizona, between Tucson and Phoenix, and training at Darr Aero Tech, a civilian contract school with civilian pilot instructors.

We started our training in a Super Cub PA-18. It was a distinctly yellow plane that looked like a Piper Cub, but it had a little bigger engine and was fully aerobatic. It was the airplane we would solo in – eventually. To get to that point, however, we had to average about eight hours of dual flying with our civilian flight instructor, Skip Henderson. After we soloed and flew the required flight hours in the Cub, and after we gained valuable experience, we transitioned to the T-6 "Texan", a World War II vintage training aircraft with a radial engine and retractable landing gear, quite a handful after the cub.

Aviation Cadet Class 54G at Marana Air Base, Arizona May 1953 (L-R) Marve Whitman, Gerald Hilton, Ebb Harris, Instructor "Skip" Henderson (kneeling) and the author with PA-18

Four of us – Marv Whiteman, Ebb Harris, Gerald "Jug" Hilton, and I – were Skip's students, and that bond has lasted 60 years now. The four of us have renewed our friendships at each class reunion, starting at our 25th in Las Vegas and continuing every five years since then. The four of us sit together, have our pictures taken, and reminisce about our early flying careers. Ebb retired as a pilot for Lockheed Aircraft Corporation in Burbank, California; he and his wife, June, now live in Southern California. Gerald retired, and he and his wife, Gloria, run a bed and breakfast on Highway 6 & 34 half way between Omaha and Denver in Cambridge, Nebraska. Marv took over his father's manufacturing company and after retiring lives with his wife, Carol, in McCall, Idaho, and live close to Ebb and June in Southern California during wintertime.

(L-R) Gerald Hilton, Marve Whitman, Ebb Harris and author Bob Wearley in front of Korean War era F-86 Jet Fighter during USAF Cadet Class 54G reunion at Luke Air Force Base in April, 2004

The instrument flying portion of our training took place in the backseat of the.T-6, which had a retractable hood that covered the canopy, so you couldn't see out and instead had to rely solely on the instruments. The instructor sat in the front seat and observed your performance, acting as a safety pilot to ensure that you didn't get into trouble. The T-6 was a handful to fly, by anyone's standards. But I really took to the instruments. It was a fun airplane, even though it was a tail dragger and accomplishing a clean, three-point landing was a challenge. My instructors decided I had completed this part of the instruction so well that I should consider going into the Air Defense Command (ADC) after I graduated and got my wings. In the ADC, flying an F-86D or other "all-weather interceptor", a pilot had to (as the name implies) intercept incoming bombers in all types of weather. I wasn't so sure about getting assigned to the ADC, but because of my knack for instruments, they really pushed me to try. This advice was encouraging to say the least.

Romance in the USAF

Handling the plane's instruments wasn't the only thing I took to like a duck takes to water. It was also during my hitch in Marana that Ruth and I rekindled the passing interest we'd once held for each other.

I received a call from my sister, Doris, who told me that she, her friends Joan and Dorothy Roemke, and Ruth Meyer were going to San Diego to visit Ruth's brother, Fritz, who was in the Marines. They intended to travel there by train. A brilliant idea came to me: I realized that I could arrange to see Ruth again if they took the train to Tucson first. So I invited them to borrow my car and drive the rest of the way to California. The plan worked. I managed to line up three cadets as dates for the other girls. I saved Ruth for myself.

Ruth must have been impressed with polished looks, and being in uniform certainly allowed me to present a striking image rather than that of just a boy from Woodburn. She immediately gravitated toward me. Maybe she saw this hometown boy in a new light – no longer just the kid from down the street, but soon to be an Air Force officer flying jets. Ruth and I had dated a bit in high school, but nothing serious had ever come out of it. It must have been this stop at the base that changed her mind about me.

Things heated up between us in the months to follow, and we wrote back and forth and saw each other when I was home in Woodburn on leave.

After I finished training at Marana, I was sent to Williams Air Force Base ("Willy", as we fondly referred to it) in Chandler, Arizona, just south of Phoenix. Willy was a training base for single-engine jets. My ambitions were high – those instructors had planted a seed when they'd suggested joining the ADC – and I was more than happy to be there, for one reason in particular: I wanted to be a fighter pilot!

When my graduation from pilot training at Willy crept up, my mother, Aunt Leona, Doris, and Ruth planned to attend. It was a beautiful ceremony held in the chapel. Clarence Gerig, father of my childhood friend Leon and now pastor of a missionary church in Phoenix, also attended with his wife. When the ceremonies were over, we were allowed to put on our bars and our wings. I asked my mother to put on my wings, and Doris put on one bar. Ruth put on the other, just as if she were already family. I was in love. What Ruth didn't know was that I was planning to ask her that evening to marry me.

Doris and I drove in to the town of Chandler, where she helped me pick out the engagement ring. She cautioned me that I shouldn't just give it to Ruth outright, that first I should romance her a bit. So Ruth and I had dinner at a local steakhouse, and like most couples in love would do at the time, we later drove to a remote area atop a peak called A Mountain and parked. It was a beautiful view overlooking Phoenix. I asked Ruth to reach into the glove box, where I'd hidden the engagement ring. She gave a squeal of delight—I think she was truly surprised. For my part, I was thrilled (and to be honest, a bit relieved) that she accepted.

Back when I'd joined the Air Force, Ruth had been interested in becoming a flight attendant. Once we were engaged, though, she forgot all about that ambition. We both really wanted to get married, but at first we didn't agree on the timing. I had little doubt that the wedding would happen one day, but I wanted to save some money and pay off my debts first. Ruth, of course, had other ideas. She often said to me that all she dreamed about was having a little house with a white picket fence and two children.

I encouraged her to follow my plan, saying, "Ruth, go into flight attendant school. I'll continue in the USAF. We can save some money, and then we can get married." But that didn't sit too well with my new fiancée. She cried. I gave in. Making her happy was my primary goal, as it would be for the next 41 years.

Ruth went back home to Woodburn and immediately started planning our wedding. I was sent to Nellis AFB in Las Vegas to start gunnery training in the F-86, which was the fighter predominately used during the Korean War. We wrote to each other every day.

I had a break from F-86 gunnery training that following Memorial Day 1954, so I drove home in my 1950 Club Coupe for a short visit. We worked on our wedding plans, and before I returned to Nellis AFB, I bought another Chevy, a 1954 Bel Air, from my brother-in-law Ben Closson, a sales manager for Parent Chevrolet in nearby New Haven. My father used to buy his cars from Harry Parent, back when the business was in Woodburn. In fact, just months before he died, he purchased a new 1936 Chevrolet, which I "cut my teeth on" as a 16-year-old when I got my driver's license. I was pleased to continue the tradition.

I graduated from fighter gunnery in early July. I had a month off to get married before I had to report to West Palm Beach AFB in Florida for C-54 (DC-4) training at the Military Air Transport Service (MATS) training base. I was a fighter pilot, albeit a disgruntled one. Since we were trained to fly fighters, I was not a happy camper flying multiengine aircraft. Half our class at Nellis, including me, had been sent to MATS to supply pilots for MATS' ability to support brushfire wars before they spread – a lesson learned from Korea.

2nd Lt. Bob Nass, Instructor, 1st Lt. Don Pape former Korean War POW, 2nd Lt. Ron Hutchinson, and author 2nd Lt. Bob Wearley

Life as a Husband, a Pilot, and a Father

Ruth and I were married July 24, 1954, in Christ Lutheran Church in Woodburn. We decided to honeymoon in Michigan and spend a few days there; our trip would be shorter than we would have liked, but at least we could take our time driving to West Palm Beach. First we drove to Houghton Lake in Michigan, where Ben and his wife, Eileen (my half sister), had a cottage. Ruth and I found a motel. We spent our time visiting with family and waterskiing, until our planned three-day trip had turned into a weeklong adventure.

Eventually we did move on. I had to report back to the base. On our way down to Florida, we stayed two nights with Don Glockner in Portsmouth. Don's dad was a Chevrolet dealer there and so, of course, Don had a brand-new 1955 Chevy. He decided to follow us down to West Palm, where he was also assigned. That way, we could stop in Charleston, South Carolina, to look over the Air Force base there – because after our C-54 training in West Palm, we'd be relocating to Charleston AFB.

During my two months of training in West Palm, Ruth and I rented a neat apartment in Palm Beach, just a block and a half from the ocean. It was off-season, and the apartment was reasonably priced. Ruth went down to the beach every day. I was the only married one out of the group, so the guys usually came to our apartment to hang out. In fact, one time they planned a party and forgot to tell us. People just started showing up! What could we do? So we gathered up some hot dogs and buns and a case of beer, and we headed for the beach, where we built a fire, (those were the days before environmental restrictions) and drank the beer, and sang songs, with Keith Hall playing his ukulele (this was before he became a tee-totaling Christian). Ruth was in seventh heaven. She was the only woman in the group, and the guys treated her like a princess.

After graduation from our training as C-54 co-pilots, we moved to Charleston, where we flew primarily to Africa and Europe with the C-54 and later the C-121 Constellation – the Connie aircraft that would become so pivotal in my life. Life at Charleston AFB in 1955 was idyllic. I was a second lieutenant, and with her great social skills, Ruth became treasurer of the Wives' Club.

Not long after we arrived, the Troop Carrier squadron (formerly located across the field from the MATS squadron) moved overseas, and the 41st Air Transport Squadron took over the entire base. Lieutenant Jim Irvine, a proficient pilot who flew C-119s, was a short-timer who didn't have enough service time left to make it worthwhile for the Air Force to deploy him overseas, so he was transferred to our squadron, the 41st ATS. When the squadron commander held his next monthly Commander's Call in the Operations area, Jim was quietly standing alone. I didn't recognize him at the time (although I thought he looked familiar somehow), but I saw that he was new to the squadron. I had plenty of buddies there, guys who had been through pilot training with me. In fact, most of us had been airmen together and were in pilot training together, too. Here I was, surrounded by my friends, while Jim looked so lonely all by himself. I went over to introduce myself.

Jim and his wife, Joan, became our fast friends. We lived very near each other, and the one thing we had in common at the time was that neither of us had children yet ... just dogs. Ruth and I were the proud owners of a Boxer named Penny, and the Irvines had a Boston terrier named Doosie. We started inviting each other over for dinner and cards, and the friendship immediately took off.

It wasn't until later, when Jim was ready to leave the Air Force and become a pilot for American Airlines, that it dawned on me: We had met quite a few years earlier, long before he was transferred to my MATS squadron. Jim and Joan were all packed up and ready to leave, and they had come over to our house to say good-bye. During the course of our conversation, it suddenly hit me how and where we had met before. I excused myself, went into the bedroom, and rummaged through my jewelry box. Cufflinks, military bars, wings ... There it was! The card that had been handed to me along with a dollar bill – three years before, when I gave the recently graduated officer his first salute. It read:

Lieutenant Jim Irvine, United States Air Force

Even when I brought the card to Jim, he remembered the person from that incident as just some scrawny airman who had walked up and saluted him. He was very surprised to realize it was me. Somehow fate had made our paths cross … twice. Side bar here; when Jim told his boys he was going to be in a book they ask the title and Jim said; "why the Jim Irvine story of course".

After the Irvine's moved on, Ruth gave birth to our first child, Scott Alan, at Charleston Naval Hospital in February 1956. Twenty-four hours after his birth, though, little Scott lost his battle with toxemia. We buried him in the Christ Lutheran Church cemetery in Woodburn. Not long after we lost Scott, we found out that Ruth was pregnant again, and in March 1957 we were overjoyed when our first daughter, Robin, was born.

Just before Robin's birth, I was involved in that fateful Connie accident in Saudi Arabia. Like a newborn, it took me nine months to get back to flying status, and during that time, I started reconsidering my future in the Air Force.

American Airlines Beckons

Jim encouraged me to join him at American Airlines if I decided to leave the Air Force. The idea of ending up a retired airline captain and later having the opportunity to pursue my entrepreneurial instincts, while not flying in my off time, as some Airline Pilots do. This was very appealing. I wouldn't make a lot of money, at first as a co-pilot in the airlines. But I'd known I was interested in flying for an airline since the day Jim and I had crossed the field to look over an Eastern Airlines Connie that was sitting there, ready for an engine change.

During that time, Charleston was a joint military/civilian base. The civilian side of the field was also home to several commercial airlines. So Jim and I just walked out on the ramp and over to the other side, striking up a conversation with the mechanics who were working on an Eastern Airlines Constellation type aircraft. I will never forget them joking with us about how captains only flew commercial planes to pay their income taxes – how they all had other jobs, too. Back then, airline captains flying the slower propeller aircraft would need to take only several trips a month to reach their maximum monthly limit on flying time. In fact, I later met a TWA captain living in Bermuda who would hop a plane to New York to pilot his flights to Europe once or twice a month, just to get his time in. He probably had at least two weeks off every month.

I suppose that kind of luxury and the opportunity to make a lot more money are what beckoned me to apply at American Airlines. I could visualize myself starting a business while I kept a "part-time job" flying for a commercial airline. Ruth wasn't so sure, but still we geared up in preparation for that move. I was only making about $7,000 a year as a first lieutenant. In the Air Force, you could easily live on that. I even bought a cheaper car to lower our operating costs. We spent $60 a month on an apartment, and $30 worth of groceries could go a long way. Civilian life, however, would be different.

In the fall of 1956, when I was 23 years old, I applied to and was interviewed by American Airlines. I was hired – pending a physical. Once again, a doctor was all that was standing between me and my heart's desire. All that was left to do was pass my physical, which was scheduled for after the first of the year.

I was a very favorable candidate to become an American Airlines pilot, considering my multiengine experience and the many hours of flight time I had racked up at my young age. For this final step in the application process, I took a commercial flight to Fort Wayne, and my brother-in-law Ben loaned me his brand-new 1957 Chevy to drive up to Chicago's Midway Airport. I checked into a motel near the airport and went in the next morning for my physical. I was supposed to be wearing my back brace because of the back injuries I'd sustained in the Connie accident, but I had intentionally left it in the motel room.

During the physical, the American Airlines doctor was taking my blood pressure, a stethoscope in his ears, when he looked up and noticed the relatively fresh scars on my forehead. He asked me if I had been recently hospitalized. I confessed that I'd been in an accident. He said he would need to see my records. That's when my heart started pounding so hard, I probably blew his ears off. I couldn't help it – I came clean.

"Doc," I said, "I suffered a broken back and had multiple lacerations on my forehead that required extensive sutures."

The doctor practically blew his top. He grabbed my medical records and exclaimed, "You didn't say anything about that in here!"

When I'd filled out the medical history form, I'd skipped the part about the back injury, on the advice of the doctor who had treated me at Charleston Naval Hospital. Well aware of the fact that I was going to apply at American Airlines, the Navy doctor had suggested that I omit this information on the medical history form. By the time I'd start flying for the airline, he explained, my back would be healed. He even made me an offer: If there were any problems with my American Airlines physical, his family had stock in the company and might be able to help me out.

So much for following that recommendation.

My pounding heart soon started to sink. I left the American Airlines doctor and, as instructed, went immediately to the Human Resources department, where I told them the whole story. Their reply: Don't worry about it. My acceptance would be based exclusively on the medical exam and not on what I had failed to write down on the medical history form. I felt better but still a bit guilty. I had a notion that my dishonesty would come back to bite me later.

What could I do? I headed back to Charleston and waited. A few days later, I received the "Dear John" letter from American Airlines. The letter stated that, because of the recession, the airline had consolidated three classes into one, and they simply had too many applicants. I was devastated. After all, I'd thought of myself as a prime candidate.

At this point, I could do one of two things: get out of the United States Air Force and reapply at American Airlines when the recession ended and when I was in top physical form, or stay in the Air Force. I decided that the latter choice would be prudent, primarily because I did not know if complications with my health would surface later on as a result of the Connie accident. So I stayed on at Charleston AFB.

And then I was reassigned ... to Bermuda.

Bermuda Bound

As is the case for many people, there are certain milestones that changed my life – this way or that? This choice or the other? The Connie accident was one of them. That accident kept me from working for a commercial airline, from making a decision that would have taken me in an entirely different direction in life.

When I did get back on flying status, I was number one on the base as a first lieutenant and could be considered for an overseas assignment. When an assignment came in for Bermuda, my squadron commander, now–Lieutenant Colonel Bickford, said, "Bob, a bird in the hand is better than two in the bush."

I nearly turned down Bermuda for personal reasons. Ruth was pregnant again! But I took the squadron commander's advice and accepted the Bermuda assignment. Who knew? Perhaps if I waited, I would end up with some awful assignment in a place like Thule, Greenland, on a one-year unaccompanied tour!

As I would soon find out, Bermuda, on the other hand, offered not only warm beaches but a world of opportunity for the entire family.

ASSIGNMENT: BERMUDA

FIVE OF US – all base operations duty officers – arrived in Bermuda approximately at the same time. I was assigned to the 1604 Air Base Group, Kindley Air Force Base, as an assistant base operations officer on a three-year assignment.

I arrived that first time without my family. Ruth, who was pregnant with our second daughter, Roxanne, could not travel long distances. But living in Bermuda sounded glamorous and exciting, so she agreed to stay back in the States for the time being, with her mother in Woodburn, while I made my temporary home at the bachelor officers' quarters (BOQ) on base. We would make a real home as soon as she and our daughters could join me.

One evening while on duty at base operations, after I'd been in Bermuda only a short time, I received a call from Woodburn. It was my sister-in-law, Darlene Meyer. Ruth had had the baby – another daughter, just fifteen months younger than Robin. But our Roxanne was not doing well. The doctor had given Ruth a shot of Demerol but had misjudged the dosage or timing and as a result Roxie was experiencing breathing problems. I immediately started to make arrangements for an emergency leave. I learned that there was a military C-121, a Connie, inbound from Lajes Air Base in the Azores. After refueling at our base, it would be on its way to Charleston, South Carolina. I caught that flight and then boarded a commercial flight to Fort Wayne. When I arrived in Indiana, I was so very grateful to find that Ruth and Roxanne were doing just fine. Still, this scare showed me how important it was to have my family near.

When it came time to return to Bermuda, Ruth's brother Fritz, Darlene, and Ruth drove me down to Wright Patterson Air Force Base in Dayton, Ohio, where I caught a military flight to McGuire AFB in New Jersey. The C-54 from Kindley AFB – the military version of the civilian DC-4 – was there, ready to return to Bermuda. Colonel Cole, Kindley's deputy wing commander, was the aircraft commander; he would be the one to transmit a flight plan to the FAA for clearance of our route back to Bermuda. When I walked up and, without introducing myself, asked the colonel for permission to hitch a ride back to Bermuda, his reply was; "Sure, Bob." Then, without another word, Colonel Cole scribbled my name, rank, and serial number on the flight plan form.

I was stunned. I thought, *What in the world did I do wrong? Why did the deputy wing commander know my name, rank, and serial number?* Later I found out that he had a photographic memory – he knew the names and serial numbers of all the people in his command. He remembered frequencies, courses, etc. from all the routes he had ever flown. Colonel Cole eventually became General Cole, for obvious reasons.

I went back to my duties in Bermuda and found a house for the four of us off North Road in the Devonshire Parish, with a lovely view of the ocean. Bermuda looked like a dream come true: The duty was light, the weather was perfect, and soon I would have my family with me again. Thanks to my shift work, once Ruth and our daughters joined me, we spent a significant amount of time just enjoying life: making new friends, partying, snorkeling, water skiing, and taking advantage of the subtropical climate.

Of course, I had to work, too. As a first lieutenant and duty officer, I reported to base ops, the hub of activity at any U.S. Air Force base. It's the pilot's first stop after a flight. Once he is transported from his aircraft to base ops, the pilot closes out the existing flight plan and either files a new plan for his next flight out or makes RON arrangements (to "remain over night"). I was responsible (along with my counterparts) for signing the clearance for pilots after we approved the flight plan.

Base ops also housed the navigation department, along with a weather station that would query the pilots who came in from the States or the Azores, for example, to learn about the weather they had encountered during their flight. The crew navigator's weather reports were critical information that would be given to other pilots going out.

Unlike the technology we're used to today, where we get the weather in a heartbeat via satellite, crew navigators at that time had to draw the weather on paper by hand. They take note of the winds aloft, the air pressures, the temperatures, etc., and radioed in from their aircraft while in flight. In an era before the spread of computers, this was a painstaking procedure; with only two hours of ground time, the crew navigator typically did not have time to make up a flight plan for the outbound flight. So the navigators assigned to base ops would take that data and make up a handwritten flight plan with the necessary alternate requirements, fuel load, etc.

Some of the navigators were quite clever and creative, and some were very artistic. They sketched weather drawings that depicted clouds and lightning. One man in particular could draw clouds so that, if you looked at them closely, you could see the outline of a nude woman. One suchcreation was posted in the weather office, where all the crews got to enjoy the fruits of his efforts, and it stayed there for some time. Of course, there were no female pilots or navigators back then. I wonder how long that type of sketch would stay posted on the wall today. Would this now be considered sexual harassment? Probably, but no harm was meant. It was just a bit of fun.

At Kindley, the base ops office layout consisted of a desk and chair behind an operations counter where the dispatcher sat. The control towered call the dispatcher, who notified the duty officer of an inbound plane or an aircraft that was "running up" before takeoff, which could possibly throw coral rocks out on the runway. When that occurred, one of the duty officer's responsibilities was to hop in a truck and take a look at the situation, calling in the sweepers to clean it up if necessary. While the job wasn't exactly glamorous, it did allow for some downtime on slow nights – time to read, sleep, etc. Just as flying multiengine aircraft has been described as hours and hours of boredom followed by a few moments of stark terror, so too was a day in the life of a base ops duty officer: lots of mundane stuff punctuated with an occasional emergency incident.

Case in point: Kindley AFB, like Charleston, was a joint military/civilian base, with the civilian terminal on the opposite side of the field. One evening, a civilian airliner landed with an emergency. As a result, the runways had to be shut down, leaving other passengers stranded on the runway. I responded right away by calling the tower to get some buses out there to transport those passengers to the civilian terminal. Then I dispatched emergency vehicles to the scene to tow the aircraft off the runway, out of the path of incoming military aircraft. These were the types of situations where, as the wing commander's representative, you were expected to step up to the plate until the proper authorities could get to the scene and take over.

At the other end of the spectrum were those long stretches of downtime, such as one calm evening when I was on duty. It was unusually quiet and there were no aircraft moving anywhere, so I had some time to read while at my post. I just happened to pick up a magazine whose cover featured Howard Hughes.

It was the late fifties, and this was a first glimpse into Hughes's strange and interesting life. The article talked about his money, his movies, his flying, and the speed records he'd set in the H-1 Racer. It said he was a handsome man, considered by some the most eligible bachelor in America. All this piqued my interest. I was fascinated by his vast achievements in aviation. According to the article, Hughes was a self-made aviator, much like Burt Rutan, except that Hughes had the financial resources to buy the talent required to achieve great things, whereas Rutan had to scrape together what finances he could to achieve what he did, becoming a pioneer designer of unique aircraft, the record breaking, Voyager that flew around the world without refueling, and the sub-orbital space plane SpaceShipOne, which won the Asari X-Prize in 2004. Unlike Hughes, Rutan was a hands-on type of guy, his own aeronautical engineer. He did the best he could with what he had. Hughes, on the other hand, was larger than life.

After reading the article, I regarded Howard Hughes as an enigma. He was one of the "big boys" in the world of aviation, and I was impressed and inspired. And so it was that I first became intrigued by the multibillionaire. In my wildest dreams, I had no idea I would one day be working for the man.

Seeking a Challenge

For the time being, however, I had my responsibilities as a base operations duty officer, which was not very challenging and certainly not a résumé enhancer. I was always looking for greater challenges, for opportunities to expand beyond this role and to make myself more marketable in the civilian life to which I would one day return. Base operations duty officers were assigned various additional duties; mine was as officer in charge (OIC) of the base photography lab. I took the job very seriously and, during the slow evenings at base ops, I took the photo officers' correspondence course, completing it and becoming certified.

Now, during the day, when I was not on duty, I sometimes went out with a speed-graphic camera and took pictures for the base newspaper. When the evening was slow, I called the control tower and left the number to the base photo lab, telling the crew where I'd be in case they needed me. I asked the noncommissioned officer in charge (NCOIC) of the base photo lab, Tech Sergeant Mitz, to leave out any outdated paper and not to throw out the used chemicals at night. That way I could go down there and print pictures, without using "tax payers money for new chemicals and paper".

I shot a wedding for an enlisted man who was in the chapel choir, and I obviously didn't charge him since I was" essentially in training", and using a government camera – it was good experience for me. I used the outdated papers and chemicals, which were still perfectly serviceable although they were deemed unfit for official government use. I put together an impressive photo album for this particular bride and groom, who would not otherwise have been able to afford wedding photos.

Then someone criticized me for using government materials for private use. I informed this person that I was doing on-the-job training – that I did use a government camera and that the outdatedpaper, film, and chemicals all were going to be thrown away. Though it was logical to me, I knew I could be reprimanded officially for taking home even a pen that had *U.S. Government Property* printed on it. There was a saying in the military that "stealing" from the government was part of our "fringe benefits", Just like any company, the Air Force needed to stop pilferage, but I wasn't pilfering anything except the use of the camera, and I did, indeed, consider that on-the-job training. Using the camera as often as I could made me a much better photo officer. When I initially became a photo lab OIC, I was a young, very green First Lieutentant, doing my best to manage personnel. The enlisted men pulled every trick in the book on me.

That soon changed. I figured out what was going on and quickly gained the confidence I needed. In addition to my position at the photo lab, I became the decontamination officer, which meant that if there was an accident involving an aircraft that carried a nuclear weapon – a type of incident that would be code-named "Broken Arrow" – I had to leap into action. With the possibility of radiation leakage, people might have to undergo a decontamination process to mitigate exposure to radiation. We'd have to set up a portable shower – a decontamination booth. I took that job seriously, writing up an ops plan and ordering materials so that we would be able to respond decisively. Sometimes a transport aircraft – for example, a C-124 (propeller-driven aircraft nicknamed "Big Shaky") –come in with an engine out or some other emergency. If it were carrying a nuclear weapon or transporting nuclear materials, we'd have to be prepared for any contingency. In the event that Big Shaky had an accident, we had to be prepared to set up instantly for decontamination.

When the base protocol officer, a friend of mine, was being reassigned back in the States I became interested in the protocol position. He recommended me to the wing commander, who interviewed me. Then I was reassigned from base operations to being the officer in charge of protocol – aide-de-camp to the wing commander.

Protocol is very important in the military. We never knew what high-ranking military or civilian person we might meet, yet each had to be treated with the appropriate respect and deference. The protocol office had an NCOIC by the name of Sergeant Art Royce and a group of airmen who functioned as our staff car drivers. We had four to six staff cars on call, always available for the many VIPs who would land unexpectedly. My job was to meet these VIPs at any hour of the day or night. If the VIP on board was a congressman or a four-star general, I notified the wing commander and he came with me to meet the aircraft; if the VIP didn't have a high enough rank, the wing commander didn't bother getting up during the night. Many times, I was awakened at 3:00 in the morning with the message that a Code 4 was due within the hour – a general was arriving. I immediately jumped out of bed like a fireman, sliped into my fresh, clean uniform and highly polished shoes, and raced to the base, where I met Sergeant Royce. We positioned ourselves at the bottom of the aircraft steps, in front of a staff car that was waiting to do whatever the general wanted.

If it was the middle of the night, often the VIP chose to stay on board the aircraft and sleep. We stood there the entire time the aircraft was being refueled and until it was on its way. At other times the general might come down and say, "I'd like to go to breakfast, Captain." One particular early morning incident, Major General Kaliber, a native of Lafayette, Indiana, came down the steps and said, "Let's go to breakfast." There were no cell phones back then. In fact, we didn't even have "bricks" yet (the heavy two-way walkie-talkies that key personnel carried around in the years that followed). So I just whispered to Sergeant Royce, telling him to call the Officers' Club and inform them that the general was on his way.

The conversation at breakfast was quite interesting. General Kaliber lectured me on politics: "If we don't find a way to contain communism, Captain, you'll end up working the salt mines in Detroit." He also referred to the rivalry between the Navy and the Air Force, criticizing about how the Air Force flew its planes over aircraft carriers surrounded by support ships, all of which made a perfect 'bull's eye'. That's how vulnerable he thought aircraft carriers were, how easy he thought it would be for any bomber to drop a nuclear bomb on one of them. It just goes to show that not all strategic plans take into account the rapid advance of technology. General Kaliber was simply rehashing an issue that arose in the mid-1920s, when the Air Force and the Navy were constantly at odds over budgeting: The Navy wanted more battleships and aircraft carriers, and the Air Force wanted more airplanes. Back then, Air Force General Billy Mitchell, much to the chagrin of the Navy, proved his point by bombing and sinking some old World War I battleships.

General Kaliber wasn't the only tough cookie to pass through Kindley. Bermuda was an ideal stop for congressman and generals looking to take a short vacation. We had half a dozen cottages on the base for their use, always immaculately kept and prepared for arrival at any time, since these guests always seemed to require VIP treatment. In fact, in many ways the protocol job prepared me to deal with pretentious people and not to be awestruck or intimidated by them. I'll admit, I did notice that the politicians were a bit more conciliatory than the generals. They were used to pandering to the voters, whereas the generals felt they had to demonstrate results and respond to a higher command (if only to secure a promotion). I'm reminded of the movie *Strategic Air Command*, starring Jimmy Stewart as a colonel, the aircraft commander of a B-36 bomber. When the actor portraying four-star general Curtis LeMay (the real-life "father" of the Strategic Air Command) walks up to an airplane with a cigar in his mouth, a mechanic says to the colonel, "Sir, he's not supposed to smoke within 50 feet of the aircraft. The airplane might blow up." The colonel replied, "It wouldn't dare!" The generals and some of the politicians we saw at Kindley inspired that same kind of strict deference.

One politician was clearly an exception to this rule: Harry Truman. Before I became a protocol officer, the former president flew in to vacation on the island. He was staying at a friend's cottage – not a glamorous or elaborate home, but a simple, ordinary cottage. One of our protocol drivers, Airman Klackley, a well-liked gentleman from Kentucky, was assigned to drive President Truman whenever and wherever he wanted. Klackley later showed us a much-prized picture of himself with the president, who was standing by the car and waving his hat. He appeared to be like a very personable man. In fact, he threw out an invitation to anyone on the base who would like to walk with him early in the mornings. One of my biggest regrets in life is that I did not take the opportunity, that I never went over to his cottage and took him up on that offer. Several of the base's doctors did, and one of them recalled a conversation where he asked, "Mr. Truman, how do you make decisions?"

The president responded, "Young man, don't they teach you that in the military?"

Taking a Stand

In Bermuda, there were plenty of avenues to explore, plenty of opportunities to broaden and sharpen my entrepreneurial instincts, plenty of ways to hone my management skills. From a very early age, I was always in the midst of organizing some event or group. While I was stationed in Bermuda, I had the time to enhance these particular qualities.

Although various religions were well represented by a number of Bermudan churches, there was no church of the Lutheran denomination, which my family had always followed. When I first arrived in Bermuda, I was receiving correspondence from the Lutheran Armed Service Commission. The materials explained how to conduct church services and offered daily devotional booklets to people serving in the military in isolated areas. The organization was always asking for feedback, so I wrote some letters explaining that there were no Lutheran churches on the island and that the base chapel had only one Protestant chaplain (who was not a Lutheran) and one Catholic chaplain assigned to it.

The next thing I knew, I was in a meeting with the wing commander. He said sternly, "Bob, I see you've been writing letters ... again."

He was referring to an earlier letter I had written that was published in *Aviation Weekly*; it defended Francis Gary Powers, the U-2 pilot who was shot down over Russia in 1960, raising havoc and jeopardizing the planned summit in Paris between President Eisenhower and Premier Khrushchev. My letter to the magazine was in response to a previous writer's criticism of Powers' actions and suggestion that Powers should have used the "poison pin" (a pin laden with curare) to commit suicide after he was captured rather than submit to interrogation. I also took issue with the writer's opinion that Powers was overpaid for information he gave to intelligence agencies.

Had Powers acted inappropriately? I found the very suggestion offensive. First of all, nobody knew what Powers' instructions were with regard to being shot down, and second, there was no way you could put a monetary value on the information that was collected by flights over Russia during the Cold War.

The earlier discussion also proposed giving an award to one particular intelligence agency for its handling of the Powers issue. But when there are a number of intelligence agencies involved in an incident like this, and by necessity many of them are operating in secret, how can you possibly single out just one to be worthy of an award?

All in all, I thought this armchair intelligence "expert" was way off base, and I was itching to tell him so. When I finished writing the letter, I signed it *Bob Wearley, Captain, USAF* (a dumb, naïve thing to do, I might add). I did receive a message from a gentleman somewhere in the United States, saying, "Thank you, Bob, for doing what all of us should have done ... speak up!" My wing commander, however, was not of the same mind. He objected to the way I had signed the letter. It appeared, he said, as though I were speaking on behalf of the Air Force. At the time – remember, the Cold War was just reaching fever pitch – the government placed a lot of emphasis on "muzzling" the military in order to avoid any such impropriety. Luckily for me, higher command did not notice this (or at least did not force the issue), or I could have been in serious trouble.

As it turned out, I got into more trouble for the letter I sent requesting a Lutheran chaplain than for my response to the Powers incident. I soon learned that religious activities were not all that high on the wing commander's agenda. He was very specific in his reply: We had enough chaplains on the island. He likened my actions to a complaint that we didn't have enough lawyers in the advocates office!

My response was clear and to the point: "Sir, it isn't quite like that." I explained that I had been receiving literature about how to serve Lutheran worshippers, since our needs were not being met at the base or anywhere on the island. Certainly any other faith might put forth the same legitimate request. I suggested a new arrangement: Chaplain Chris Thearle, who was stationed at my former base in Charleston, South Carolina, could come to Bermuda via the regular Connie flights between Charleston, Bermuda, and the Azores. If he were sent over on a monthly schedule, he could conduct church services and offer Holy Communion before catching a return flight home.

I felt this was an issue between me and the Lutheran Armed Service Commission, and I explained this to the wing commander. Nothing more was said about the incident. But shortly afterward, Chaplain Chris (as we fondly referred to him) was assigned to Bermuda. We became lifelong friends, staying in touch even when he was later assigned to the Air Force Academy. Years later, while I was marketing director for Fort Wayne International Airport, I found myself at an air cargo conference in Portland, Oregon. Chaplain Chris was living nearby in Salem, and I made contact with him. We had not seen each other since 1962. Today, retired USAFR Colonel Chris Thearle is also a retired Lutheran minister.

Getting into Trouble

Of course, I wasn't always taking a stand or kneeling for worship. In a place like Bermuda, there were plenty of opportunities to get into trouble.

No question about it: Like every couple, Ruth and I had dozens of arguments and fights during our 41 years of marriage. But in Bermuda, we did our fair share of partying, which laid the groundwork for greater discord.

It seems as though I knew Ruth Meyer all my life. Born January 9, 1933, in Fort Wayne, Indiana, she was the youngest child and only daughter of Adena and Fred W. Meyer. Her brother Harry was nine years older, and Fritz was seven years older. At first Ruth was "just one of the neighborhood kids". She played in the same backyards, attended the same schools as me. She was always a bit of a tomboy, though she went on to become Woodburn High School's first homecoming queen. She was my partner on the cheerleading squad, the little darling of Woodburn High. She had it all: poise, good looks, personality. She was smart and pretty and a loved to dance – always the hit of the party.

"Ruth was our little princess," says Fritz now, "and Harry and I did everything we could to protect her. I vividly recall playing basketball in our yard. We'd always block the other players so she could get a shot in. Our father was especially fond of her, and even bought her a frilly little dress when we were smack dab in the middle of the Great Depression. Our family surely could not afford such an extravagance, but if Ruth wanted something, Daddy made sure she got it." As her husband, I tried to do the same.

We'd been married five good years when things became difficult. We had two little girls, and maybe we'd married too young. Or maybe it was just a difference in our personalities. Either way, we began to argue a lot.

In the Air Force, I knew of situations where guys sowed their wild oats early and *then* got married; perhaps they had not attended church initially, but later they became good family men and solid, devoted husbands. More often, though I saw guys who were straight arrows like me, who had always attended church and had strong family values – but in later years they started fooling around. Never in my wildest dreams did I think I would become one of them. I could not believe that I, too, had fallen into that "PRODIGAL" lifestyle.

I've observed that sometimes, the people who are too vocal in their professions of virtue and too sanctimonious in their attitude are the ones who fall the farthest and the hardest. I've since thought that perhaps this was my problem. In cadet training, some of my fellow cadets used to call me the "Hoosier virgin". It didn't bother me at the time, but years later when I succumbed to temptation, I could not help thinking that these same people would have been very disappointed in me.

At our 50th pilot training reunion at Williams Air Force Base in Phoenix, where we'd been commissioned and received our wings, six of us veteran pilots and our wives were seated around a table. When someone suggested we pray before our meal, I jumped in and volunteered. No one seemed surprised; everyone knew about my years of commitment to my faith. And yet during our meal I also shared with those at the table that I had a pretty dark side to my life, a side that I was not proud of. Marv Whiteman and his wife, Carol, exchanged a look of shock, and Marv blurted out, deadly serious, "I cannot believe that! Not you, Bob!"

That kind of remark cut me deeply. I guess it was hard, even for some of the people closest to me, to put the light and the dark sides together and see the whole person. While in the military, when I stayed the course, I'd had a very positive influence on those people. But when a holy attitude is fake, only skin deep, it becomes hypocritical and sanctimonious, and it does no good. Too often my holiness was just that, and in my personal life it offered nothing but hurt.

Eventually I talked with Chaplain Chris about our problems, and he tried to help Ruth and me work out our differences. The lesson might be that my faith was in fact weak. I had not allowed the Holy Spirit to live within me. If the Holy Spirit really does permeate every fiber in your body, you don't have a problem resisting temptation. When we have that faith, God gives us even more strength. "Yield not to temptation, for yielding is sin," said an old hymn I remember from my early years. And once I learned to keep this saying alive in my heart and soul, I never cheated again. Ruth died, at the age of 62, on August 20, 1995.

Moving On Up

When we were reassigned to Travis Air Force Base, a Military Air Transport Service (MATS) base in northern California, near Vacaville and Fairfield, I consulted with the pastor of our new church, who was no Chaplain Chris but still offered some reasonable counseling. I was just 29 years old and looking forward to my next step in the Air Force. Since MATS didn't offer training for jet transports, we went over to Cassel Air Force Base in Merced, which was a Strategic Air Command (SAC) training school and home to B-52 bombers and the air refueling KC-135s. SAC training was a pain because you had to wear a parachute and a helmet, both of which I found very uncomfortable.

Was this a move up? Definitely. At Travis, I was a C-135B pilot, flying on the civilian version of the Boeing 707/720B, a very short period of time before being upgraded to captain/instructor, then flight examiner. I took what I learned in Bermuda and put it to good use at Travis. There were numerous opportunities to share my experience in exercising my protocol abilities – and in having fun and throwing parties, too.

Practical Jokes and "Wearley's Girlies"

Major Henry G. "Guice" Tinsley and his wife, Nancy – Hoosiers like us, from Porter, Indiana – became really good friends of ours at Travis. Guice was a Purdue alumni who had joined the Air Force following graduation. We met the Tinsleys when they were transferred and began looking for a house in Vacaville. When Guice heard we were from Indiana, he sought us out and asked if we were Lutheran. When I answered, "Yes," he said they would see us in church on Sunday morning. From that Sunday on, we made a habit of attending church services and going to the Officers' Club for lunch afterward.

The Tinsley's and Wearley's frequently socialized together, particularly during religious celebrations, and later with the Johnson's. Al and Arlene Johnson arrived at Travis, from Minnesota, after Al's return from an assignment in Iceland. The Johnson's attended the same Lutheran Church that we were attending and the three families became good friends, attending parties at the Officers Club on base etc. On one occasion Al, and I tried to steal a papier-mâché pony – part of the officers' wives' Christmas decorations – out of the Officers' Club. We got caught, of course, and although the squadron commander just thought we were a couple of crazy guys and did his best to protect us, he had to make us pay somehow. We ended up organizing bond drives and other events that boosted morale in our squadron.

Part of our great kinship with the Tinsley's was the fact that we used to pull practical jokes on each other. One of the most memorable was the incident of the rabbit droppings. We had moved on to Tinker AFB in Oklahoma and were living in on-base housing at the time, while Guice was still based at Travis. Our doorbell rang one Saturday evening around 8:00 – it was the day before Easter. There on the doorstep was a box with three rabbits inside. One was brown, one was white, and the third was black. There were rabbit droppings in the bottom of the box mixed with the multicolored Trix cereal. I immediately suspected that Guice had sent the bunnies.

I called the command post and asked if any aircraft had come in from the West Coast that day. Nothing had. Still, I suspected Guise. Perhaps he had put someone on the base up to it? But Guice and I had taken a silent oath: You never admitted that you'd had a practical joke pulled on you. So our hands were tied as we tried to find out who put the rabbits on our doorstep for Guice. We couldn't overtly ask about the prank, and no one in our neighborhood came forward – until one day the silence got to the couple who did it, and the wife spilled the beans at a cocktail party.

Our daughters enjoyed the rabbits during Easter, and then we gave them away. But I saved the rabbit droppings and put them in an official 8" x 12" Air Force envelope and sent it to Major Tinsley at 22nd Air Force Headquarters, where he worked. As he was opening the envelope, his boss – a colonel, no less –walked up, so he was standing there when all the rabbit droppings and Trix cereal dropped out on the desk. It was an embarrassing moment for Guice but a fitting end to his own practical joke ... or so I thought.

Some months later I flew to Travis from Tinker in a C-141 and stayed overnight with Guice and Nancy. The next morning, Guice dropped me off at base operations on his way to work. I got on the crew bus and headed out to the airplane. As was normal practice, I sat down at the navigator's table to review Form #5, the aircraft maintenance log, to make sure the maintenance officer had signed off on it. When I looked up, there was a Styrofoam cup on the navigator's panel. It read "Smart Pills for Stupid Pilots." In it were the rabbit droppings and the Trix. The joke was back on me.

Practical jokes weren't the only fun we had at Travis. Back in Bermuda different squadrons had put on skits for evening entertainment, and some of them had been fantastic. So when our squadron commander at Travis, Colonel Barney Hartnet, tasked me with putting on a show at the Officer's Club, giving me carte blanche to proceed, I borrowed those ideas, and that's how "Wearley's Girlies" were born.

We planned a Gay '90s dress-up evening, and to put the party together I picked people who had a lot of talent. These pilots and crew members were intentionally kept off the flight schedule for that evening, but there was a catch: At midnight, we had to man a flight over the Pacific, which meant we could not drink any alcohol at the party.

I called up Harold's Club in Reno, later owned by none other than Howard Hughes, which offered free gambling tabletops for blackjack, dice, and such. We also procured old green visors, arm garters, and fake money for the dealers. Anyone not in theme costume was put in our make-believe jail, and someone would have to bail out the offender with the play money. The gals were waltzing around in their old-fashioned outfits, sweet-talking the men into giving them all the money, and winning all the door prizes that I had collected from merchants over in Vacaville and Fairfield.

I picked Bob Hazeleaf to be the MC for the evening. I also chose a pilot and a navigator who put on a hilarious *"Smothers Brothers"*–style skit that had us roaring. Pilot Charlie Colvin did a Jackie Gleason skit, playing the Joe the bartender, and the navigator played Crazy Guggenheim. Charlie had an apron pulled up to his chest, and his hair was slicked back as he belted out the song Gleason used to sing at the bar. The audience was in stitches. Charlie threw barb after barb at Colonel Hartnet and the ops officer, and I got them both (along with their wives) to dress up like a bunch of hillbillies with liquor jugs and taught them to sing the "Good Ole Mountain Dew" song. I had picked out six of the really good-looking wives and located a choreographer who taught them the can-can dance. We ordered their costumes all the way from San Francisco. For my part, I was dressed like Chief Wahoo in the *Li'l Abner* comic strip from the Sunday funnies. I wore a derby with a feather in it, a vest, a breechcloth (I did have long pants underneath!),and moccasins. A photographer from the local newspaper came out and took pictures of our party; he named the can-can gals "Wearley's Girlies," and that tag stuck. Those gals were the hit of the party! Two colonels who had crashed the party insisted on having their pictures taken with me. We got away with it all, because it was within a party atmosphere.

Everyone on the base had a good time, and morale was high. We showed everyone (and ourselves) that we were a gung ho, "can do" squadron – a reputation that would work both for us and against us.

Life at Travis Air Force Base

One day I was scheduled for a flight to the Air Force Academy at Peterson Field in Colorado to pick up a group of cadets and fly them out into the Pacific for training. We were delayed throughout because of engine trouble. After taking off hours late, we finally arrived at Hickam Air Force Base in Hawaii, where we could "crew rest." But I still had crew duty time available to get us back to Travis AFB, just 50 miles east of San Francisco – a five-hour flight. Due to late loading of some cargo, it was well into the next afternoon before we got airborne. We had been up all night and day, and we were absolutely exhausted on that flight home. I let everyone sleep for a while – even my co-pilot, so he would be fresh when I woke him to make our landing back at Travis. At one time, I was the only one of the entire crew who was awake, until I roused the navigator to give me a fix. We had to be sure to hit our air defense identification zone (ADIZ) right on the money. Missing that checkpoint meant a violation – the authorities might think you're a Russian threatening American airspace.

The next day I went in to see the squadron commander and told him, The gung ho spirit of the squadron actually could get us in trouble. We could crew rested in the interest of flight safety, legally, but who was going to pull that maneuver in

Hawaii and get away with it? It would have seemed as though all we wanted to do was go down to Waikiki and party. Colonel Hartnet put through a phone call to Hickam about the situation. He agreed that the crew needed to rest and assured me that we would not be criticized for doing it next time. Our squadron had proved that with our high morale and can-do attitude, we could do more than just party hard – we could get the job done.

Eventually, after gaining the necessary experience and becoming capable of assuming the greater responsibility, I was promoted from instructor to flight examiner in the C-135. I was selected to go on the embassy flight, which was literally a flight around the world heading west from Travis AFB. I was assigned to fly with Colonel Hartnet and Colonel T. C. Weir (the Military Airlift Command chief pilot). I was in the right-hand seat while the two colonels alternated making all the takeoffs and landings, after which they would go in the back and play cards while I and a co-pilot did all the work of flying the airplane. This didn't bother me; I loved flying. The journey took us from Travis AFB to Honolulu to the Philippines, where we stayed overnight, and then on to Saigon, Bangkok, Karachi, New Delhi, Dhahran, and up to Madrid. After 24 hours in Madrid, we flew to Charleston and then back to Travis.

The trip took about one week, during which time Colonel Weir got to know me pretty well. So when he was selecting pilots for the initial cadre to establish the C141 program at Tinker Air Force Base in Oklahoma City, he recognized my name on the list of candidates, and I was selected during the second draft. At first I wasn't too happy with the assignment. But once again, in retrospect I saw that it was God's hand at work, continuing to direct my life. My time at Tinker was my segue into the Hughes organization.

From Travis to Tinker

My initial two-month temporary duty (TDY) at Tinker, where I went through ground school simulator training and flight checkout to become a qualified captain in the C-141, lasted two months. Then, in the summer of 1965, I decided to obtain more college credits so that I would qualify for the military's Bootstrap program, allowing me to finish my degree. I made arrangements to go back home and attend three courses – civics, calculus, and history – at Indiana University–Purdue University Fort Wayne (IPFW).

Today IPFW has an enrollment of more than 12,000 students and is a very complex campus housing the Indiana School of Medicine and offering an elaborate sports program. At that time, however, IPFW consisted of just one building, Kettler Hall. Was there a method to my madness? Yes. My plan allowed me to continue my college education while spending six to eight weeks with my family in Woodburn, courtesy of the United States Air Force. I thought it was a very clever move on my part.

Little did I know, even this brief summer was a step toward that big change that would soon come in my life. I learned more about the illustrious, somewhat enviable and yet also pitiable Howard Hughes. During one civics class, my instructor told us about how the City of Tucson wanted to lure Howard Hughes there to build a helicopter factory. As an incentive, Hughes had been given options on an abundance of land in Tucson. Hughes was a visionary: The property soon became very valuable. That class provided yet another glimpse of Howard Hughes's power and tenacity.

Decades later, when I was marketing manager for Fort Wayne International Airport, we were hosting a customer service event. The airport staff positioned themselves so that they could greet passengers embarking on their flights after going through security, and pass out coffee, donuts, cookies, and calendars for the upcoming year. One gentleman traveler stopped in front of me and said, "Bob, I have been following your career." He was my civics instructor from that IPFW summer session almost thirty-five years earlier. During the remainder of his tenure at IPFW and later at Indiana Tech, I tried to see him whenever I was in Fort Wayne, finding out what time his classes were and stationing myself outside the classroom door. Once he saw me, he announced to the class that an emergency had come up, gave them their assignment, and dismissed them. Then he would invited me to go for a drink with him. This former professor became another constant in my life: No matter where my next orders took me, where I next found myself drifting and bobbing in the sea of life, people from home anchored me.

After that summer session in 1965, Ruth and I returned to Travis AFB with the girls. I assumed we would be based there indefinitely. We owned a four-plex apartment building off the base in Vacaville, but it was totally rented out, so we couldn't return to the three-bedroom, two-bath apartment we had occupied before my TDY assignment. Fortunately, the house next door was available, so we rented it instead.

Although my primary duty was as officer in charge of the flight simulator section, I had made a couple of Middle East trips as an aircraft commander on the C-141. I thought I had a nice career ahead of me in California. Everything looked very promising. But it was only a few months later that I came home from work early one afternoon and walked into our kitchen where my wife was fixing dinner. I took my hat off and threw it on the floor, and Ruth instinctively knew what I was about to say.

"We're going to Tinker?" she asked.

My answer was "Yes."

Life at Tinker Air Force Base

I went to Tinker AFB as a captain and, during my four years there, was promoted to major. I continued my education with the University of Oklahoma, completing courses in economics, accounting, and management. After a year or so, I lobbied for the officer in charge of the flight simulator section in order to gain experience managing personnel and resources. I was in my early 30s, and would be eligible for retirement at the ripe old age of 39. I felt that this would make me more marketable in civilian life. The thought of owning my own business after my Air Force career had ended was always in the back of my mind.

Being hired as an airline pilot was not an option for me at that time. Due to union restrictions, the age limit for starting in the airlines was twenty-something; you were required to start as a co-pilot or flight engineer. I knew if I wanted to work for an airline when I got out of the Air Force, I'd probably have to work for a contract carrier or a cargo carrier – someone who who'd hire me as a captain.

In the meantime, Tinker became my permanent change of station (PCS). Oklahoma was a far cry from California, but we did enjoy living there. At first, we lived in temporary quarters until the house assigned to us was ready. We had never lived in on-base housing before. It meant that we had to put Penny, our Boxer (who was by then nine years old), in a kennel. It was January, and an inside/outside kennel was the best we could find in the area. A month later our permanent housing came through and we brought Penny home but unfortunately, she had already contracted pneumonia. Our beloved Penny died at home a short time after we had settled in.

Losing Penny was a difficult adjustment for our family. I was no longer surprised, though, at how quickly Ruth and I adapted to a new base and new surroundings. The day we moved in at Tinker, a formal party was planned at the Officers' Club. Our clothes and belongings were spread out all over the house in crates and boxes, yet we knew exactly where our formal clothes were. We found a babysitter, opened the crates, got dressed, and went to the party.

Our experience at Tinker turned out to be memorable for our daughters, too. While we were stationed at Travis, they were very young – in kindergarten and first grade. A little older now, they adapted well and thoroughly enjoyed all that the base had to offer, most of it free or reasonably priced. When summer came, they got up in the morning and caught the free shuttle bus to the Officers' Club, where they spent the entire day swimming (the college kids working as lifeguards sort of adopted them). Or they went to see a movie for just a quarter. We gave each girl an extra quarter to pay for lunch. They made many friends at Tinker, some of whom they still correspond with to this day.

While at Tinker I finally moved out of flight instruction to become the officer in charge of the flight simulator section. The C-141 flight simulator was operated by a newer digital computer along with an older, analog-operated non-motion C124 simulator, because the C124 Globemaster pilot and in-flight transition school was still based there. Today, the state-of-the-art C-17 workhorse of the Air Mobility Command is a follow-up to the old propeller-driven C-124, which we knew as Big Shaky.

When the staff position opened up for chief of pilot training and analysis, I was able to move up and take over that fantastic opportunity, working for a civilian with his rank equal to a full colonel. Our school's job was to turn out knowledgeable, well-trained pilots. These men would be essentially "diamonds in the rough"; the finishing touches, so to speak, would be added once they were placed in their squadron. All the squadrons wanted was for us to teach a pilot what he needed to know in order to leave training as a qualified co-pilot. It didn't matter if these pilots were aircraft commanders before coming to us for instruction; before they could transition to the next airplane, they had to start over as a co-pilot again. Of course, the more experience they had, the faster their transition from co-pilot to captain to aircraft commander to instructor.

Some of the guys loved the instructing side of things because they could put in an early morning flight, be done by noon, and play golf the rest of the day. For me, however, that was not the motivation. I was an eight-to-five type of guy. I enjoyed learning staff work and being creative and innovative in training. One man in particular really made a difference to my job in pilot training and analysis: Senior Chief Master Sergeant Walter Grundwald.

The "Need to Know" Theory

Walter Grundwald had immigrated to the United States from Austria and joined the Air Force, accumulating about 10,000 hours in flying time as a flight engineer before he started college and earned a PhD in educational systems. At Tinker, he was my NCOIC at pilot training and analysis, and I learned a great deal from him. I took him along to an Air Force conference, where representatives from various commands discussed training methods, and he ended up being the only enlisted man sitting around the table with generals and colonels, and me as a major. Sergeant Grundwald was very bright and held his own in spite of his rank, much to the chagrin of the brass.

One of the things Sergeant Grundwald taught me was his special theory of instruction: the "Need to Know" theory. Think of a classroom setting, where an instructor talks about a variety of issues. From the students' viewpoint, the question is, "Do I need to know this? Will that be on the test?" They simply want to pass the course. Sergeant Grundwald helped me establish the criteria for Need to Know information and taught me not to confuse this with everything else – the "Gee Whiz" information, facts that are interesting and helpful but would not be on a basic classroom test or quiz.

Much like a licensed physician who still learns after he has earned the title of doctor, after military pilots have they checked out in an airplane (or civilians have earned their private license), they then have a license to learn. They need to know enough to pass the test so they can get out into the field and get their experience. Our students were like vessels ready to be filled to the brim with information. But even an empty vacuum can only hold so much material. They could learn Gee Whiz stuff when they returned to their squadron; for now, we focused on the Need to Know stuff. Other instructors taught in the Gee Whiz style, but this led to one major problem: When students start to remember all the Gee Whiz information, they forget about the Need to Know items.

How do you teach Need to Know? Grundwald was a pro at it. One way is to use descriptive words – *push, twist, pull,* etc. – for each task in the cockpit as you go through the checklist. If you *flip* this switch, what was supposed to take place? If you *pull* this knob, what would happen? You didn't need to be an aeronautical engineer or an electronics engineer to analyze it; you just needed to know what would happen if you pushed a button or turned a knob. That's the basis for Need to Know instruction. The Gee Whiz stuff was all superfluous information: how many windows are on the left side of the aircraft, how many rivets are on a wing, and so forth. All these questions did was intimidate the student (and inflate the instructor's ego).

Teaching was a wonderful and useful experience, one that I was happy to add to my repertoire. With every student I instructed, I learned a little bit more myself.

Family and Worship

The whole family really enjoyed life at Tinker AFB. The girls were typical pre-teenagers, and Ruth did an outstanding job of raising them. They took many classes: dance class, ballet, White Gloves and Party Manners. This last was an etiquette school where they learned how to fold napkins, set a formal table, use the proper dinner utensils, and such. To this day, they remember all that and appreciate it.

Guice and Nancy Tinsley stayed back at Travis AFB, but we kept in touch as best we could. When Guice later volunteered for duty in Vietnam, he made arrangements for his family to rent a house in Porter, Indiana, their hometown, during his one-year tour. Guice then drove down to Tinker in his camper and parked it in our driveway while he went on to Victorville, California, to transition into the F-4 fighter he'd be flying in Vietnam. (While doing the yard work one morning, I clunked my head on the camper's gigantic side view mirror, ripping open a large gash on my forehead. We were lucky to have a doctor as a neighbor, though. I just walked next door to with blood gushing from my head, and he drove me to the hospital. Once they sewed me up, I went back and finished the yard work. Al Johnson and his family – his wife, Arlene, and their two boys, Tom and Tate – were now based at Tinker, too. After I left the Air Force for the Hughes Organization at Las Vegas, Al took my job at wing headquarters, and he moved from there to Scott AFB near St. Louis, becoming a full Colonel and the chief pilot of what amounts to the largest airline in the world the; Military Air Command (MAC),(later the Mobility Cimmand) which replaced MATS in 1966. After Al retired from the Air Force, the family moved to Houston, where Al became manager of FlightSafety International's training center at Houston Hobby airport, for corporate jet pilots and Arlene became a scratch golfer, winning many club championships (including a hole in one!). The boys went into the military: Tom is now retired from the Coast Guard, and Tate is a retired full colonel from the Air Force. Al and I remained good friends until, unfortunately, he passed away from a massive heart attack at the age of 62, in an Atlanta hotel while on business, and sadly Arlene lost her battle with cancer, over 10 years later, shortly after my wife, Sherry and I had visited in Houston. Sunday school was great fun for our daughters. Unlike a lot of military families who arrive at a new base and shop around for the right church, Ruth and I always tried to find the closest Missouri Synod Lutheran Church (LCMS) in the nearby community, and that's where we worshiped. Once we settled in at Tinker, I used the Yellow Pages to find a Lutheran minister with counseling credentials so we could continue to work on our marriage.

Initially, Art Prizinger was the pastor of the church we attended while at Tinker. We became close friends, and he asked me to teach Sunday school to the teenagers. He thought I would relate to them, but if truth be told, I just was not a good Sunday school teacher (probably because I was usually pretty hungover on Sunday mornings!). That's not to say I didn't want to be involved in church activities. When Pastor Prizinger accepted a call to another parish, our parish suddenly faced a vacancy. The way it works in the LCMS, you put out a call to another pastor and wait to see if the Holy Spirit will guide this pastor to your church. I put forth the name of a friend of mine, Ken Young.

Pastor Young had been pastor in South Carolina when I'd been stationed at Charleston. We used to fish together at the end of the dock where my family lived, on the Ashley River. It was on that dock that he got an important message across to me: *You are saved by faith through the grace of God.*

A Biology major in college, he also liked to collect snakes. When our dog Penny cornered a black snake, Ruth called me at work and I went home and caught the snake and put it in a gunnysack. Then I called Pastor Young to come and retrieve the snake. Why? So he could keep it as a pet. I suppose this is kind of strange, but perhaps he simply lived by the creed "We are all God's creatures."

When I put forward Pastor Young's name, he was working in inner-city Chicago at the time, having taken over a church with a very mixed, urban congregation – blacks, whites, Asians, people of all different races and cultures. At Tinker, on the other hand, we were surrounded by small towns: Oklahoma City, Dell City, Midwest City (where we lived and attended church, right outside of the base gates). We didn't have that crossover of ethnicity in our area, much less in our church. Still, I recommended him because of his experience with integration and different cultures.

The first pastor who got the call from us turned us down. I assumed Ken Young would be called since he'd come in second when the congregation had voted. However, at the next meeting, we took a vote and he came in second again. This was frustrating. I could not understand why the congregation would not take this willing and wonderful pastor. Was there something funny going on? This was in the late '60s; perhaps they thought I was trying to integrate the congregation. I addressed the members of the congregation, challenging them to lay down their prejudice, but they dug in against a pastor who they feared might foster integration.

Soon after, I was nominated as chairman of the congregation, but I lost out to someone else. I believed all of this had a lot to do with me not being elected. In fact, the parishioner who was elected to that office confessed to me that he felt that I should have had it, that he'd been railroaded in because of my strong beliefs and the fact that the congregation could not control me. Who says you can't mix religion with politics?

The new chairman was a permanent resident in town, and because I was in the Air Force it was felt that I would be moving on and was not committed to the congregation. This was not true. When Ruth and I were members of a congregation, we were good members. We got involved and never acted as though we were transient. We always jumped in with both feet. So when the parishioners decided to make me the church's financial secretary, I did my best, although this was a big mistake. Handling finances was the last thing I wanted to do. Suddenly, it was my responsibility to initiate fund-raising for a building project. I talked to the banks and financial institutions and finally went with a church-sponsored program of bonds. Members of the congregation bought bonds on time, and the church then bought the bonds back at maturity. We called on all of our strongest supporters for our membership drive. Warren Bachelor was one of my strongest supporters in our fund-raising attempt. He would soon be working with me on a much larger project in Vegas.

The Neighborhood Hangout

At Tinker, Ruth and I continued not only with counseling but with parties, too. We threw one wild party over the holidays, between Christmas and New Year's, and we were credited with hosting the "social event of the year". After that, our house became the staple for the really fun parties. We would make a punch called French 75: pink champagne, vodka, and powdered sugar. It was a very smooth drink – and a lethal one. A guest at one of our parties, a rather refined lady, kept partaking of this concoction throughout the night and when she finally decided to get up from her seat, she executed a graceful pirouette and fell to the floor face first.

The house had a carport that we transformed into a bar. I built it myself for all of $15. The design came from a home decorating magazine Ruth found, and I picked up the materials in the base's salvage yard. We hung a bamboo blind across the large entrance and strung up Oriental-style paper lanterns. I was instructing in the mornings, but on my afternoons off, Ruth and I worked on this project and on any number of others. The house turned out to be a bit of a fixer-upper, but we enjoyed the challenge.

My pride and joy was the lawn. I was trying for the weekly Green Thumb Award, given out to the best-kept lawn on the base. Rather than play golf with the guys at the local course on Saturday mornings, I preferred to take care of the lawn. Of course, in the afternoon when I had finished with the yard and had washed and waxed the cars, the guys came over from the golf course and I offered them a beer

Soon our house was considered the neighborhood hangout. When I was at Wing level, we were transitioning into the gigantic C-5A, the Air Force's new jumbo jet that was the size of a Boeing 747. I was involved in selecting the pilots who transitioned into this program. Guys were always stopping by our little bar to quiz me about who was on the confidential C-5A list; of course, they never found out from me. In the end, building the bar may have cost us only $15, but buying the beer for our guests cost me a lot more over the years.

Ruth and I did a lot of things well together. We were great partiers, but we also had wonderful children and were very devoted to our church. Ruth was a great Air Force wife and a good cook, but she didn't particularly care about cooking. So when she volunteered as a church secretary, I started to learn how, and she was happy to let me do it. I got up at 4:00 in the morning, arrived at base operations by 5:00, briefed for an hour, and was off the ground by 6:00 for my early morning flight. We flew for approximately four hours, debriefed, and were done by noon. Ruth was working, so I went home, took a nap, and then got up and started reading cookbooks and making dinner. By the time Ruth got home, I would have the table ready. The entire family were buying me cookbooks and offering tips and advice. I thoroughly enjoyed it.

The Job of a Lifetime?

One day, quite unexpectedly, I received a call from retired Colonel Jerry Triola, formerly the 443rd Military Airlift Command's training wing commander at Tinker. I had been on his staff as chief of pilot training and analysis. Colonel Triola wanted to know if I would be interested in working for the Hughes organization in Las Vegas. I would be the chief pilot of a newly purchased twin-engine corporate jet, a British built de Havilland DH-125.

I couldn't believe it. I had heard so much about Howard Hughes and his organization over the years, and now I might have a chance to work for the man himself. Part of me hoped I would receive that job offer … but I worried about leaving the Air Force. I had been in the military for 17 years, had reached the rank of major, and had met the criteria to be promoted to lieutenant colonel. I was just three years away from retiring. I knew full well that if I stayed put, I'd enjoy my military retirement benefits, which would provide a more conservative and secure future. Yet the opportunity to work within the Hughes organization was a nagging temptation.

"Bob, what do you want to do?" the Lutheran counselor asked me one day.

At that moment, I didn't realize that God's hand was guiding my life again. Today, however, I am sure I was put in that position for a reason. I struggled with the decision to leave the Air Force, naturally. But I knew the position with the Howard Hughes organization would be a unique and wonderful opportunity, and it wouldn't necessarily be there when I got out of the service.

"I want that job," I answered.

THE HAND OF GOD

I FIRMLY BELIEVE THAT the call I received from Colonel Triola was God's way of guiding my life. Once again, as had happened many times over the course of my career, a number of things came into play – things I had nothing to do with – that led to an important opportunity for me and my family.

When it came time for reassignment to the States from Bermuda, many of my friends were automatically assigned to McGuire, the MATS base in New Jersey. But because I had expressed my interest in becoming a general's aide, my personnel records were pulled and scrutinized at MATS headquarters at Scott Air Force Base in Illinois, just east of St. Louis. The timing was perfect: The Air Force was looking to send pilots on another plum assignment, to the first jet transport squadron out on the West Coast – and I ended up at Travis Air Force Base, near San Francisco, between Vacaville and Fairfield. First Bermuda, then California, and now Las Vegas, this opportunity to work for one of the most powerful men in the universe – some might call it luck. To me, though, these circumstances wouldn't have come together without God's hand in my life.

Some of the things that I had experienced in Bermuda now seemed nearly to have been orchestrated to give me the credentials I needed to get into the Hughes organization. Evidently my protocol background, my staff work, and my flying experience impressed Colonel Triola. I guess he recalled the duties he had personally assigned to me at Tinker – the planning of various VIP escorts, ceremonies and dinners. On one occasion, an Air Force captain from Mexico whose father held a high-level cabinet position in the Mexican government arrived at Tinker and was assigned as an observer of U.S. Air Force training procedures. He stayed several days, during which I treated him to an inside look at all facets of the Air Force ground school (the flight simulator training), walking him through the same process the students go through from the time they arrive until they are checked out. Colonel Triola, as the wing commander, requested that I set up a reception and dinner in the captain's name. After that, I flew the captain on to his next destination on a C-141 training flight.

I couldn't help but think that Colonel Triola remembered his former protocol officer's respectful nature ... my eager, willing attitude ... my decency and decorum. Now, facing another crossroads in my life, I shared the facts with him: I only had a short time left in the Air Force. I was up for lieutenant colonel. I had USAF approval to finish my degree at the University of Omaha through the military's Bootstrap program. How could I rationalize leaving the military now, just as I neared completion of a successful career? I was not trying to play hard to get, but in retrospect my candidness may have worked in my favor. The colonel acknowledged my struggle and suggested that I come out to Vegas and look over the situation, no strings attached. He offered me an airline ticket, and within a few short days I was on my way.

My curiosity had gotten the better of me.

A Glimpse of the Life to Come

When I arrived in Las Vegas, the Hughes organization put me up at the Castaways hotel on the Strip, just across the street from the Sands hotel. (Both of these are now demolished.) That evening, Colonel Triola and his wife took me to the Sammy Davis Jr. show at the Sands. Over the course of a delightful evening, we talked a lot about what I could expect the following day when I was scheduled to meet with Triola's boss, retired general Ed Nigro, a former fighter pilot who had worked in the Pentagon. Triola was obviously enamored with General Nigro, using his name reverently whenever he spoke about him. I, on the other hand, wasn't quite sure what to expect.

When I entered General Nigro's offices the next afternoon, I was duly prepared to be in awe of the man. He had an ex-military aide, a retired lieutenant colonel, posted outside his door, at the ready in case he needed anything, and two secretaries awaiting his every order. Inside, the carpeting was thick and the decor opulent, further proof of the man's status. The general had a presence, all right. His size, his handshake – he was absolutely overpowering. He was brief and curt in keeping with military fashion, which I found interesting because he had been in civilian life for a couple of years already.

It was immediately clear that General Nigro, too, was very interested in hiring me. When I asked about what kind of contract might be necessary, he blew me off like yesterday's news.

"No, we don't give contracts here," he said in a booming voice. "A handshake is good enough." He then told me that a handshake was all that had been necessary when he first came to work for Hughes. He'd been hired on the spot, he explained proudly.

I gulped. Considering all I was on the brink of giving up, was a handshake good enough for *me*?

It would have to be. The selection process narrowed it down to two of us, and in January 1969 Hughes Nevada Operations (as the corporation was known at the time) offered me the job. I took it.

According to Triola, it was my protocol experience that had tilted the decision in my favor. The other person they were considering, the wing chief of standardization back at Tinker, did not have a protocol background; I got the impression that perhaps he lacked my people skills. These attributes were essential to working within the Hughes organization, primarily for reasons of discretion, respect, and deference:

I would be flying high-ranking personnel, national political figures, famous entertainers, and some of Hughes's closest confidents.

There was, however, a catch: General Nigro wanted me to start immediately.

But I was still an officer in the United States Air Force! If I wanted the job, I would have to find a way to get out of the Air Force – gracefully.

Getting Out of the Air Force

How on earth was I going to get out of the service? Colonel Triola's recommendation was to fake "humanitarian reasons" – a sick mother who had to be taken care of, or a death in the family that left a business needing to be run.

"Make up something," he said. "Just get out of the Air Force and get over here so we can put you to work flying for Howard Hughes."

It had a great ring to it. I wanted the job – badly – but did I want it badly enough to lie about it?

The money certainly wasn't worth lying for. I had been advised by fellow officer and pilot Keith Garland, whom I knew while we were young lieutenants at Charleston in the '50s and with whom I had stayed in touch, to ask for a three-year contract and at least $30,000. What I got was a $17,000-a-year job without a contract. But there were a lot of perks, and I knew the long-term possibilities it could bring. Most of all, I was hoping that it would turn into a lifelong career. General Nigro had indicated that when he became president of Hughes Air West, he would take me along as vice president of training and/or operations – an opportunity that would be hard to turn down. (In retrospect, it never would have worked. I probably would have had more than my fair share of headaches working with union pilots. Not to mention the fact that the general was out of a job – after he and Las Vegas head honcho Bob Maheu had a falling out, regardless of the "firm" handshake – within the year.)

When I told him about my dilemma, Keith (who later ended up as Vice President Spiro Agnew's Air Force aide), said, "Bob, I wouldn't do that if they gave me a dozen gold-plated Cadillacs!" What Keith was saying was, *Stay where you are, retire out of the Air Force, and forget this baloney with Howard Hughes.* It was sound advice.

But I didn't listen.

I knew I was gambling on the future by taking this job. I also knew it was going to take something clever to get out of the military early. But I didn't want to be dishonest. I didn't want to burn any bridges by coming up with some phony "humanitarian" excuse.

I started contemplating another way of getting out, an honorable reason. During a search of one of our USAF regulation manuals, I found a paragraph that referred to the "convenience of the Air Force." The regulation wasn't specific. It was a "catch-all" for things not covered elsewhere. It was my ticket out and I just ask to be released from active duty to pursue other interests.

I wrote my letter of resignation. While on a training flight up to Scott Air Force Base, I hand-carried that letter into the office of a two-star general, who was quite happy to accept my resignation as a favor to General Nigro – an example of the "good ol' boy" network among high-ranking officers. It was so easy, I even picked my own release date.

In March 1969, as I drove past the gate and pulled out of Tinker AFB, I looked back over my shoulder and questioned my sanity.

What in the world am I doing? I thought. I had just walked away from a 17-year career with the Air Force, with only three years left before retirement as a lieutenant colonel, to join an organization I knew very little about. The only thing I did know about the man heading it up was what I'd read long ago in that magazine I picked up in Bermuda. I was plowing some new and very unfamiliar turf, and right then I was not entirely convinced the job opportunity was going to work.

The Elusive Mr. Hughes

My paychecks were issued now from Hughes Tool Company's West Coast offices. I was chief pilot for Howard Hughes's personal fleet of aircraft. But there was a lot of speculation back home in Indiana about what I was really doing for the organization. The folks in Woodburn believed I lived under a cloak of secrecy. Even my brother-in-law Fritz was curious, but he never asked specific questions.

"There was this impression back home that Bob was actually flying Howard Hughes around the world," Fritz recalls when asked today. "But Bob was pretty protective of his situation all the while he worked for Hughes, even when he came home. He never talked about Howard Hughes or what he did for the Hughes organization. Still, I always had this vision of Bob flying around the continent with Hughes sitting in the co-pilot's seat, and the two of them chatting back and forth to each other."

I was very tight-lipped about what I knew about the man, his people, and his organizations. In fact, as Hughes became more and more reclusive, few people ever saw him, even Bob Maheu, his man in Las Vegas. And anyway, as one of his aides once told me, Hughes would never have allowed a pilot in the co-pilot seat when he was flying. He didn't want anyone in the cockpit who might criticize his flying ability.

Hughes was not a pragmatic person when it came to piloting an aircraft any more than he was about getting his way in other things. Roy Crawford, another of Hughes's aides, told me about the time Hughes took a TWA Constellation out of the lineup, causing total chaos at the airline he partially owned. The plane had been scheduled for a passenger trip, but Hughes put a girlfriend in the right-hand seat and ordered Crawford, who was a Navy training pilot during World War II and knew a little bit about airplanes and reciprocating engines, to sit at the engineer's panel. They flew to the Bahamas. Just imagine the excuses TWA had to concoct for the paying passengers who were supposed to be on that plane!

During that flight, Crawford noticed that the temperature on one of the engine's cylinder heads was approaching the red line: too hot.

"Would you like me to crack the cowl flaps?" he asked Mr. Hughes. On the Connie you could open and close those flaps depending on the temperature of the cylinder head.

But Hughes's response? "No, it'll be all right."

Later in the flight Hughes turned around in his seat and said, "Roy, you better crack the cowl flaps." Hughes always wanted to be in control in an aircraft. It was as understood that no one better question his flying ability in even the slightest way.

There was just one situation in my time with the organization that could have put me in the cockpit with the man himself. While living in London, Hughes decided to start flying again (he had quit when he became a recluse and people were trying to subpoena him for various lawsuits). Arrangements were made with Hawker Siddeley for him to fly an HS-748 turbo prop, which at that time was a type used by some regional carriers in the United States. Some of Hughes's aides suggested that I be chosen to fly along with Hughes. My boss, Jack Real, who was making the arrangements for Hughes to fly from Hatfield Airport near London, requested a man named Tony Blackman instead.

I immediately took to Blackman. He was perfect for Howard: well educated, a Cambridge graduate, a former college professor. Later he took up flying and became an aeronautical engineer, eventually working for Hawker Siddeley. He was very familiar with that particular airplane.

Even if Jack Real hadn't nixed the idea of me flying with Howard Hughes, I probably would have had to decline the offer. At that time I had never flown a turbo prop airplane. Curious as he was about the aerodynamics and the eccentricities of every aircraft he flew, Hughes would have wanted to know every minute engineering detail, every particular term, and props were just not my area of expertise.

So I never did fly with Howard Hughes, and from what I gathered, the stress of sharing cockpit space with him was something I could do without. But Tony Blackman is another story. He and I would become friends and share some rare experiences flying Hughes's airplanes. In fact, we actually flew together the first time I met him.

Life in the Fast Lane

Jack Real proposed that Hughes enter into a lease-purchase agreement for a Hawker Siddeley demonstrator, the HS-748M. There was some reluctance on the part of the aircraft manufacturer, which may have feared adverse publicity because of media attention to Hughes's return to the air. Once it was decided that Hawker Siddeley would indeed provide the airplane, we discussed how long Mr. Hughes could use the Hatfield Airport without being seen – and without the British press leaking the news. As always, the boss was demanding secrecy.

Some time after Hughes left London, I received a call from Jack Real, who instructed me to go over to London in order to make contact with the Hawker Siddeley folks. Modifications were made to a DH-125 (similar to the one I had flown back from Vegas) so Hughes could get in and out of the cockpit a little easier; it was anticipated that he'd transition to the twin engine jet after he regained his flying skills in the HS 178M, so I would be exercising the purchase option on the DH-125. In my pocket I had a check for close to $1 million. After completing the inventory and reviewing the maintenance records, I took the plane up on a test-top. Satisfied, I signed the purchase agreement and handed over the check. Tony Blackman was the Hawker Siddeley pilot who accompanied me.

I stayed at the Skyline Hotel near Heathrow Airport while I met with the folks at Hatfield. Once I had purchased the aircraft, I was to rendezvous with Chester Davis, Hughes's chief counsel who was also in London at the time, and fly him to some location yet unnamed. I called Davis from the Skyline and asked what he wanted me to do next. He said he'd let me know, and I didn't question him. (He used to call me "general" if I disagreed with him about a flight itinerary.) So I stayed in that hotel room for about a week, waiting for further instructions.

Finally Davis called and said he wanted to go to Vienna for lunch, so Tony and I flew him there, along with his wife and a younger couple related in some way to the Rothschild family, who had apparently streamlined the immigration procedure for Hughes's arrival in London. It was the young Rothschild gentleman who helped me recoup our expenses without anyone back home being the wiser. I just told him my predicament and wrote out my expenses on a yellow legal pad, and he issued me a check to take care of it.

We waited for them in Vienna, and when they finished lunch, Davis had a new destination in mind: He wanted to fly down to Rome.

Once we arrived in Rome, Tony said he couldn't stay any longer, so he returned to Hatfield and sent over another DH-125 pilot to fly with me. Next, Davis told me that he wanted to fly over to Sardinia to look at some property. I wondered about this; rumor had it that Chester Davis was originally from nearby Sicily and that his name was not really Davis.

Whatever his real name, he had changed it and then married the heir to the Ferry Seed Company.

The Davises had a 3,300-acre racehorse and dairy farm in upstate New York. It was known as the Ferry Mansion to local folks, but it was hardly a mansion at all – just an old, well-preserved brick farmhouse. I stayed there several times over the years when we flew Chester to his "farm." It was my job to play tennis with Chester. On a hot afternoon, Mrs. Davis brought out homemade cookies for us, then went for a swim in the ancient swimming pool. We nicknamed it the "cee-ment pond," a quip taken from the TV show *The Beverly Hillbillies*, and it was filled with ice-cold water. Unbearable, but invigorating!

I always found it amusing that even though the Davises could well afford the nicer things in life – Chester had flamboyant and prestigious law offices at One State Street Plaza in Manhattan, a yacht in the Bahamas, a private jet at his disposal, and many other perks – in their primary home they lived somewhat frugally. Though maybe it wasn't so amusing after all; there was another rumor about Chester Davis, that he could also be a very cruel man. I saw this side of him once, on that trip in the DH-125.

From Rome, we took off for Sardinia, a little island off the coast of Italy, and not a very long flight. Basically, it was up and down. Davis wanted to fly along the coast, I dropped down to an altitude of 1,000 feet and slowed the aircraft down to a much slower speed so that he could get a better look at whatever he was looking for. When we landed at the airport, a gentleman picked him up and they went about their business.

My new co-pilot and I decided to take a little tour, and we found a taxi. As it turned out, this Sardinian city on a Sunday afternoon was basically vacant. The streets were rolled up, and it was a very dull tour. We finished and went back to the airplane, where we waited a considerable amount of time before Davis returned and we headed back to Rome.

Davis was in no hurry to return to the States, While I was waiting, I decided to take a chance on another tour – of Rome this time. Things looked up a bit when, at the tour desk in the hotel, I met a very nice lady from Los Angeles who was intent on doing the same thing. I suggested that we take the tour together. She agreed. I soon found out that she was the wife of a wealthy Italian contractor, and they lived in Los Angeles. She mentioned during our conversation that she was a friend of Dean Martin's (or was it Jerry Lewis's?) wife.

The tour this time was wonderful. As we were walking along, we ran into Chester Davis and the young Rothschild gentleman. I guess Davis thought I had picked up a streetwalker, because he made some unkind remarks in front of my female companion. I was appalled, apologized to her, and we continued our tour. Afterward I made it a point to tell Davis who she was and explained that we just happened to meet and were only touring the Vatican together.

After completing his business in Rome, Davis wanted to go up to Amsterdam and then on home. I took him there and bought him and his wife an airline ticket, charged to my personal American Express card. Then I flew the airplane back to London's Heathrow Airport, so the Hawker Siddeley pilots could later fly it back to Hatfield, and hopped a TWA flight back to the States. I rented a car at Newark airport and drove down to Atlantic Aviation on the New Jersey coast, where another DH-125 was kept. Jack Real had bought this one from the Telex Corporation in Tulsa, Oklahoma, for Chester's exclusive use. It was being retrofitted with a new interior– and it was my job to check on the progress.

All in all, this was but one very odd trip. Working for Hughes, one could always expect the bizarre. It always meant excepting the unexpected.

What I didn't expect during that trip was to find out I had contacted a serious disease.

Taking One for the Team

It was on my return trip to the States aboard that TWA flight that I started feeling unwell. I was flying first class as usual, and the flight attendant brought me a mixed drink. I complained that it just didn't taste very good. I then ordered a glass of wine, but that didn't taste good either. Nor did my glass of milk. I was feeling restless, I sent my card up to the cockpit and was able to sit with the crew for a lot of the flight from London to Newark.

That evening, after checking on the newly purchased airplane, I went over to the hotel bar with the mechanic and we ordered a drink. Yet again, the alcohol tasted terrible – which was a blessing in disguise. This was nature's way of telling me that something was terribly wrong, but I still didn't quite get the message. I just switched to Coke.

The next day I flew down to the Bahamas to brief Jack Real on the trip with Chester Davis and give him an update on Davis's DH-125. The day after that, I was back in the air, flying to New Orleans to attend a National Business Aircraft Association convention. While sitting in a seminar, I became delirious. I telephoned my doctor in Las Vegas and confessed that my urine was turning red and my stools were almost white. He told me to get back to Las Vegas and go directly to the hospital. Even over the phone, he could diagnose hepatitis.

I can only surmise that I contracted the virus when I ate a hot dog bought from a sidewalk vendor in Rome. Imagine it: There I was in the Bahamas, up at the Xanadu penthouse where Howard Hughes was living, with a highly contagious illness and neither of us any the wiser. Had the world's most famous germaphobe known, it's not hard to tell what he would have done. But for starters, he would have had my head on a platter! My wife met me upon my arrival back in Las Vegas and took me directly to the hospital. In the morning I was setting on the bed with my brief case open and doing some paper work when the Dr. Wolever arrived and said; 'you got it lay back down and rest'. I recuperated at home and it took several weeks for me to regain my strength to be able to get back to.

Life in Vegas

Mr. Hughes never did find out about my illness, of course, and while I never flew with him, my move to Las Vegas led to plenty of other adventures. The FBO at McCarran Field was my base of operations throughout the time that I worked for the Hughes organization. Little did I know when I first arrived what an interesting experience it would turn out to be.

When I arrived with my family in Las Vegas to start working for the Hughes organization, they put us up in two rooms in the Castaways hotel. Our short time living on the Strip was especially interesting for our two daughters. They were introduced quite suddenly to a very different life: maid service, room service, taking all our meals in restaurants. For one, they grew to loathe the abundance of food in the school lunches the hotel chef fixed each morning. Robin always opened up the lunch bags and removed one of the sandwiches from each. She explained that the school principal, Mr. Stageman, the principal at the Lutheran School they attended, made the students eat *all* their lunch, and that two big sandwiches were way too much for each little girl to eat.

After two weeks at the Castaways, life started to unfold for the four of us in Vegas in a way that we all thought would be very positive. We found a house to rent while we hunted for one to purchase. We enrolled our daughters in a Lutheran elementary school, and it was my responsibility to get Robin and Roxie to school each morning. Colonel Triola had promised me a company car when I signed on with the Hughes organization, and I held him to that. I think he had some trouble pulling that one off, but ultimately he kept his promise.

In the end, we decided to build instead of buy. Our spectacular home went up very quickly – a fabulous, 3,300-square-foot house designed in a Spanish motif with an in-ground pool. The price tag: an amazingly low $60,000. What would that home be worth on the Las Vegas market today? Things were definitely going well on the home front.

Meanwhile, within the Hughes organization there was a certain "boys will be boys" attitude, an acceptance of the excuse *I'm having a midlife crisis*, a wink and a nod at infidelity. Not the best thing to be surrounded by in my life.

When we left Oklahoma, the counselor had given me the name of a gentleman in Vegas who could help us continue marriage counseling. This counselor turned out to be a former professor of psychology, an academic with little hands-on experience in counseling. In actuality, he knew zip about either marriage or counseling.

But I trod these new waters very carefully in the beginning and was able to resist the temptation of being "one of the guys". In the Air Force, other pilots' wives had told Ruth they were glad their husbands were flying with me because it meant they would stay out of trouble. That's the reputation I had, and I was flattered by it. I clung as tightly as I could to my religious values and my staunch upbringing.

One Easter morning in the early '60s, while flying C-135Bs at Clark Air Force Base in the Philippines, I awoke the crew for services at the base chapel. We had a flight out of the Philippines that very morning, and we attended the Easter service in our flight suits, then across the International Date Line to Hickam AFB in Honolulu. We were flying into the sun, so we had a short night and when we landed it was morning for us again – in fact, it was Easter Sunday again. I laughed inwardly.

"Well, crew," I said in a light-hearted tone, "I guess we should probably attend Easter services again."

The only reply was a low groan. In truth, we were exhausted from the long flight, and I had no intention of attending services, it was time to get some much needed crew rest. My piety went only so far.

I hoped it would be with me, though, now that we were living in Sin City. Luckily, our new city offered more than just adult fun and games; there was also a family-oriented social scene to get involved with. When I joined the Hughes organization, I certainly was not a novice at partying and having a good time in all sorts of social situations. One of the first things Colonel Triola did when Ruth and I arrived in Las Vegas was invite us to a dinner party at his home. There we met Pete and Rosemary Maheu, Bob Maheu's son and daughter-in-law. Well, I didn't need to "meet" Rosemary. We were already acquainted.

When Triola told Pete and Rosemary the name of the person he'd hired out of the Air Force to head up Hughes's fleet of aircraft, Rosemary had surprised him by saying, "Not *the* Bob Wearley? From Woodburn, Indiana?"

I couldn't believe the irony: Rosemary Maheu (née Gustin) was also from Woodburn. Although when I had left for the Air Force she'd been much younger than me, we had known each other back home. The world truly is a small place.

Becoming Indispensible

Pete Maheu and I quickly got to know each other. I liked him, and we ended up working a lot together over the course of the next two years. Pete obviously ingratiated himself to the organization because of his father, Bob, who was referred to time and again as Mr. Hughes's alter ego. When Hughes wanted something done, he picked up the phone and called Bob Maheu, or wrote him a memo on one of the yellow legal pads he always used. Many times the things Mr. Hughes wanted done were nearly impossible, and in the eyes of the other staff members, Bob Maheu became somewhat of a miracle worker.

Maheu was hired by Howard Hughes in a very uncustomary manner. He had been a counterspy during World War II, working his way to the top echelon of the FBI before leaving to start his own private consulting firm in Washington, D.C. He worked as a consultant for Howard Hughes but kept his firm available to other clients until 1966. That's when Howard Hughes decided he wanted Maheu at his beck and call full-time.

We were always picking up little tidbits of information from the aides, and I heard from one of them that, to test Maheu's loyalty when he was considering hiring him, Hughes asked Maheu to fly to Tucson, Arizona, stay in a particular motel, and wait for his call. Maheu waited there a week without hearing from Hughes. Finally, Hughes called and told him he could start working for him, and Maheu immediately proceeded to Las Vegas and formed Hughes Nevada Operations (HNO). This was so typical of Hughes – to test and retest people until he was absolutely sure of their loyalty to him.

When Maheu formed HNO, he hired General Ed Nigro to be his second-in-command. Although Hughes had any number of jets stored in various places around the country, it would have been very difficult for the general to get his hands on them without Hughes's permission, since he'd had them prepared for storage, they were not ready for flying. The general and Bob Maheu were able to purchase a de Havilland DH-125. Nigro had a former aide in mind to serve as the company pilot and tried desperately to get him out of Vietnam. When that plan didn't work, he asked Colonel Triola to find a MAC pilot. That's when Colonel Triola called me.

Even though Triola chose me for the job largely because of my protocol background and my experience handling VIPs and dignitaries while stationed in Bermuda, it was this very experience that he seemed to grate against. It was obvious to me that what Colonel Triola wanted more than anything was to be in charge of Howard Hughes's entire flight department. Triola, who applied typical military structure to his business practices, thought the flight department should be run his way and his way only. Whoever wanted us to fly them in the company plane had to ask him first, and he in turn notified me – this was his "chain of command". When Triola called, he'd typically say, "Well Bob, we have a big one," or "We have to fly to Washington first thing tomorrow morning". When I queried him about details for this or that flight – how many people we'd be flying, which airport to land at, what sort of food the passengers might be expecting – he would bark at me, "I don't know!" Apparently he thought questioning him about these things was inappropriate.

Despite Triola's best efforts to act as a barrier to our mutual success, my protocol training in the Air Force paid off, in the instances when we were flying guests or members of the Hughes organization. I made sure that they had appetizing food on board and that there were real place settings – linens and china, not paper and plastic. I appropriated all the amenities necessary to provide the very best for our passengers. This was called job security. My crew and I were making ourselves indispensable.

More times than not, when we could not get any realistic answers from Triola about how many passengers would be flying with us, we just put on seven breakfasts or lunches, because the plane could hold only seven passengers. My attempts to be frugal went nowhere; over the years we put on hundreds of meals that were never eaten, simply because we could never get a straight answer from Triola. The attitude by some within the organization was *Who cares if we waste Hughes's money. He has a ton of it!*

Triola even appeared to be impressed with this largesse. The comment he was likely to make was, "You just take five hundred bucks and go." Ironically, what he was referring to was when Pete Maheu, who acted as his father's aide, gave Triola $500 and told him to take care of all the expenses (taxis, meals, etc.) during a particular trip – I believe it was to Mexico. Now, Pete was in his 20s and Triola was in his 50s, and in the military there was no way Triola would have tolerated that lack of respect from a young officer. It was an about-face from military life, where senior officers could expect deference – and where we had a per diem. In the military we had to be accountable for every penny … and alcohol was not considered a legitimate expense. But at the Hughes organization, Triola seemed to eat up this sort of behavior.

Bob Maheu may have set the tone; he was generous with $20 tips to limo drivers, line boys (who meet the aircraft at refueling stops or destinations, and arrange the limos, load the luggage, and service the aircraft), and such. The Mormon faction of the Hughes organization (which was not insignificant) was critical of Maheu's extravagant lifestyle. In my opinion, though, he felt it was necessary for his image, so that he could accomplish the almost impossible tasks assigned to him by Hughes. There were times when Joe Williams (a retired USAF fighter pilot hired by General Triola to fly with me) and I felt that Maheu's generosity was a liability, but not for the same reasons. We worried that it could be taken for granted in the future when we would transit an FBO and could not be quite as generous with our tips as we had been previously. In fact, in many cases, a six-pack of Coors beer, which at the time was not available east of the Mississippi, went a long way and got us a far greater return on the investment than a generous cash tip.

I heard several conversations among Hughes's staff about Bob Maheu that painted him as an arrogant, conniving person, but I never saw him act the way. He was always very generous and sensitive to the "little guy". For instance, the Maheus brought their nanny, Missy, and her husband, Roscoe, to Las Vegas with them when they moved. Missy was more than a nanny to the Maheus; she was entrenched in the family as a confidante and a friend. Bob assigned Roscoe the job of assistant manager of the FBO, and eventually gave him a high-up position at the Frontier Hotel.

Missy and Roscoe flew on the airplane quite often, and I got to know both of them very well. Missy enjoyed gossiping, and it was clear that she was not very fond of Triola at all. In my opinion, Missy probably had more to do with Triola getting fired than anyone.

Fortunately, Missy and I got along great.

Mutiny among the Ranks

The rub between Triola and me began when Hughes's people stopped involving the colonel in their flight scheduling. After Pete Maheu got to know me, he called me directly instead of going through Triola when his father wanted to schedule a flight. Triola become furious, and I got caught in the middle. I was open with him, always telling him when Pete had called me about a flight for Bob.

Triola just bark at me, "Why did he call you? He's supposed to go through me."

One time, in an attempt to defuse the situation, I picked up the telephone and called Pete. I asked him to please call Colonel Triola with the details about any upcoming trips. Pete's response was, "Why would I have to do that? I'm telling *you*. You're the pilot."

As these incidents continued, they started to draw a line in the sand as far as Triola and I were concerned. In his mind, I was trying to undermine him. In fact, I was just doing my job and trying to play the diplomacy game.

Six months went by, and Triola's paranoia still had me in a no-win situation. During this time I was frequently flying from Las Vegas to Los Angeles and Burbank, and I decided to look up my friend Ebb Harris, the corporate pilot for Lockheed who had started out in pilot training along with Marv Whiteman, Jug Hilton, and me, at Marana Air Base in Arizona in April 1953. When I related my problems with Triola, Ebb introduced me to Tony Levier, a famous aviator back in the golden years of aviation. Tony had been a test pilot on Lockheed's very successful XP-80. Now he was director of flight operations for Lockheed at Burbank, and he was Ebb's boss. Tony said he could use someone like me – someone with C-141 experience – because they were building the L-1011, the Lockheed TriStar, a medium-size jumbo jet.

When word filtered back through the aviation grapevine that I was talking to Lockheed about a job – back to Bob Maheu, in particular – he took me aside before a flight one day. He told me he understood the problems I was having with Triola, and he assured me that he would put me on his personal staff and payroll if that would get me to stay.

So Pete called me in to visit their Vegas offices in the Frontier hotel and showed me where I would be working if I accepted the job on Bob's staff. I guess it was one way to handle the situation, but I wasn't sure that sitting in an office all day was really what I wanted to be doing. I'd have to be there at the crack of dawn, have to answer to someone at every turn. I really didn't think this was the best position to put myself in. After all, I was an aviator. On the other hand, prestige-wise it sounded great: big office overlooking the hotel pool, a nice secretary, and a place at the heart of the Hughes-Maheu organization!

I thought about it for some time, but before the Maheus could put me on their payroll or set me up in that exclusive office, the Hughes-Maheu relationship started to unravel. According to Richard Hack, author of *Hughes, The Private Diaries, Memos and Letters*, Hughes demanded absolute loyalty.

The problem, as Hughes saw it, was that his alter ego was "thinking." Robert Maheu, his consummate problem-solver, seemed to be operating on his own agenda, "having opinions," even arguing, for crying out loud! It was a situation that Hughes could no more understand than he could tolerate.

After all, he'd given Maheu everything Bob had requested – the yacht, the penthouse in Newport Beach, two Cadillacs, a $500,000 mansion in Las Vegas, and a $10,000-per-week salary and unlimited expense account.

Some men just can't be bought – at any price. Hughes didn't seem to understand this – any more than he realized that for some men, the price was always right for buying false loyalty.

Howard Hughes: The Truth and the Myth

By the time I joined the company in early 1969, Howard Hughes's past was intriguing, even legendary. I was soon to learn that Hughes was a bigger enigma then I had ever imagined. I would not attempt to recount all his legacy here, since many other authors have already researched and recorded that legacy thoroughly, from birth to death. Perhaps Jack Real, a close associate of Hughes's for 20 years and my boss for several years, came closest to the real story in his worthwhile 2003 biography, *The Asylum of Howard Hughes.* But having been so close to the organization, I can tell you this: In my opinion, some of the stories in the many books written about Howard Hughes are true, and some of it is myth.

It's true that Howard Hughes isolated himself from the public later in life, beginning around the time he suffered near-fatal burns and injuries when he crashed the XF-11, in the spring of 1946. It's definitely true that Hughes was a brilliant man with a whole lot of money that he initially inherited from his father and Hughes Tool Company. It was the kind of money that could earn him fame, and name in the world of aviation, by flying around the globe in record-setting time, and by designing experimental aircraft that outstripped some of the best inventions in aviation history.

But to obtain this sort of success, he also took a lot of risks, and the outcomes were not always positive. Buying and subsequently losing TWA. Spending excessively on movie productions that caused pandemonium among his financial gurus. Building the Hercules, which would come to be known as the infamous "Spruce Goose," which he only flew once before it was mothballed and placed in a museum. (After he died, it was given to a Southern California aviation museum, along with $1 million to build a dome and a reflective pool where it was housed alongside the *Queen Mary* in Long Beach harbor.) These spectacular failures were just that: painful, public spectacles.

Then, of course, there was the debacle that was his personal life. Hughes loved women, but he had a tough time keeping them. It is well documented that, after he married Jean Peters, he had barely any contact with her. He shipped his wife from hotel to hotel, while he lived in quarters just down the hall. Even when the Hughes's purchased homes, the husband isolated himself from his wife – though not from his aides, who, on the rare occasions when the Hughes's were sharing the same bed, were ordered into the bedroom suite to take instructions and notes.

Eventually Mrs. Hughes demanded to be treated like a wife, provided with a home of their own where she could foster her great love for gardening. But none of that happened. Elizabeth Jean Peters had already suffered extreme mental and emotional cruelty in her first marriage, to Stuart W. Cramer III, which lasted a little more than a month. In the end, she finally left Hughes, too, and went back to her roots in Ohio. It was rumored that Hughes blamed Bill Gay, a member of his own "inner circle," for breaking up his marriage.

Rumors and gossip about the aides themselves spread quickly throughout the organization, with some of it becoming kind of a joke among us pilots. I was privy to certain conversations that took place among the aides, sometimes while we were flying and sometimes during other activities such as tennis games, which we often played at the same hotels where Hughes was living (especially in the Bahamas).

It is unfortunate that the dark side of Hughes's life eventually swallowed up the aviation genius. In his later years, he was addicted to drugs, suffered from malnutrition, and cloistered himself in hotel rooms with windows draped in black to shield him from sunlight. He lay in a bed or in his famous Berkline lounge chair, stark naked at times, for most of the end of his life.

It is true that his personal hygiene was atrocious. According to reports, Mr. Hughes did in fact store his urine in Mason jars. He had an incurable need to avoid germs and stacked dozens of Kleenex boxes next to his bed where he could easily reach them; he used Kleenex as a barrier between any germs he might touch from incoming mail, memos, and especially the doorknobs. In those same Kleenex boxes he hid his drugs, primarily codeine, which he purportedly injected. Many times throughout my tenure with the Hughes organization, I heard his aides refer to his stash as "goodies". It is said that he weighed far less than 100 pounds at the end of his life and no longer had the ability to inject himself with drugs. He didn't have the strength to drive the plunger into his arm; on many occasions, the needles would break off and remain under his skin.

Those of us who worked for Mr. Hughes heard the stories circulating within the organization too many times not to believe that there was some truth to them. However, there are hundreds of tales about Howard Hughes that are just plain lies. It's not difficult to imagine the selfish, money-grabbing types who spread such rumors. I dealt with some of them on a daily basis.

Hughes's Worst Nightmare: A Self-fulfilling Prophecy

When I started working for Hughes, he was living on the Las Vegas Strip, on the top floor of the Desert Inn. For many years he had employed a handful of men to be his drivers. Eventually, as he became more reclusive and more dependent on those in his immediate circle, these men became his personal aides. I knew many of them, including John Holmes, Roy Crawford, George Francom, Levar Myler, and Howard Eckersley. Later there were Jim Rickard, who replaced Roy Crawford when Hughes left Las Vegas, and Gordon Margulis, a fitness buff who was assigned to carry Hughes when he needed to be transported somewhere. Hughes's barber, Mel Stewart, was one of our favorites. Of these men, only Holmes, Crawford, and Margulis did not belong to the Mormon faith.

Hughes handpicked his aides. He preferred men who didn't smoke or drink, men he believed to be trustworthy; he believed he could accomplish this by hiring mainly Mormons. Some of his aides wound up being paid extremely well for unnecessary services. For instance, a number of men were paid handsomely for babysitting airplanes that were decayed and no longer airworthy. All these employees did was sit, read, watch, and wait – and in some cases make phone calls to raise money for the Mormon church.

A man by the name of Kay Glenn was in charge of the office on Romaine Street in Los Angeles, which was often referred to as the Hughes's "fortress". It was the center of communications for all Hughes's activities. When I was out of touch with my family, particularly when my daughter Robin was facing some crisis that her mother couldn't quite solve, they could call the Romaine Street number in order to get a message to me, and I would get back in touch with them.

By 1975, Hughes was suffering significantly from the effects of his long-term dependency on drugs. His most trusted aides controlled almost everything he did, even placing restrictions on who was allowed near him. These people heavily criticized anyone they claimed was squandering Hughes's money. Meanwhile, Hughes was urged to sign personal employment and consultancy contracts for a number of people on his staff, including these aides. Their goal was to ensure that they would be financially secure should anything happen to Hughes.

Some betrayals of Mr. Hughes's trust were more overt than others. In September 1975, Dr. Wilbur Thain replaced Dr. Norman F. Crane as Hughes's primary physician. Dr. Thain became the newest member of Hughes's medical team after Dr. Crane apparently refused to continue providing his patient with narcotic prescriptions. It turns out that Dr. Thain was close to many of the aides, and was related to Bill Gay.

On March 16, 1978, Hughes's personal aide John Holmes and Dr. Crane were charged with illegally supplying Hughes with narcotics over a period of two decades. Following seven days of testimony, the jury finally acquitted the doctor of any wrongdoing. But the evidence that led up to the indictment in the first place prompted Will Lummis – Hughes's only surviving family member (a cousin), who took over the reins of control after Hughes died – to set in motion legal actions that nullified many of those earlier wage contracts. Lummis ended up suing for $50 million in damages.

There are volumes of documentation indicating that some of Hughes's aides manipulated the man in order to gain control and power when his defenses were down, largely due to his excessive use of narcotics. It is my belief that many of those aides were out to get as much of Mr. Hughes's wealth as possible. Everything they did, they did for money.

In my opinion, some of the aides who surrounded Howard Hughes were not all that intelligent. They did not come into the organization with a resume like that of Bob Maheu, whose experience equipped him to do the impossible tasks he was expected to perform. They did not have strength of character like George Francom, one of Hughes's top aides, another exception to the rule. This was a man who looked almost malnourished. We'd be eating lobster and steak in the Bahamas on the Hughes organization's expense account, and Francom was eating the least expensive entrée on the menu. He just couldn't stand to waste Hughes's money like that. George was simply a good guy, a guy who was very loyal to Hughes and to Jack Real. He knew what Hughes's intentions were and what he wanted from his employees. Francom was very frugal, and he was grateful for his job; he appeared to have no ulterior motives.

Employees like Bob and George, who had intelligence and fortitude, could walk away from the Hughes organization and still have the ability to make money and be successful elsewhere. What could those lesser men do after Mr. Hughes was gone?

Howard Who?

If there was one thing each of us understood while we worked for Mr. Hughes – whom the staff commonly referred to as "The Man" – it was that his existence was always to be shrouded in secrecy. We never told anyone where he was living, where he might be traveling, what he ate, when or where he slept, or who he confided in. It was an unwritten rule that his name was never, ever to be mentioned.

I was made keenly aware of this "unwritten rule" one evening when Ruth and I accompanied Pete and Rosemary Maheu to the dinner show at the Frontier hotel to see the Supremes. When we exited, I made the mistake of nodding toward the top floor of the Desert Inn, directly across the street from the Frontier. Mr. Hughes was believed to be residing there at the time.

"So, he's up there?" I foolishly said.

In response, Pete gave me an alarmed look and walked away. It was his signal to me that we were never to discuss Mr. Hughes – in public or otherwise. I got the message.

As chief pilot for his personal fleet of aircraft, I had the responsibility of being at the ready whenever anyone in the Hughes organization needed to fly or needed to send something by air. Most of the time I was shuttling his aides to and from wher- ever Hughes was living at the time – any of a number of places during my nine-year tenure. But some of these flights were a pure embarrassment, laughable to the greatest degree imaginable, especially while Hughes was living in the Bahamas, at the Britannia. Once I flew a single envelope from Los Angeles to the Bahamas. He was so perpetually fearful of germs, bugs, and contact with other human beings that his aides had me and my co-pilot fly paper towels, certain movies, Kleenex, and a particular brand of water bottled produced by a company in New Hampshire. This happened many times at a moment's notice, often in the middle of the night. These products were so important to him that flight time, fuel, and labor expenses were meaningless.

Each year that I worked for the Hughes organization, the man became more impossible, more demanding, more invisible, and more profoundly frustrated with and untrusting of the people around him – except, of course, for his closest aides, some of whom perhaps deserved his suspicion more than anyone else. The truth is, I never met Howard Hughes face to face. But as his chief pilot, I learned a lot about him – sometimes more than I wanted to know.

GENIUS OR ROGUE?

HOWARD ROBARD HUGHES – some loved him, some envied him, and others just plain loathed him. But no one can deny his worldwide celebrity, his methodical approach to aviation, and his very strange and elusive lifestyle. Even today, more than 35 years after his death, Hughes is still an enigma worthy of the celebrity he devised for himself.

Some say Howard Hughes was a genius; others, a rogue. I fall somewhere in between these two schools of thought. To my mind, when you have great ideas – plus enough money to pick from the best brains in the country and demand results – yes, you can effectively be branded a genius, so to speak. And Hughes did have some great ideas. For instance, in 1935 he was determined to set the speed record in his H-1, the airplane that is now on display at the Smithsonian Institute in Washington, DC. Then in 1936 he set his famous transcontinental speed record, flying from Los Angeles to New York in 9 hours, 37 minutes, and 10 seconds.

After making a name for himself in aviation by setting a world distance record, however, he broke almost every bone in his body when his 1946 flight of the XF-11 prototype (a photo reconnaissance plane and a fast airplane for its time) ended badly: He crashed the plane into a neighborhood in Beverly Hills, California. This was in fact the beginning of his infamous addiction to painkillers.

Hughes is also credited with several aviation innovations, including flush-mounted rivets to get rid of parasitic drag, and hydraulically operated landing gear that quickly snap the gear up into the wheel well after tale off. In reality, however, no one knows for sure if these were his ideas or his engineer's.

He did build the Hercules HK-1 flying boat, nicknamed the "Spruce Goose" (which flew only once, in 1947), but that was essentially the ship-builder's idea. Henry J. Kaiser approached Hughes about building an airplane that had the capacity to negate the threat from the German U-boats, which were sinking our Liberty ships as they crossed the Atlantic, picking them off like flies. According to Jack Real's *The Asylum of Howard Hughes*, "Kaiser commanded considerable confidence in Washington at the time because his West Coast shipyards were efficiently and economically turning out transport ships by the dozen to support the American war effort. Entrusting Kaiser to get a job done was considered a sure thing." Kaiser came up with the idea of building a gigantic flying boat that would be out of the submarines' reach. He went to Hughes with the idea, and Hughes bought into it.

The only problem with the HK-1 ("Hughes-Kaiser, first prototype") was the funding. During wartime, aluminum was at a premium since it was listed as a "strategic material". Ultimately the HK-1 was built with wood – primarily birch –

spawning the name "Spruce Goose". Because of the war effort, Hughes had trouble getting engines for the plane – they were needed for fighter aircraft and bombers. But eventually he was able to procure the largest engine available at that time: a Pratt & Whitney 4360. In fact, he purchased eight of them.

Taken February 20, 1978, the author in the left seat of the "Spruce Goose" with David Grant in the co-pilot seat. David sat in the co-pilot seat when Hughes flew the giant airplane in 1947

Of all the aircraft Hughes built, there was one contraption that he never flew himself: an experimental heavy-lift helicopter nicknamed the "Flying Crane". This was an XH-17 helicopter of sorts, built by Kellett Aircraft and funded by the Air Force. In 1949 Hughes paid $250,000 for it. In his 2004 article "Howard Hughes' Top Ten," Lerner describes it as follows:

After Hughes bought it, it was equipped with a 130-foot, two-blade rotor. Two Allison J-35 jet engines, modified by General Electric to act as compressors and designated TG-180s, fed compressed air through the hollow rotor blades to the tips, where the fuel was ignited in burners to produce thrust. The rotors turned at a leisurely 88 rpm, but the effect was monstrous.

For the aircraft's first official flight off the Hughes runway in Culver City, California, Gale Moore was the pilot.

Moore accumulated 10 hours of flight time before the program ended in the mid-1950s. Although a follow-on Flying Crane program failed for lack of funds, helicopters turned out to be the key to a profitable future for Hughes Aircraft. Hughes himself, though, had no interest in rotary-wing technology, and the first flight of the XH-17 was the last time he visited the helicopter factory.

According to my observations, and in my humble opinion, despite all these innovations Mr. Hughes was not so much a genius as he was crafty enough (and manipulative enough) to hire the really smart people to get the job done. The true geniuses in his camp were those people like Bob Maheu and Mickey West, Hughes's tax attorney. I flew West numerous times, and we got to know each other and really hit it off. West told me once that when Mr. Hughes called him for direction on what the tax laws required, he had him on the telephone for three hours. After all that time talking, West could not even remember his own name!

Playing Politics

In his pursuit to be immortalized as the brightest, most inventive, richest man in the universe, Howard Hughes risked bold moves in the political arena and made huge investments in some innovations that may have put him in the history books but ultimately flopped miserably in execution. Perhaps his problem was that he was too much of a dabbler. It was when he attempted to delve into areas with which he was less familiar that his inventions (historical though they would become) did not turn out positively.

The Spruce Goose project was one such downer that dragged on, like so many Hughes initiated, until the aircraft was no longer needed by the military. The war was over. Many people had profited from it, and the Spruce Goose became the subject of Senate hearings into such allegations. The hearings, aimed at uncovering Hughes's misuse of federal funds, were chaired by Senator Ralph Owen Brewster, a Republican from Maine. According to journalist Preston Lerner of *Air & Space* magazine, when he was exonerated, "Hughes crowed to the press, 'I designed every nut and bolt that went into this airplane … I have stated that if it fails to fly, I will leave the country. And I mean it.'" Hounded by subpoenas to appear in court, he left Las Vegas around Thanksgiving 1970 for the Bahamas. He never did return, dying six years later en route to a U.S. hospital.

Senator Brewster was not unfamiliar to Hughes, who had suffered persecution at the senator's hand only the previous year. Shortly after Hughes's airline TWA had introduced flights to Europe in 1946, a bill was introduced in Congress that would have taken away its overseas routes. Called the "Chosen Instrument" bill, if passed it would have required all United States airlines flying abroad to give up their overseas routes to a new consolidated international airline corporation. Pan American, the largest overseas carrier at the time, operating under the control of a Republican crony, would have had controlling interest. Senator Brewster was the author of that bill.

Hughes was at odds with the federal government more often than not. Still, the government was only too happy to use him when they needed him, as was the case with "Project Jennifer", where he was positioned as a ruse to fool the public.

Some, like Andrew Toppan on his Scientific Military Naval FAQs website, have theorized about Hughes's involvement in the U.S. Navy's efforts to recover a lost Soviet sub from the Pacific Ocean floor. As the story goes, Global Marine, a Hughes company, built the Glomar Explorer in the early 1970s at an astronomical price under contract to the U.S. government, and under the guise of mining manganese and other useful metals. It certainly does add mystique to the Hughes enigma, and after all, there could be no monetary value put on projects of this nature when it came to the Cold War. Hughes seemed to be the logical choice for the CIA to use as a cover.

The "deep-sea mining" operation located the sub in June 1974, and as the Soviets watched, certain nuclear missiles and highly sensitive code materials were recovered while others were lost. Following the recovery, and just months after Hughes's death, the Hughes Glomar Explorer was transferred on September 3, 1976, to the Navy and then to the Maritime Administration, which had it laid up in Suisun Bay, California. Eventually the craft ended up in the mothballed fleet before it was reconditioned and converted to a drill-testing ship for operation in the Gulf of Mexico.

With the capital to finance a project of this magnitude and to see potentially high returns on the supposed investment, and with his reputation as a daring entrepreneur, Hughes made a very believable "wallet" behind this covert operation. He was extremely wealthy and had government ties; why shouldn't he have been the person to finance Project Jennifer?

Taking Risks and Cheating Death

As I have said before, much has been written about the eccentric billionaire, some of it true while other yarns were undoubtedly spun out of suspicion and jealousy. The elusive, exclusive, often irritable, and totally unpredictable Howard Hughes was nonetheless a person to be reckoned with.

Hughes in the early years was a risk taker. Consider the crash of the XF-11, which almost cost him his life! One of Hughes's mechanics also related a story to me about the time Howard, while piloting a twin-engine Convair from New Orleans to Santa Monica, was warned that, according to the fuel gages, the propeller plane was getting extremely low on fuel. But instead of calling in an emergency or making a straight-in approach, Hughes flew clear out over the Pacific and came in on a long, low approach. After he landed, when the ground crew dipped the tanks to determine how much fuel was actually left, there wasn't even enough to wet the dipstick. Like a daredevil, he had flown perilously close to a condition called "fuel starvation."

That was pretty typical of some of the pilots of that generation. Hughes was a wealthy man with a big ego, and he didn't like to be told what to do. He practiced very dangerous maneuvers and took chances as though he intended to cheat death.

Some would say that the Grim Reaper wasn't the only one to be cheated by Howard Hughes …

Watergate: My Unwitting Role

In the later years of Mr. Hughes's life, on numerous occasions I played a minor yet memorable role in his personal aviation business activities. I am grateful for that experience, though at times it was just as sad as it was exciting. One incident that will go down in political infamy is Hughes's reported involvement in Watergate.

Throughout the Watergate investigation two *Washington Post* reporters, Bob Woodward and Carl Bernstein, beat the pavement for sources who could contribute to the stories they unraveled about who was responsible for the break-in. Both Bernstein and Woodward claimed to have one key witness to the entire mess. They referred to him as "Deep Throat" and kept his true identity secret.

For years speculation spun about who Deep Throat really was, or if he or she even existed. Then, on May 31, 2005, the *Washington Post* confirmed that now-91-year-old W. Mark Felt, a former "number two" official at the FBI, was indeed Deep Throat. This was confirmed by both Bernstein and Woodward.

So much has been written about the Watergate scandal, yet when it comes to Hughes's indirect involvement so few truths have been revealed. It has been reported and thoroughly documented that the break-in was perpetrated under the direct orders of Nixon himself. Some have speculated that Howard Hughes was the kingpin behind thousands of dollars he donated surreptitiously to President Richard Nixon's reelection campaign – his contribution to Nixon's "dirty tricks" slush fund. This money could even have been used to finance the Watergate break-in. Although it has never been proven, I know for a fact that money did exchange hands between Hughes and Nixon. How do I know this? Because I was the pilot of the plane that carried it between Las Vegas and Miami.

Why didn't I object to carrying that loot? Why didn't I question what was going on? When you work for an organization as powerful as Hughes's was, you don't ask questions. You do what you are told. Besides, I didn't actually handle the money.

Many of Hughes's closest confidants conveyed to me Hughes's blatant ambition to "buy" a president. It was also a well-known fact that Hughes was playing favorites on both sides of the party line by making campaign contributions to Democratic candidates as well as Republicans. But was Hughes personally involved in the break-in at the Democratic National Committee headquarters at the Watergate Hotel in Washington, DC, on June 17, 1972? This question has been debated ever since.

When the Watergate story broke, there was no doubt in my mind about one thing at least: I had made several flights between Las Vegas and Miami with deliv eries for Charles "Bebe" Rebozo, who has been labeled the bag man for Hughes's famous $100,000 contribution to Nixon's campaign. I acted as a conduit unknowingly, however, and had little knowledge of what was actually being delivered. I had no idea that those flights would trigger a string of corruptive activities that I'd eventually have to answer for, regardless how small my part in them was. While the flights figured prominently in the Watergate scandal, I really was quite innocent of any wrongdoing in Watergate. The appropriate people and the money may have been on board, but in reality all I did was fly the airplane.

Here is what happened: I had been instructed by Dick Danner, general manager of the Frontier hotel and Bebe Rebozo's brother-in-law, to fly down to Miami. Danner was Miami's former city manager and ran Nixon's campaign there, though he continually turned down Nixon's offers of various jobs within his administration. Danner was the middleman; he orchestrated the friendship between President Nixon and Rebozo, who owned a bank in Key Biscayne. The setup was perfect. When Mr. Hughes instructed Bob Maheu to make a campaign contribution to Nixon, Maheu must have thought of Danner and his connection to Rebozo, whose bank presumably was where the "contribution" would be laid to rest in a lock box.

After one particular flight down to Miami, I flew Danner and Rebozo to the Bahamas and stayed overnight at the Britannia Hotel in Nassau, then flew back to Miami the next day with Danner and Rebozo on board once again. While I can never be sure what that trip was all about, I believe now that it could have been the delivery of Mr. Hughes's $100,000 contribution to Nixon's reelection campaign.

From Miami that day I flew Danner and Rebozo to Washington, DC, a trip we made on more than one occasion. During these flights I got to know the two men very well, as we shared many tidbits of conversation. I especially remember the enormous amount of food that was packed on board. Rebozo, a Cuban-American, always took care of the catering, and he always overdid it.

Rebozo, who was also a pilot, liked to sit in the cockpit with me, and on one particular flight he told me that he had owned a seaplane. He was reminiscing about his very own near-death experience – how he had crashed the seaplane and woken up under 20 feet of water. He recalled just lying there as everything became very serene, beautiful, and fantastic, until suddenly he woke up, came to the realization of where he was, and somehow made his way to the surface. He must have been a very lucky man, since he also managed to stay afloat in 1973, in the midst of the Watergate scandal.

During this Miami trip, around February the 5th 1970, I met a very interesting aviation legend, Captain Dick Merrill. Dick was retired from Eastern Airlines and liked to "hang out" at Miami International and in particular the Fixed Base Operator, to see who might be in town, since corporate aircraft used this particular FBO. Our aircraft was there waiting on our passengers and Dick strolled up and started a conversation. At the time I did not have any idea who he was, other than a retired Airline Pilot. Dick claimed he knew Howard Hughes and I'm sure he would have had some great stories if we had had more time to talk. Recently I found a book written about Dick titled, "Wings of Man", The Legend of Captain Dick Merrill. A very interesting excerpt from the book tells, about in 1927, when Dick was made aware of the Orteig prize money for flying the Atlantic, he was able to find a backer and a Bellanca aircraft suitable for long range. However, the newspapers picked up the story and warned that it would be a "suicide mission" and his backer withdrew his offer. The rest is history with Charles Lindbergh winning the "prize". Dick went on to set many records with flights for Eastern Airlines including a round the world flight with Arthur Godfrey in Godfrey's Jet Commander, N1966J.

Corruption at the Highest Level

Historically there has been a great deal of speculation concerning Howard Hughes and his possible involvement with the infamous Watergate fiasco. In my opinion, one of the best collections of facts on this subject is *The Ends of Power*, written by H. R. Haldeman, Nixon's chief of staff, who had a stern reputation as the president's gatekeeper. The controversial 18-and-a-half-minute gap in Nixon's Oval Office recordings was found later to include a conversation between the president and Haldeman. Haldeman was also involved in a conversation recorded on what was referred to as the "smoking gun" tape, in which Nixon discussed using the CIA to divert the FBI's Watergate probe.

Haldeman was forced to resign on April 30, 1973, and was convicted of conspiracy and obstruction of justice on January 1, 1975. He served 18 months in prison for his role in Watergate, after which he wrote *The Ends of Power* (with Joseph DiMona). Several chapters of this book, which was published in 1978, implicated my boss, Howard Hughes, as being indirectly involved in the scandal, using his money, power, and personnel to get a foothold in the White House. In particular, there is one poignant commentary about Nixon's take on Hughes:

In the case of [DNC strategist and probable Watergate target Larry O'Brien, Nixon was acting very much like Captain Queeg in his search for the strawberries. He knew the strawberries had been stolen, but he just couldn't get anyone to take the event seriously.

And yet, as Nixon had often said to me, how the press took after him on any possible connection to Howard Hughes! He strongly felt that the build-up to the $205,000 loan to his brother was a typical "cheap shot" by the press. Now he felt he had a scandal of his own to reveal which could turn the tables on the Democrats. He called me into his cabin in Air Force One and laid out the program. 'We're going to nail O'Brien on this, one way or the other.'

Haldeman died of cancer at his home in Santa Barbara on November 12, 1993, at the age of 67 – less than six months before the death of Nixon himself.

Dirty Tricks

Shortly after it was signed on November 8, 1973, a summons arrived at my Las Vegas home, indicating that my presence was required in Washington, DC – in room G-308 of the New Senate Office Building, to be precise. I was to testify on December 3, 1973, before the Senate Select Committee on Presidential Campaign Activities about what I may have known relative to the subject matters under consideration – namely, whether a large sum of Howard Hughes's money had made it into President Nixon's war chest.

Attached to the subpoena was a lengthy list of directives I was to follow with regard to the hearings. It read:

And bring with you the following:

Any and all documents and records and copies thereof including; but not limited to, books, files, ledgers, books of accounts, correspondence, receipts, appointment books, diaries, memoranda, checks, check stubs, deposit slips, bank statements, petty cash records, photographs and negatives, recordings, notes, telephone records, credit card vouchers and bills, airline and railroad records, relating directly or indirectly, in whole or in part, to the Presidential Campaign of 1972 and related events prior and subsequent thereto, including but not limited to any and all activities of January 1, 1969, to the present which involve:

1. The break-ins on or about May 27, 1972, and on or about June 17, 1972, and electronic surveillance at the Democratic National Committee Headquarters;
2. The planning, execution, or discussion of any break-in or illegal entry into the office, home, or any other premises of Herman Greenspun and the planning, execution, or discussion of any electronic surveillance therein;
3. The Presidential Primaries of 1972;
4. Any and all contributions, compensations, payments, or loans to any individuals who were candidates for the offices of the President and Vice President of the United States of America, or to any agent, relative, representative, designee, or employee of any such candidate, including but not limited to Robert Abplanalp, Vincent Andrews, Arthur Blech, Frank DeMarco, Thomas Evans, Kenneth Gemmill, William Griffin, Herbert Kalmbach, Donald A. Nixon, F. Donald Nixon, Edward Nixon, Frances Raine, Charles G. Rebozo, Thomas Wakefield, Rose Mary Woods, by any of the following: **Hughes Tool Company, Hughes Air Corp., Summa Corporation, Air West Airlines,** Robert A. Maheu Associates, Robert Mullen and Co., Toledo Mining Company, Basic Industries, Inc., Maatschappii Intermovie, N.V., Inriego License, N.V., Hallomar Homes, San Bar Corporation, Resorts International, Meier-Murray Productions, Georgetown Resources, Ogden Foods, Charles Adams, Robert Bennett, Gene Bowen, Howard Cerny, E.L. "Jack" Cleveland, James Crosby, Richard Danner, Chester Davis, I.G. "Jack" Davis, Virgil Gladieux, Louis Gonzales, Nadine Henley, Anthony Hatsis, Patrick Hillings, **Howard Hughes,** E. Howard Hunt, Paul

Laxalt, G. Gordon Liddy, Peter Maheu, Robert A. Maheu, John Meier, Edward P. Morgan, Charles G. Rebozo, John Suckling, Robert Vesco, or any persons representing themselves to be employees, agents, designees, or representatives of any of the aforementioned companies;

5. The employment of or any compensation paid to or on behalf of John Meier, his employees, representatives, agents, or designees, including but not limited to F. Donald Nixon;

6. Any relationship between F. Donald Nixon and any of the following individuals: Charles Adams, Arthur Blech, E. L. "Jack" Cleveland, Gene Bowen, Howard Cerny, James Crosby, I. G. "Jack" Davis, John Dean, John Ehrlichman, Robert Finch, Virgil Gladieux, Louis Gonzalez, Rolando Gonzalez, Herman Greenspun, William Haddad, Anthony Hatsis, Patrick Hillings, Lloyd Hallomare, William Hallomare, **Howard Hughes,** Herbert Klein, Robert Maheu, John Meier, Cliff Miller, John Mitchell, Thomas Murray, Charles G. Rebozo, John Suckling, Robert Versco;

7. Any files of correspondence to or from F. Donald Nixon, Robert Maheu, Richard Danner, C.G. Rebozo, **Howard Hughes,** John Meier, Chester Davis, Herman Greenspun, Herbert Kalmbach, or Kenneth Gemmill or any agent, representative, designee or employee of any Presidential candidate;

8. Any memoranda or reports on the activities of F. Donald Nixon, Donald A. Nixon, or Edward Nixon, including but not limited to any memoranda or reports drafted by John Ehrlichman, Stanley McKiernan, Cliff Miller or anyone else;

9. Any documents between or relating to F. Donald Nixon and **the Hughes Tool Company or the Summa Corporation;**

10. The solicitation, negotiation, delivery, and/or storage of two $50,000 contributions to the Presidential Campaign of 1972 from **Howard Hughes** or the **Hughes Tool Company** delivered to Charles G. Rebozo and/or the return of said contributions to **Howard Hughes, the Hughes Tool Company, theSumma Corporation,** Kenneth Gemmill, Chester Davis, or any individual associated with the law firm of Davis and Cox;

11. The use, dispersal, and accounting of any funds given as contributions, compensations, payments, or loans to any persons who were candidates for President or Vice President of the United States of America in 1972 or to any agents, relatives, representatives, designees, or employees of any such candidate;

12. Negotiations or contracts between any federal agency or department, or employee thereof and **the Hughes Tool Company, the Summa Corporation, or any employees, agents, representatives, or designees thereof** including but not limited to:

a) Negotiations between former Attorney General John Mitchell, his agents, employees, representatives, or designees and **the Hughes Tool Company, the Summa Corporation, or any employee, agent, representative, or designee**

thereof relating to proposed hotel acquisitions from January 1, 1969, to the present;

b) Negotiations or contracts between **the Hughes Tool Company, the Summa Corporation, or any employee, agent, representative, or designee thereof** and any and all individuals in the federal government relating to the acquisition of Air West by the Hughes Tool Company from January 1, 1969, to the present; or

c) Any and all discussions of **the Hughes Tool Company, the Summa Corporation, or any employee, agent, representative, or designee thereof** and any and all individuals in the federal government concerning atomic testing in Nevada from January 1, 1969, to the present;

13. Lawrence O'Brien and any corporation, partnership, or business entity owned in whole or in part by Lawrence O'Brien.

The summons also indicated: *"And bring with you all materials and documents in your possession, custody, or control as listed on the attached sheet."* It was signed by the committee chairman, North Carolina senator Sam J. Ervin, Jr.

Had the money Hughes contributed to Nixon's campaign been lying in wait to be used for "dirty tricks"? And was I responsible for flying it down to Miami in one of Mr. Hughes's personal corporate jets? Finding the answers to these questions was undoubtedly one of the reasons that Senator Ervin had subpoenaed ten of us from the Hughes organization into his chambers.

This meeting on Capitol Hill did not include any of the Maheu people at that time, and I was the only one from the aviation entities of the Hughes organization subpoenaed to appear. Hughes's chief counsel, Chester Davis, joined us. Once we were paraded into Ervin's office, Sam Dash appeared. While some might be familiar with Dash from his involvement in the Clinton impeachment hearings decades later, at this point he was chief counsel for the Senate Watergate Committee. Senator Ervin was hard of hearing, and it was curious to see Dash sitting behind him, periodically whispering in his ear, presumably explaining what was being said and advising him.

Even more interesting was watching Chester Davis at his best, taking on a man of Sam Ervin's stature in such a high-profile Senate hearing. I sat there watching as Davis's juices just ran. He was rocking in his chair and would look at us and grin whenever he made a point. And when Ervin talked about the $100,000 and asked Davis if he could produce it, he retorted that yeah, sure, he could get the *$#% money!

After we left Ervin's chambers that first time, we went to the Mayflower Hotel. Chester Davis had a suite, and in that suite we peons sat at one end of the room while the heavy hitters (Davis and his lieutenants) gathered at the other, strategizing about what to do in response to the directive from Sam Ervin. We at the other end of the hotel room sat there trying to be very quiet – eavesdropping on the conversation, naturally. Who was in that group, I can't quite recall, but I know that I was the only pilot.

Finally, Davis summoned me to his end of the room and said, "Bob, can you get up to New York and pick up the money?"

I nodded, though I was not sure how I would accomplish this.

He looked pleased. "Go up to LaGuardia, head into New York, and pick up the money."

I said, "Yes, sir. When do you want it?"

His reply was "By tomorrow morning."

I had initially flown to DC on a commercial flight. How was I going to get up to New York and back by the next morning? Then it came to me: Charlie Wilson and Warren Bachelor were standing by at another hotel in town, and they had the Jet-Star.

During my tenure with the Hughes organization I worked with several co-pilots, flight mechanics, and stewards, including Carroll "Smitty" Smith; Jan Moore, who could fine-tune a Cessna 421 and make it run like a Swiss watch; Jim Hogan, the son of a casino manager at the Frontier hotel; and Joe Williams, a retired Air Force major and an F-105 pilot in Vietnam. Then there were Charlie Wilson, a former B-47 co-pilot and C-141 pilot in the Air Force, and Warren Bachelor, a retired Air Force sergeant flight engineer with a commercial instrument multiengine pilot rating, who later received his type rating in the JetStar, joined me in flying Robert Goulet, and became Wayne Newton's pilot. These were guys I could trust.

I called Charlie and Warren and said, "Guys, you have to go up to LaGuardia." I gave them the contact information. "First thing tomorrow morning, come back here and bring the package you'll get there."

Charlie and Warren did exactly as they were told, and the next day we witnessed Chester Davis very unceremoniously walking into Senator Ervin's office and, using some strong language, plunking the money down on Ervin's desk. Ervin and his group immediately looked at the serial numbers. Why? To be sure the money had been printed before the date we claimed the $100,000 went to Bebe Rebozo. This would reinforce Rebozo's statement that it had been in his bank's safety deposit box all that time rather than exchanging hands in the name of "dirty tricks". There was no way of truly knowing whether that cash was the actual money from the lock box or different money, printed after the Watergate scandal broke and not retrieved from the lock box at all.

During that trip in December I was called back again with the other nine to appear before one of the subcommittees. Back at home a few weeks later, I received another letter from the United States Senate Select Committee, requesting further information. This letter was dated January 7, 1974, and addressed to Solomon Freedman, an attorney with the Davis and Cox at One State Street Plaza in Manhattan, who was retained by the Hughes organization to represent me. It read:

Dear Mr. Freedman:

At Mr. Robert Wearley's Executive Session before the Senate Select Committee, he agreed to provide certain records to the Committee which were not available at the time.

Specifically, Mr. Wearley agreed to reconstruct the 7.2 hours not reflected in the logs of the DeHavilland 125 between March and June of 1973.

Secondly, Mr. Wearley agreed to forward a list of passengers and their travels noted on the accounting records after the new procedures were instituted in the spring of 1971.

We would appreciate very much receiving this information as soon as possible. Thank you for your cooperation.

Sincerely,

Mark E. Lackritz

Of course, I complied with everything the Senate Select Committee requested of me. But the hearings were not at all what I expected. In fact, there were moments of levity – and some that were downright comical.

Humor at the Hearing

During my last "summons" to appear before the committee, Freedman and I were called into another room, separate from the large committee room where the television cameras and reporters were stationed. In that smaller room were a different set of lawyers, a court reporter talking into a dictating machine, and three or four people on the other side of a long desk. The people seated at the desk started interrogating me. I had my flight records right there with me and could have told them anything they wanted to know, but they just were not asking the right questions. They were fishing around but nothing was rising to the bait. I wanted to say, "Why don't you ask me *this question*?"

Instead, they asked, "Did you ever fly any large sums of money for the Hughes organization that you know of?"

I replied, "Yes."

Then they perked up like they were on to something, asking, "Where did you go?"

I told them that we were instructed to go down to Palomar Airport near LaCosta, Califonia. They perked up again because that airport was so close to San Clemente – Richard Nixon's personal residence.

"Well, what did you do?" they asked.

"We flew down there, and because there was some cloud cover, we could not get into the airport visually or with the circling instrument approach, so we diverted to San Diego and rented a car, drove up to La Costa, and picked up a package from a gentleman at the La Costa Country Club."

"What was in the package?"

I told them that I didn't know at the time but later found out it was a $50,000 payment on a gambling debt, an IOU to the Sands hotel in Las Vegas.

They weren't interested. "Skip that. That's not relevant."

They were obviously looking for some connection between the money I flew and Nixon's "dirty tricks", but couldn't find anything with their line of questioning.

When Freedman, my attorney, got up from his seat to take a phone call, he leaned over to me and said, "Now, Bob, don't say anything while I'm gone."

"Yes sir," I replied. The Watergate attorneys in the room overheard what he said to me and, having worked with Freedman before and being very familiar with him, decided to play a joke on him.

"When he comes back," someone told the court reporter, "act like you're taking something down, but don't really record it. We're going to pull our own trick on him."

Even at the time, I thought this was rather humorous. Here we are in a serious hearing concerning Howard Hughes, my boss and one of the country's most influential men, and the possible impeachment of the president of the United States, and they're playing courtroom tricks.

When Freedman returned and took his chair, he resumed his comfortable, slouched-down position while chewing on his cigar.

The next question came: "Now, Mr. Wearley, would you go into a little more detail about what you were telling us while your attorney was gone? About this money that you flew down to San Clemente?"

The court reporter acted as though she were taking it down. I didn't have to say a word before Solomon Freedman literally came out of his chair, glaring at me as he said, "What in the world have you done? This is going to take some undoing to get this straightened out, young man." But when the room broke out in laughter, he realized that the joke was on him.

In the end, I gave Sam Ervin and his committee what they needed to know and no more. Despite having no actual knowledge of any illegal activity (though I had my suspicions), I could have given them a lot more information had they asked the right questions. For instance, I could have told them about all the flights I made with Bebe Rebozo, how many times I flew to Miami, and why I flew to the Bahamas with Rebozo and Dick Danner. But they never asked those questions. I waited and waited for them, thinking that any good investigator would have smelled some innuendo regarding those flights and would start to ask enough questions to smoke out the information they were looking for. But no one ever did. They even subpoenaed my log books, but they never went through them with a fine-toothed comb.

To see Bob Wearley's entire Watergate transcript, go to Prodigal Pilot dot-com [http://www.prodigalpilot.com/].

The one person the committee could not serve with a subpoena was Howard Hughes himself, who was conveniently living out of the country during those days. I didn't know to what extent Howard Hughes was involved in Watergate until much later, when I heard Bob Maheu's

statement: "He had both sides of the Strip covered." Larry O'Brien of the DNC was on the

payroll of the Sands hotel; Hughes reportedly paid him $180,000 a year as a part-time consultant. Meanwhile, Republican and Nixon man Dick Danner was general manager of the Frontier, right across the street. Employing these two men with opposing political motivations, both so closely linked to the scandal, was no coincidence.

H. R. Haldeman was one of the few men Nixon confided in during the Watergate scandal, and he may have penetrated the secrecy surrounding Hughes's contributions to Nixon's campaign. In *The Ends of Power*, he says:

Rose Mary Woods and the president's brothers denied they had received money from Rebozo. And the investigators who probed Bebe's finances never found any such payments, although they did find that Bebe had paid for such items as personal gifts for Pat Nixon as well as improvements to Nixon's Key Biscayne home. But there was no evidence that this came from the Hughes money.

In fact, Bebe Rebozo told FBI investigators that the $100,000 from Hughes had been kept untouched in the safe deposit box for years. But when an agent opened the box to count the "untouched" $100,000, he found it had at least been nudged. There was an extra $100 bill.

Now in San Clemente, Nixon told me the full story for the first time.

He said that Bebe also kept his own money in that box, mingled with the "campaign contributions," and that's where the extra $100 came from. The $100,000 was apparently only part of a much larger cash kitty kept in a safe deposit box.

How much money was really in that box, or other bank accounts, for the president's use?

Nevertheless, despite all the rumors, I can say that in all my years with Nixon, I never knew him to do any special favors for Hughes. Quite the contrary, when Hughes objected violently to the nuclear testing in Nevada, Nixon ordered the testing to go forward, even though Hughes was enraged.

Years later, in 1976, I asked Nixon about that $100,000, which by then had been the subject of vigorous investigation for years. The investigation had finally petered out with no results. Rebozo explained that the $100,000 was a campaign contribution, and the reason it never reached the Campaign Committee was that an internecine war had broken out in the Hughes empire. Rebozo said he was afraid the president would be embarrassed by one side or another in the Hughes war if the campaign contribution was revealed.

The investigators couldn't find the evidence to refute this. But I had questions in 1976 – based on a personal experience.

In 1973 when Nixon "requested" [John] Ehrlichman and me to resign, he softened the blow by offering us money for our legal fees. The amount he cited was $200,000 on one occasion, $300,000 on another. We had refused it. But I had always wondered about that offer. In 1976 I asked Nixon where that money would have come from.

We were sitting in the den of his San Clemente residence. Nixon had his feet on a hassock, piles of paper on either side of him. He said, "Bebe had it."

But I reminded him that Bebe had only $100,000 of the Hughes money. Where would the rest of the two or three hundred thousand have come from? Nixon told me this interesting news. There was much more money in Bebe's "tin box" than the Hughes $100,000. For example, Dwayne Andreas, a Minnesota financier, who had also been inadvertently and unknowingly connected to the Watergate money, had contributed another $100,000. That, Nixon said, made the $200,000.

From time to time over the years *Playboy* magazine has published some less-than-credible articles about Howard Hughes and his involvement with Watergate, articles with information I can refute because it was during my tenure with the Hughes organization that some of these incidents occurred. In a September 1976 article titled *The Puppet: Uncovering the Secret World of Nixon, Hughes, and the CIA*, by Larry DuBois and Laurence Gonzales, the authors succinctly track the relationship between Howard Hughes and President Richard Nixon, giving a possible motivation for Hughes in depositing the so-called "dirty tricks" money in Bebe Rebozo's lock box.

The relationship between Hughes and Nixon goes back at least to 1956. That year Hughes lent Donald Nixon [Richard Nixon's brother] $205,000 to save a failing restaurant business. Right after that loan – in a coincidence investigators have been suspicious of for years – while Nixon was vice president, the Hughes Medical Institute was suddenly granted a tax-exempt status after prior refusals by the IRS. The loan to Donald was kept secret for obvious reasons. But four years later, one week before the 1960 Kennedy-Nixon election, columnist Drew Pearson got the story and printed it. The press flashed it across the country and to this day, Nixon and his friends believe it was the news of that loan that was partly responsible for his defeat by Kennedy.

In 1962, Nixon was running for governor of California. The loan again became a campaign issue, and [this time] Nixon was called on to explain it publicly. Again he lost the race. Later Rebozo's attorney, William Frates, was to say that Rebozo felt the story "had materially affected the outcome of the 1960 presidential election and the 1962 governor's race in California." So not once but twice Nixon's relationship with Hughes was connected, at least in his mind and in the minds of his friends, with agonizing political setbacks.

It was assumed from the Donald Nixon loan that Hughes was giving money in exchange for potential political favors. According to the article, "Some important pieces of the puzzle were put in place by a few of the investigators on Sam Ervin's Senate Watergate committee. But the puzzle was never made whole; the pieces never seemed to fit."

Regardless, Nixon resigned the presidency on August 9, 1974.

Those with Clout and Those Without

Someone once commented that I probably didn't know the power I had when I was in the Hughes organization. I'm not sure I would call it "power"; perhaps "clout" is a better word, because of the secrecy and how some people within the organization capitalized on that. Their secretiveness evolved into making people believe that what they were doing for "The Man" was routine.

For example, one time after a flight to Los Angeles, I was staying at the Airport Marina Hotel near LAX and John Seymour and I went down to Long Beach look at the Spruce Goose. Formerly the manager of Hughes's FBO in Las Vegas, Seymour was pushed out of that job by General Nigro to make room for Colonel Triola. When Bob Maheu was fired in late 1970, Seymour wormed his way back into the organization as one of Bill Gay's trusted lieutenants. That time in L.A., Seymour was on an assignment for Hughes, to ensure that his fleet of JetStars and other aircraft were secure and properly cared for in storage. He used this "mission" to get us into the dry dock where the Spruce Goose was stored.

It was also during this time that Jack Real entered the picture. Real was Hughes's friend and confidant right up until Hughes died. As an aeronautical engineer for Lockheed, he became friends with Hughes primarily because of two things: Real's vast knowledge of aviation and Hughes's romance with Lockheed. Real died in 2005, but not before authoring his book *The Asylum of Howard Hughes* (with Bill Yenne). Long after Howard Hughes's death, Real writes about his invitation into the Hughes organization.

In February 1971, less than three months after Howard left Las Vegas, I received a call from the Hughes Tool Company's chief executive, Raymond Holliday, inviting me to be his guest at the tool company factory in Houston. I flew down and spent two days reviewing all of the phases of the oil drill bit manufacturing operation ... On the way to the airport to catch my flight back to Los Angeles, I finally asked Raymond why he had invited me to visit the Hughes Tool Company. He replied that it was at Howard's request and he then added: "Someday the whole operation will be ours to operate. Howard wants you to look after the whole Hughes organization."

As a result of that meeting, Real was offered an annual salary of $100,000. Real refused the offer, saying, "I told him that I'd accept $60,000, which was $10,000 more than I was getting at Lockheed." Perhaps he would have taken the larger salary if he'd known when he resigned from Lockheed and entered into his first personal meeting with Bill Gay that it was the start of years of turbulence and hostility. Real writes:

[Bill Gay] chided me for accepting Raymond Holliday's offer to be his number two man, blasting Raymond as a drunk and saying that the offer was just a means for Raymond to get to Howard through me ... While he was in my office that night, Gay showed me a new organization chart that he had recently conceived. It showed Howard at the top and the Hughes Tool Company over to one side. In the main part of the chart was the "Howard Hughes Corporation," with two executive vice presidents in the same box – Gay and myself. I was to have the title of vice president of aviation, and I would have everything that had to do with aviation, including the Aircraft Division of the Hughes Tool Company (Hughes Helicopters), the fixed base operation at McCarran Airport in Las Vegas, and, I assumed, Hughes AirWest. Under this plan, Bill Gay would have control of the Las Vegas Hotels. I made one of the major mistakes of my life. I accepted Gay's proposal. Gay was delighted and said he would start building me a suite of offices in the morning. I got an office a year later."

Jack Real eventually took over all of Howard Hughes's aviation interests; he became my boss after John Seymour was ousted from the Las Vegas FBO. However, our relationship never really solidified and I believe Bill Gay was at least partially responsible for that.

HOUSE OF CARDS

WHEN I LOOK BACK on my days with the Hughes organization, it is easy to see that those years are where the phoniness of my life first started—when it became all about power and prestige. A lot of people involved in the Hughes organization had an arrogance about them. Some acted self-important simply because they were supposedly "insiders". Others were into name dropping and celebrity. Still others simply slacked off, knowing they wouldn't be reprimanded.

Some of Bill Gay's lieutenants took great pride in turning their wine glasses upside down—that is, making it clear to everyone sitting at the table that they didn't drink alcohol. They made a big deal over their desserts instead, even tasting each other's desserts. Their hypocrisy, at times, struck me as insane. If Howard Hughes employed men of the Mormon faith because they did not drink and were said to live a straight and clean life, what did he make of the clannish, self-righteous attitude of some of his own aides? Certainly that was neither trustworthy nor in the Christian spirit—it did not epitomize what it meant to be a true Mormon, in my opinion.

In some ways that type of behavior and the highfalutin lifestyle was expected. It was as though if you didn't play "the game" you were not considered a team player.

Guys like John Seymour, for example, played the game better than most—or at least, he thought he did. Seymour managed to find his way from Culver City and Hughes Aircraft (in Los Angeles) to Las Vegas in the late 1960s when Howard Hughes arrived, somehow finagling his way up the ladder so he could be close to his idol. I am not sure why Bill Gay had allowed this—perhaps it wasn't even his decision—but somehow Seymour was put in charge of the FBO at McCarran Field. He was a big man, and impressive to a certain degree. And he loved to emulate Howard Hughes.

Seymour would come out of the executive offices and head to the men's room—you had to walk by Jim Hildegard's desk, in an office just off the lobby, to get there. Seymour would say imperiously, "Jim, follow me in here. I want to talk to you." And Hildegard—a Cessna charter pilot—would jump up and follow Seymour into the john. Seymour was playing him, though—taking his cue from Hughes, who at times carried on business while in the bathroom, sitting on the "john".

That's the way things worked: One of the "bigwigs" told a subordinate to jump, and the immediate response was "How high?" Personally, I would have refused such a demeaning request and waited for Seymour in the lobby, probably pacing while muttering a few choice words under my breath. But this was so typical of some people who worked for the Hughes organization. To them, getting to the top rung of the ladder meant copying the outrageousness of the boss—and it didn't get much more outrageous than Howard Hughes!

When Hughes went into seclusion in 1966, he had a half dozen or so mechanics who were his favorites. It was comical. Each of his mechanics had one job, and that was all they did. One guy drove a tug to pull an airplane, another was Howard's exclusive sheet metal man, another was an electrician, another worked with hydraulics … All these guys had their one specialty, and each was Hughes's personally handpicked man for that job. When he wanted something done to one of his airplanes, they were the "chosen ones" who worked on it. According to John Seymour, that's the way the system worked for those single-job mechanics—and later, for me: "You have a job for life—a guaranteed paycheck—but we won't have anything for you to do." Now, that's a flimsy way to run a business!

These mechanics—like many others in the organization, I'm sure—continued to bilk Hughes's money in various ways. One of them went home and built a machine shop in his garage, where he spent most of his time working for himself. Bill Gay eventually ordered the aides to test Hughes on it: Did he remember any of the mechanics? Of course he didn't. After that, Gay told these mechanics that they had to go back to work—the game was up. The threat of getting fired was thinly veiled, but he wasn't worried about repercussions. Gay had covered his butt in case anyone tried to bring a lawsuit claiming they were told that they had a job for life. He knew he could say, "Howard Hughes doesn't even remember your name," and the original promise would never hold up in court.

So these mechanics were back to work, and guess who they were working for? Jack Real, my new boss, who was based in Los Angeles. Meanwhile, here I was in Las Vegas, the chief pilot for Howard Hughes's personal fleet of aircraft, but the mechanics were only talking to Real, 250 miles away. And their reasoning? These mechanics were in their 60s, and they were not about to work for a 40-year-old upstart pilot who was born of the "jet age".

These mechanics maintained a fleet of aircraft out of Van Nuys and various other places, while my mechanics, Smitty and Jan—who reported directly to me—maintained the JetStar that was based in Las Vegas, along with the C-90 King Air and the Cessna 421. Whenever a flight was scheduled out of Southern California, though, we had to fly down commercially, then use one of the Burbank or Van Nuys JetStars, which the mechanics would get ready for us.

The irrational methods and total lack of communication were, as I pointed out to Jack Real, becoming a little difficult. In fact, the situation could have been disastrous. There was some dissension among the mechanics, which spilled over into their relationship with the pilots. The leader of the Van Nuys mechanics actually told Real that we were doing a poor job of maintaining the Las Vegas airplanes and that we were violating regulations. Real explained, almost apologetically, that he was a Johnny-come-lately to the organization; he listened, but there was no resolution to the problem.

It was true; he had come from Lockheed after I had joined the Hughes organization. Prior to his arrival, Bill Gay and the rest were coming directly to me for their flights. But things were no longer as clear-cut as they once were, and Real wanted everything to go through him first. Now, there was no way Gay was going to Real for permission, getting him to tell me every time he needed to fly someplace. I was caught in the middle, and I told Jack Real in no uncertain terms: "They come to me, I go to you, you get upset, and I get caught in the middle. This arrangement isn't working!" I wanted to work with him, but how exactly could I do that when there was this apparent enmity between Jack and Bill. Jack did know that I had Bill's ear, which annoyed him, but this was the only leverage available to me for getting issues of this nature resolved.

Eventually Jack understood and tried to simplify the lines of communication, but the Van Nuys head mechanic kept pestering him about what he thought was our lack of maintenance procedures. In every organization I had ever worked in, the chief pilot worked closely with the mechanics. That's how it has to be. It just makes sense. These mechanics didn't have to "salute" me. They didn't have to report to me. But they needed to work with us. We needed to be a team, and at that point we were far from it—except for the flight department in Las Vegas, where Jan and Smitty worked with us pilots harmoniously.

The Van Nuys mechanics had their own approach to an aircraft preflight inspection, and it was overkill. Following standard procedure, no major items needed to be taken care of during each preflight inspection; however, in Van Nuys they were doing scheduled maintenance inspections only as required periodically, depending on the hours flown or on calendar requirements, such as annual inspections. For instance, they would flatten the hydraulic accumulators to check the air pressure load—but that wasn't a requirement for a normal preflight inspection, according to the Lockheed JetStar manual, and that wasn't the way other JetStar operators did things. It was a task that was only supposed to be performed after so many hours in the air—not for every flight. And as we found out, unorthodox methods within the organization didn't mean just a difference of opinions—they had the potential to become disastrous.

An Accident Waiting to Happen

On one occasion at Van Nuys jet center, where we always departed from, my co-pilot Brent Neal and I had just completed the routine checklists and were in the process of starting the number three and number four engines, on the right side of the aircraft (which, by the way, was routine according to the operation manual). We were out on the ramp with the plane pointed toward a hangar full of corporate jets. The doors of the hangar were open. As our number four engine began winding up, a powerful rush of air came through the aircraft pressurization system, indicating that an engine had gone to full power.

What the ... ? I thought, startled—until I saw that engine number three had gone to full power with the throttle in idle.

I immediately shut off the fuel to both engines. Then I began to troubleshoot the situation. We started number three again, and once again it went to 100 percent power. We still had the brakes on, and the chocks were in place. What had happened? As it turns out, the fuel control unit had failed upon starting and allowed the engine to reach 100 percent power. We had to delay the flight while we changed the fuel control unit on the number three engine. Finally we took off, and it was an uneventful flight.

Not long after this, at the Van Nuys jet center again, I found myself in a very similar situation. I started up the number three engine first, then the number four. Through the open window on the co-pilot's side, we could hear the jet center lineman who was attending to our departure yelling, "Stop, stop!" He was pushing the front of the airplane as if to hold it there, trying to keep it from moving. The plane was heading for the mobile auxiliary electrical power unit that was plugged into our external receptacle and positioned in front of the right wing. We used these units to supply power to our electrical engine starters—that is, to start the engines until we could switch to the aircraft's own engine-driven generators.

The parking brake had been set, but it was not holding the airplane in position.

Two alternatives immediately came to me. In order to get power to the brakes—and *fast*—either I could switch the hydraulic system that normally runs off the number two engine (which was not running yet) over to the number three engine (which was running in idle and would supply the necessary hydraulic power to the brakes), or I could turn on the switch for the auxiliary electrical pump that energizes the hydraulic system when the engines aren't running, thus giving immediate hydraulic pressure to the brake system. We managed to stop and shut down the aircraft by switching to the number three engine, and fortunately there was no damage. But when I backtracked to find out what had transpired, I discovered a comedy of errors.

When the lineman had asked Brent Neal, the co-pilot who did the preflight inspection, if the parking brake was set, Neal's answer was "Yes," so (unbeknownst to us) the line guy pulled the chocks. But the brakes had not held.

Earlier, when Neal had preflighted the airplane and came to the *Set parking brakes* item on the checklist, he had followed the correct procedure: To set the brakes, it was necessary to press the brake pedals, then move the parking brake handle to the "locked" position, and if the handle stayed in the locked position, you could assume it would stay that way. What we didn't know, however, was that there was no air pressure in the hydraulic accumulator to actually hold the brakes even though the parking brake handle stayed in the locked position, the brakes did not lock. And why was there no air pressure? The pressure had been released in order to check the charge, after which the proper charge of air would later be reintroduced.

So the Van Nuys mechanics had flattened it during their "necessary" preflight inspections, which Lockheed did not advise for this aircraft.

I broke out in a cold sweat. How could we have known that the parking brake handle would indicate that the brakes were set even though there was no pressure? What if this had happened the day the number three engine went to 100 percent? We would have been unable to stop the airplane fast enough. It would have gone right into that hangar full of jets, and it would have been a total disaster. In just seconds, 100 percent power on one engine will move that plane quite a distance. That whole scenario proved the point I had made to Jack Real: Standard procedures had to be implemented to prevent further occurrences that could be serious.

I went to Jack Real and told him about the incident. Some common sense would put things in motion—necessary changes that would prevent this kind of thing from happening in the future. I shared my ideas and instituted new procedures. But it didn't change anything with the lead mechanic at Van Nuys. He continued to run his own show.

It was at this point that I saw things clearly—and wondered how we could work more closely with the older mechanics.

These weren't the first instances of near disaster. I could trace the problem all the way back to when I had just arrived in Las Vegas to start my new job with the Hughes organization. The DH-125 was coming in from the East Coast, dropping passengers off in Las Vegas before proceeding to Burbank. Colonel Triola suggested that I ride along down to Burbank to drop off the last passenger. On the return to Vegas, we delayed takeoff due to a heavy rain shower in Burbank. After the rain there was a lot of standing water still on the runway, about midfield. When the water sprayed up and obscured the pilot's view, he rejected the takeoff and taxied back for another attempt. To me, this didn't seem like a good idea.

I questioned the pilot regarding the limitations for takeoffs on wet runways. Since he had a type rating in the DH-125, he was under contract to fly as pilot in command until Joe Williams and I could get our type ratings. Yet it became obvious to me that this contract pilot didn't understand the danger of attempting to take off in these conditions. Having just come from instructing in the Military Airlift Command's transition training school for jet transports, I was very familiar with these restrictions. When I suggested that we delay takeoff until the water subsided on the runway, and that we get out the performance charts in the flight manual and review the takeoff distance before we try it again, Joe acknowledged my concern and we persuaded the pilot to wait it out. Once again, it was just plain common sense! Why had a contract pilot been hired who would make a rookie mistake like not following an aircraft's guidelines? Although I was working within one of the wealthiest organizations in the world, where the fountain of riches never seemed to run dry, in that respect we were dirt-poor. Common sense is something you just can't buy.

On another flight we stopped for fuel in Grand Isle, Nebraska—a great stopping off point back then, when airplanes didn't have coast-to-coast capability. Grand Isle was an old army base, and the staff there would spoil you. By the time a plane pulled up, the ground crew already had the fuel trucks out and the gas caps open and were pumping fuel, getting you food, and altogether making it a fast turnaround. On this particular occasion in Grand Isle, Smitty came up to the cockpit when we were already buckled up to get back in the air.

"Just a minute, Bob!" he said, and even though his voice was controlled, I recognized urgency in his tone. During Smitty's quick walk around the aircraft, he had looked under the wing and seen a small inspection panel hanging down. Looking closer, he discovered that only one screw was holding that panel on—and that single screw had loosened at the last minute, because the panel hadn't been hanging down when they brought us the airplane. In fact, a sack of screws was still sitting there. The Van Nuys mechanics had opened an inspection panel and never put all the screws back in. Sure, they had a very good system that included an inspector checking the work of each mechanic, but the system broke down that day. The inspector wasn't there—he was on vacation. Why didn't they have a Plan B? Yet again, no common sense.

A Nice Trip

Jack Real also found himself in the midst of his own communications fiasco—one where I was also drawn.

At Lockheed, Real had been an aeronautical engineer and the "man on the ground" from Hughes's perspective—the guy Hughes dealt with personally at Lockheed. But in 1971, Lockheed was on the verge of bankruptcy; the company was forced to do some restructuring. Real's position was in jeopardy. The Cheyenne Program, which he was in charge of, did not sell to the U.S. Army as planned. Real then apparently exercised his option: an open invitation from Hughes to come work for him.

Bill Gay decided to put Real in charge of all of the aviation activities, including Hughes Air West, Van Nuys, and our flight operations at McCarran Field in Vegas, and that is how he became my boss. According to Real, all flights were supposed to come through his office; Bill Gay's lieutenants, however, still went directly to me.

Like Seymour, Real seemed to be playing games. Without my knowledge or bringing me into the discussion, he bought two airplanes, and in both cases there were available on the market (in my opinion) better aircraft for the money. Real didn't want me to know he'd purchased another JetStar, but Jack Baumann (one of the owners of the Van Nuys jet center) leaked it to me. Bill Gay asked me about the JetStar, and since I wasn't supposed to know about it for whatever reason, I played innocent: "What JetStar?" Gay wasn't pleased when he found out that Real hadn't consulted me. Howard Hughes didn't even know the jet was purchased.

When the JetStar landed in Las Vegas, several of us pilots went out to look at it. It had been owned by Qualitron Aero in Texas, which had purchased it from Trans

World Airlines (TWA). TWA had reconfigured the cockpit and certain components so it would resemble a Boeing 707. Why? To give its pilots jet training. TWA took its pilots directly from the Connie propeller airplanes to its jets; this JetStar and a second one reconfigured to resemble a 727 inside the cockpit were the interim airplanes for them to train on. These training "jets" had different hydraulic pumps and different avionics and electronics from those of the Hughes personal fleet, and we weren't necessarily familiar with them. As it turned out, though, I had a 707 FAA type rating to fly the aircraft, so it wasn't a major problem for me.

We had some real problems with that airplane, though. On one of our initial flights, we were instructed to pick up three passengers at LaGuardia Airport and depart around 9:00 p.m. for Nice, France. The passengers showed up in a "gold-plated Rolls Royce"—a newlywed couple (apparently connected to the Rothschild family). They had been married just that night and were accompanied by another gentleman. After landing at Gander, Newfoundland, for fuel we flew across the North Atlantic to Shannon, Ireland for refueling. That's when the extra male passenger got off, and we proceeded on to Nice, where we assumed the couple would be honeymooning.

The aircraft was equipped with older-model Bendix flight directors, which were installed because of TWA's insistence on familiarity with their 707s. This plane was really screwed up, but with our experience and a bit of finesse, we managed to get through the flight, repairing the necessary things and the various radios that were not working properly for navigation purposes. After we landed at Nice, we were instructed to pick up someone from the organization in London (where, as far as I could tell, Howard Hughes was living at the time) and fly them back to the States. Luckily, this gave us the opportunity to get the necessary maintenance performed for the return flight to the States.

A third airplane was almost purchased without my knowledge. Jack Real was seriously considering trading in the Cessna 421 for a TurboProp Aero Commander, and it would have cost us $300,000. Real was in the midst of a deal with Jack Baumann. In the meantime, I spoke with Bob Thorn, chief pilot for MGM in Las Vegas. He was the personal pilot for Al Benedict, the president of MGM Hotels who had worked for the Hughes hotels under Bob Maheu, as president of the Sands. The MGM was buying a DH-125 jet similar to the one we were flying and had put its King Air C-90 up for sale. Bob Thorn told me they were asking $300,000 for it without a trade-in—and this meant we could keep the Cessna 421 (which was worth about $100,000).

I went to Real and asked him if it was a done deal with Baumann.

"Why?" he asked me.

"Because I'd rather have the C-90. The cockpit is more compatible with the types of aircraft we're currently flying." I lobbied hard for that plane. As pilots, we were jumping in and out of different airplanes all the time, and we needed cockpits that weren't going to throw us for a loop every time we made a switch. The Aero Commander just wasn't compatible. Plus, it was more difficult to fly.

Real argued that the Commander was faster and had greater short field capability. But we didn't need short field capability. We were flying short distances, from Miami International Airport to Freeport International Airport, and both had long runways. As for the difference in speed, it was negligible. Besides, the Commander was not as comfortable for passengers.

Well, it irritated Real quite a bit that I had talked with Bob Thorn, because he had already been in talks with Baumann, although it was not a closed deal. I continued to press my point, though, and finally Jack Real realized the sense of the deal on the C-90. At the same price, it was the more appropriate aircraft for our purposes, and on top of that, we still could turn around and sell the Cessna for a profit of $100,000. He also knew that if Bill Gay found out about the deal Jack was going to make and that we could save $100,000 on another deal, he wouldn't be happy about it. The last thing Jack needed was another source of friction between him and Bill.

I'm glad I spoke up. If Real had purchased a third plane without consulting me, it could have resulted in greater problems for all of us. In my opinion, it was the game he was playing. He didn't trust me—supposedly, I was Bill Gay's man. But in every case, we had problems with the airplanes that Real purchased. If my mechanics and I had seen these planes before he purchased them, we would have found the problems and made the seller fix them before the deal was closed. At least in this transaction, I saved the company $100,000. And I got my C-90.

And They All Fall Down...

Howard Hughes was very much alive and well, sequestered on the entire top floor of the Desert Inn, when I joined the organization in 1969. Though he remained in seclusion, hovered over by his closest aides, he certainly had his faculties about him. I know this because I received many instructions through Bill Gay, Bob Maheu, and Hughes's aides that could have come only from him. From whatever penthouse suite he was living in, Hughes managed his staff and his massive empire with a yellow ruled legal pad and a pen.

Hughes lived in a number of different places during his lifetime: his family home in Houston, Texas; the Ambassador Hotel, the Beverly Hills Hotel, and the infamous Nosseck Theater (the screening room where Hughes spent hours upon hours watching films, rumored to be stark naked) in Los Angeles; the Desert Inn and the Green House in Las Vegas; the Ritz-Carlton in Montreal; Emerald Beach in Nassau; a quaint little bungalow in Rancho Santa Fe, near San Diego; the Ritz-Carlton in Boston; Britannia Beach on Paradise Island, Bahamas; the Intercontinental Hotel in Managua; the Bayshore Inn in Vancouver; the Inn on the Park in London; the Xanadu Princess in Freeport, Bahamas; and the Acapulco Princess in Mexico. During the time that I worked for him, no one in my aviation group really knew where he was until well after the fact. Hughes moved from place to place and from country to country like a shadow. Only his closest aides and friends, like Jack Real, were privy to the details of his peregrinations. The one thing Hughes feared most (besides germs) was taxes, and as long as he stayed away from the States, he knew he could not be subpoenaed by the IRS, or in connection with other lawsuits.

As time passed, though, it was widely noted among Hughes's employees that "The Man" was becoming more and more obscure within the organization. The less we heard about him, the more things spun out of control in the company's day-to-day activities. Chaos thrives in a vacuum. People jockeyed for position, and even those who had no idea what was going on acted as though they were secretly part of Mr. Hughes's inner circle. The saying was, "Those who know don't say, and those who don't know, do."

When I initially joined the organization as Mr. Hughes's chief pilot for Hughes Nevada Operations, I was spending my days just a few miles away from the Desert Inn, at Hughes's terminal building at McCarran Field, either getting ready for flights or flying. Our passengers were Hughes's protégés, celebrity friends, and business acquaintances; many times we were flying Hughes executives and their families. But I could have been a million miles away for all the contact I had with the reclusive Hughes, and in retrospect, that is a relief. I didn't get involved in the backbiting, and I didn't get crushed when the house of cards came crashing down. I was just happy to be doing what I loved: flying.

I flew all of Hughes's personal aircraft: the de Havilland DH-125, the JetStars (my favorite), the Gulfstream I. Hughes's aircraft were outfitted to the hilt to keep his guests in comfort and luxury. We had special tables built so that we could seat six people to dine. We threw out the plastic dishes and utensils and replaced them with china and silver. I even employed the help of a company located in Syracuse, New York, to design china with the Hughes Nevada Operations insignia on it. We had access to the Gourmet Room chefs at the Sands hotel, and we shopped the best delicatessens and bakeries for delectable foods to serve during the flight. We kept the latest newspapers—*The Wall Street Journal* and such—and entertainment publications on board.

Flying powerful executives and famous people became commonplace, and I was rarely star struck. But from time to time I transported someone who really had earned his bars, so to speak, and on numerous occasions I flew people who were famous for their experiences and innovations in aviation. One such fellow was Bill Lear.

It was 1969, and Joe Williams and I were getting the DH-125 de Havilland ready to fly, without passengers, from Las Vegas up to Reno, Nevada, to pick someone up. In the meantime, a Learjet landed in Vegas and was parked at the Hughes terminal, across the airport from the main passenger terminal. As it turned out, the Lear had experienced engine failure while in the air and had to land—and ironically, the manufacturer of the jet himself was on board. With their plane disabled, Mr. Lear's pilot asked Joe and me if we could take Mr. Lear along up to Reno, their original destination. We agreed.

Apparently, while still in the air, Lear and his pilot had been in some disagreement about what to do after one of their engines failed. When they had lost oil pressure, the pilot had tried to follow procedures, but Lear thought they could continue on to Reno on just one engine. He ultimately lost that argument, and I had to side with the pilot: When you lose an engine and you have an opportunity to land at an available airport, a landing is always advised.

But I knew the stories about Bill Lear trying to squeak by and try new things when it came to an aircraft's capabilities. After all, he had built the powerful Bizjet with tiny switches and used electric motors instead of heavier hydraulic actuators in order to shed as much weight as possible! I'd heard that his engineers would show a design to Mr. Lear, and he'd say, "Reduce the weight on that. I would sell my grandmother for a pound!" The saying caught on, and when his engineers reduced weight, they'd say, "Well, I got another grandmother today ..."

Anyway, Lear didn't seem too fazed by the decision to land in Vegas as he climbed eagerly into the cockpit of our plane and took the jump seat. To me, this was comical. Here's Bill Lear sitting in our little British de Havilland, which was nicknamed the "Limey Tank" because it was built so sturdy and heavy, so much less sleek than his jet—and believe me, there were no tiny switches in that cockpit. It was an interesting flight. Mr. Lear was clearly getting a kick out of flying in our little DH-125. I can only imagine that during our flight he was comparing everything about it to his invention.

A Hughes Rival

One of the reasons Howard Hughes lived in so many different locations, in many different parts of the country, was that he was always skirting subpoenas to appear in court. He never wanted anyone catching up to him, and he'd rather rot in a hole than pay a dime in taxes. This was evident by the secrecy cloaking his eventual departure from the Desert Inn to the Bahamas.

The Desert Inn officially became Hughes's property on April 1, 1967. In reality, though, Hughes never really owned the hotel. He did own the business that ran the hotel: the Desert Inn Operating Company, for which he paid $13 million. And his arrival and subsequent purchase of much of the property on the Strip was a welcome endeavor; Las Vegas had a reputation as a place run by mobsters, and many thought that Hughes would be a factor in cleaning up the town. There was, however, an issue that had to be resolved before operations of the Desert Inn could ensue under the Hughes organization: the reclusive billionaire had to make a public appearance before the Nevada Gaming Control Board.

Once again, money talks, and Hughes received a reprieve. Paul D. Laxalt was elected governor of Nevada just prior to Hughes's arrival at the Desert Inn. It was said that Hughes "gifted" the new governor with a donation to the University Of Nevada School Of Medicine: the promise of $200,000 to $300,000 every year for the next 20 years. According to *The First 100 Persons Who Shaped Southern Nevada,* by K. J. Evans of the *Las Vegas Review-Journal,* Bob Maheu made some insightful comments on Hughes's influence with the governor: "Laxalt saw Hughes as a better option than the mob ... He was an excellent businessman, and he was totally legitimate—the kind of sugar daddy Las Vegas needed." It took less than 10 minutes for the gaming board to approve Hughes's application—no personal appearance required.

By the time I came to the company, Hughes wasn't appearing in public at all. From 1966 until November 5, 1970, he lived at the Desert Inn behind blacked-out windows, with no contact to the outside world. One of the richest men in the world, yet he lived like a pauper. His living conditions were appalling. In addition to the well-documented fact that he stored his urine in Mason jars in a closet, his closest aides reveal that his room had not been cleaned in years; layers of dust adorned his cluttered nightstand. Many say that he resembled a bum, with long, unclipped fingernails and decaying teeth. His room smelled like rubbing alcohol, which he literally bathed in from time to time. He stayed up for days watching movies, and then slept for days. His food was meager and not taken regularly, which his doctors believe contributed to his morbid malnutrition and, eventually, renal failure. Most of the time he was so constipated that he needed enemas, but he would put off that ritual as long as he possibly could.

Yet his health did not get in the way of his plans to buy up as much property as possible in Nevada while he lived there. Hughes's dream was to be the biggest and the best at whatever he did, and with his power and money, owning the lion's share of Las Vegas seemed like easy pickings—until he came up against another power mogul who wanted the same thing: Kirk Kerkorian.

In 1968, when Kerkorian built the International Hotel (which is now the Las Vegas Hilton) Hughes decided to try and renovate the Landmark hotel, a squat concrete tower with a disc on top, simply because it was slightly taller than Kerkorian's International. The tower had been vacant almost since the beginning because it was designed without enough rooms or casino space. That didn't stop Hughes from paying top dollar for it. According to K. J. Evans, Maheu said, "A lot of people have given me credit for paying 100 cents on the dollar ($17.3 million) for it. It wasn't my idea, it was his. He was on a public relations kick at the time." When Hughes claimed he would personally oversee plans for the grand opening, Maheu was concerned. "I knew from that point on that I was in trouble," he said, explaining that his boss was "completely incapable of making decisions."

Kerkorian planned to open the International on July 2, 1969, with Barbra Streisand headlining. Hughes left the Landmark's opening date flexible and wanted to orchestrate the impossible: a Bob Hope–Bing Crosby reunion. His second choice: the Rat Pack. The guest list was only slightly less fantastical.

It is well documented that Maheu, who was in charge of the extravagant event, was continually put off by Hughes, first with the guest list, and then with the ordering of food. Procrastination was in Hughes's character, and Maheu, intent on making a political and social splash with the grand opening, was at a breaking point. In order for Bob Maheu to make the opening of the Landmark a success—or at least to keep Hughes and company from looking ridiculous—he had to act quickly. He got in touch with a public relations person from RCA who was also in charge of public relations at Cape Canaveral and knew all the astronauts. Maheu made arrangements for this PR person to extend an invitation to astronauts Tom Stafford and Gene Cernan to appear at the opening of the Landmark.

Joe Williams and I flew the DH-125 to Washington National Airport and picked up Stafford and Cernan and their wives, who had enjoyed dinner the evening before with President Richard Nixon. We flew them to Chicago and picked up another guest before taking them all to Las Vegas. Joe and I offered to let Tom or Gene fly in the co-pilot seat if they wanted to. Following that initial flight with Cernan, he and I started a friendship, and I would fly him on other occasions.

The Landmark Hotel did open, and the astronauts' appearance made a big splash. The grand celebration was even attended by none other than Kirk Kerkorian. I was surprised to hear he was there; Mr. Hughes wouldn't have been pleased. But as CEO of a multibillion-dollar empire, Kerkorian liked to flex his muscles a little bit.

We flew Kerkorian several times, one night picking him up at Truckee Airport near Reno. On that particular flight, Kerkorian came forward into the cockpit, his eyes wide. He asked the other pilot and me if we had seen an airplane pass much too close to us, and of course we had seen the plane but it was too distant to be a factor. Air traffic control had already advised us of the traffic that night, but out of respect we certainly weren't about to tell a World War II pilot that he was in the wrong. Understand that for people in Kerkorian's position, a corporate airplane may be one of the only places where they don't have control. In my experience, these people test the pilots from time to time in order to flex that control. Kerkorian was no different.

After the opening ceremonies at the Landmark, we flew the Staffords and the Cernans back to Houston, and in Austin, Texas, I let Stafford land the airplane from the co-pilot's seat for refueling. As his wife was deplaning, she stuck her head into the cockpit and said to her husband, "The next time you take flying lessons, I'm staying home!"

I just chuckled to myself. Talk about answering to a higher authority!

Whisked Away in the Night

There were a lot of shake-ups in the Hughes organization during the first two years I worked for the company, while Howard Hughes was living at the Desert Inn. Notable among these were "General" Ed Nigro's departure, the dismissal of Bob Maheu and his faction, and the unsettling fight for power within the power-mongering Bill Gay faction. It got to the point where some of us really didn't know who we were reporting to.

In the fall of 1970, Joe Williams and I were in annual refresher training at Flight-Safety International at New York's LaGuardia Airport when I was called out of the Marine Air Terminal classroom by Bruce Whitman, the program's executive vice president, who was to become my good friend. Whitman told me that I had an important phone call to take. On the phone was Bob McDonald, one of Bob Maheu's aides, who started a very subtle and inquiring conversation.: "How are you doing, Bob? How is the training going?"

A call of that nature was supposed to be "important"? Maheu and his associates knew that we were in recurring training. Why would they interrupt us just to check in? It was all very puzzling—until we were watching the national news that evening and heard the announcement: Hughes had departed Las Vegas.

Immediately following our training, Joe and I boarded a commercial flight to Los Angeles International to pick up our DH-125 from Air Research, where it was undergoing a routine inspection. When we arrived at the Air Research FBO at LAX, on the tarmac we saw the Hughes Tool Company's Gulf Stream I from Houston. Bill Gay and Chester Davis and their entourages were boarding, headed for Las Vegas. As far as we knew, we were still working for Bob Maheu, but this seemed like evidence that the two factions were preparing for war.

A day or two later, at nine o'clock in the evening, I received a call at home from John Seymour, asking if he could come over and talk. It was so typical of his secretive fashion, as if he was trying too hard to be enigmatic. What was so important that it could not wait until the morning? I knew something was up. Maheu was getting sacked.

I told my wife Ruth that I'd sit there and wait until the dust settled, and then I'd know where I stood—and it'd be shortly, because Seymour was coming over. I didn't really know where he fit into this whole scheme of things. What I did know was that he was a Scotch drinker, and we were out of Scotch. So I ran down to the liquor store and bought a bottle.

When Seymour came over, he sat down at the bar in the kitchen and I poured him a drink while we made small talk. Then he came right to the point: He was authorized by the board of directors of the Hughes Tool Company West Coast Executive Offices to notify me that if I flew the airplane for Bob Maheu, I would be "liable."

I told Seymour that my paycheck was signed by the Hughes Tool Company. "Who will I be reporting to from now on?" I asked.

He said, "Well, you are reporting to me."

I figured that wasn't necessarily true. It was likely that Seymour was taking liberties with his newfound position.

The next day, Seymour got a big log chain and wrapped it around the doors of our hangar at the FBO, securing the DH-125 inside with a padlock. I couldn't believe it. He had literally chained the doors together! It seemed like overkill to me. At this point Seymour approached me and said, "Bob, you may have a job for life—without even having to work. You may never have to fly these airplanes again." There was a ring of truth to that—it was the way Hughes operated. But I still didn't give it much credibility at the time, since Hughes probably didn't even know we pilots existed—and anyway, if I stayed with the organization, there'd probably be another job for me.

That same day, Joe Williams and Charlie Wilson, the only other pilots qualified to fly the DH-125, wanted to take a commercial flight to the Los Angeles area to look at a single-engine airplane they were planning to buy together.

"Would that be OK with you?" they asked.

What could I say? "Be my guest," I told them. "We aren't going anywhere!"

Falling Apart, One Card at a Time

Hughes's house of cards really began falling apart when Bob Maheu was ousted from the organization. One faction of people in particular was working behind the scenes to bring about Maheu's demise, primarily Ray Holliday, Bill Gay, and Chester Davis—who, with a proxy signed by Hughes, provoked the firing.

According to Lewis Chester and James Phelan in *The Money: Battle for Howard Hughes' Billions*, Holliday had complained to Hughes about Maheu's spending. He questioned the need to provide any "right- or left-hand ass-wiping machine [Maheu] may require." And yet the circumstances were suspicious; with Maheu out of the way, Holliday could move up from the Hughes Tool Company leadership to become Hughes's new right-hand man. Of course, the other parties who had worked to oust Maheu had their own ideas ...

Bob Maheu was livid. But in many ways, he saw how divided he and Hughes had become during the past two years of his employment with The Man. Still, in my opinion, the split certainly was acerbated by split loyalties and personal motives of the aides. Bob Maheu's falling out with Howard Hughes was not Maheu's fault. It could not have happened, according to Jack Real, without the aides shutting off communications between Bob Maheu and Howard Hughes, and spreading lies about Maheu. And he should know: The same thing happened years later to Real himself.

Maheu was perfectly capable of handling Hughes; if the aides had been working with him instead of against him, things would've gone differently. As a team they could have done what would have been in Mr. Hughes's best interest. That is exactly what Jack Real points out in his book *The Asylum of Howard Hughes*, and later he was in a position to make it happen. However, Real alone could not compete with the leverage Bill Gay had infused in controlling the aides. How could Hughes's true desires ever be executed when the aides—with the exception of George Francom and perhaps Roy Crawford (who was edged out of the organization after Hughes was moved from Vegas to the Bahamas)—were not loyal to him? Any aides who were suspiciously loyal to Hughes were kept out of the way or summarily replaced. Take Crawford, for example: Because he was apparently loyal to Bob Maheu (or perhaps it was because he wasn't Mormon?), they made sure he wasn't on duty the night they snuck Howard out of the Desert Inn penthouse and flew him to the Bahamas.

The crumbling relationship between Maheu and Hughes broke down more and more while plans were being made for the Landmark's grand opening. Things really reached the point of disintegration on the day after the event. Ordinarily Hughes would have been on the phone with Maheu, inquiring about the event, who attended, and so forth. But it is common knowledge that not a word was spoken between the two men the following day. According to Richard Hack in *Hughes, The Private Diaries, Memos and Letters,* this was "unusual behavior for the billionaire who lived vicariously through his alter ego." Why didn't this behavior tip Maheu off? Shouldn't he have noticed how far their relationship had fallen? Hack speculates that Maheu was too caught up in his relief about the positive spin on the Landmark celebrations to notice that his ship had sailed.

Hughes read the reports printed in the Las Vegas Sun, *including the mention that Kirk Kerkorian attended the party. Ordinarily his outrage would have been channeled into an immediate phone call. This was not an ordinary time, however, and Hughes moved with methodical purpose. He had decided to leave Las Vegas, but he had yet to decide if Maheu would be joining him.*

In Hughes's mind, Maheu had committed yet another unforgivable act in his communication with Mrs. Hughes. Hughes was married to Jean Peters at the time, the longest marriage of his three. (There is skepticism that his marriage to Terry Moore, an aspiring Mormon actress, was ever legal, since it took place on board Hughes's yacht, three miles outside of international waters. But she says they were never divorced, and her claim must have been sufficiently valid, since she supposedly received a seven-figure payoff after Hughes's death to preclude any claim from his will.) According to reports, Peters was becoming increasingly distraught over the lengthy periods of time she went without seeing her husband. On January 15, 1970, after 13 years in a miserable marriage, Peters announced—not to Howard, but through Bob Maheu—that she intended to seek a divorce. Here is what Hack has to say about it:

That the confirmation of the divorce occurred through Maheu infuriated Hughes, even though he had refused to speak to his wife directly. The announcement made headlines across the world, as much to confirm that Hughes was still alive as to verify the dissolution of his marriage. The official announcement began: "Jean Peters

Hughes, wife of industrialist Howard Hughes, stated today that she and her husband have discussed a possible divorce and that she will seek to obtain one."

The one-time close business relationship Bob Maheu shared with Howard Hughes was over. Behind the scenes, the Mormon "mafia" had worked hard to put down Maheu at every turn. They pointed out his extravagant wages and spending, his luxurious privileges ... But most of all, everyone was jealous of the fact that Maheu had become a very powerful man within the organization—a man who had Hughes's ear.

The Sacking of Bob Maheu

What followed was an extraordinary chain of events. Hughes wanted out of the United States in the worst way, and Maheu was reluctant to believe that Hughes had actually fired him without proof.

On Sunday, December 6, 1970, the headline in the *Las Vegas Review-Journal* read "Maheu Claims He Still Controls Hughes Empire." The article written by Don Digilio read:

Robert Maheu, chief of the Hughes-Nevada Operations here, said Saturday he was still controlling the recluse billionaire's holdings in this state despite an attempt by another Hughes executive based in Texas to take over.

The almost unrealistic events came to the front Friday night and Saturday morning, when attorney Chester Davis from New York and Frank Gay, a vice president with the Hughes Tool Co., in Texas, came into Las Vegas, said they had Hughes "somewhere," had his proxy to take control of the state's operation, and Maheu was to be fired. Hughes supposedly gave the outsiders the right to discharge several other key Hughes executives, including security boss Jack Hooper and Al Benedict. All in all, at least 150 top heads were to roll.

However, Saturday morning Maheu said he was still in control and issued a memo to all Hughes employees. This is the text of that memo:

To all employees:

I am sure that you are all mindful of newspaper comments suggesting that an effort has been made to effect an unauthorized takeover in responsibilities for the operations of Mr. Howard Hughes's properties in the state of Nevada. In this connection I think it is timely to advise you that I continue to be responsible in all respects for such operations in this state.

It is perhaps unnecessary to comment upon those persons who have endeavored to change the status quo in these operations as Mr. Hughes has entrusted them to me. I want to assure you, however, that I intend to discharge this trust and to continue with your help to ensure a responsible stewardship on behalf of Mr. Hughes.

Unfortunately, it has come to my attention that some ill-advised actions have been taken that are distinctly prejudicial to the operations of Mr. Hughes's properties. I would, therefore, like now to call upon you to exert every effort to ensure that no unauthorized person injects himself into any phase of the activities of Hughes Nevada Operations.

Signed, Robert A. Maheu

But the proxy was real. Levar Myler had gotten Hughes to sign the affidavit sacking Maheu, and Levar's wife had taken it to the bank and put it in the Myler safety deposit box. It was a perfect setup. The Mylers lived in our neighborhood and looked for all intent and purposes like common homeowners. Levar was very good at blending in to the Las Vegas community. In fact, although he lived only about three houses from me, I had never heard of him or from him. Who would have suspected that his wife would do anything sinister? And yet she had carried that very important document to the bank. No one had paid any attention. Had someone like the flamboyant Chester Davis been seen heading into the safety deposit vault, flash-bulbs would have gone off and there would have been a big story bylined by Hank Greenspun in the morning paper. It was a brilliant plan.

The *Las Vegas Review-Journal* printed yet another story later that Sunday in December 1970, with the rebuttal from C. J. Collier, Jr., vice president and treasurer of the Hughes Tool Company.

Dear Mr. Maheu:

Pursuant to authorization from Mr. Howard R. Hughes and the boards of directors of Hughes Tool Company, The Sands Incorporated, and Hughes Sports Network Inc., this is to confirm that you have no authority to act for or on behalf of Mr. Hughes, Hughes Tool Company, The Sands Incorporated and its subsidiaries, Hughes Sports Network, Inc., the Silver Slipper, or any division, subsidiary, or other interest of any of them, and you are directed to refrain from acting for, and from causing any other person or entity to act for or on behalf of, any of them.

You are also to turn over immediately to me or my representative all property, files, and documents of the above in your position, custody, or control.

Very truly yours,

C. J. Collier, Jr.

The ruckus continued, and what followed was a barrage of court proceedings in which Nevada District Court Judge Howard Babcock upheld the Hughes Tool Company's position and rejected Maheu's request for an injunction. On Christmas Eve Judge Babcock ruled that the proxy Maheu claimed was forged was actually valid, and Robert Maheu was officially, and sadly, out of a job.

After Maheu was fired, everybody seemed to scramble and worry—everyone, that is, except Howard's personal aides (mainly the Mormons). As for me, after I gained the confidence of the new "regime", and was accepted and not deemed a part of the Maheu faction, I had access to the Romaine Street headquarters in Los Angeles, as well as the penthouse, where ever Hugh was "holed up". I survived all the coups after Bob Maheu was sacked, plus a test by some of the Kay Glenn security loyalists.

I had thoroughly enjoyed working for Bob Maheu and spoke with him several times after he was fired. A list of people were fired right along with him, and in all the commotion, it was a little hard to define who worked for whom—and whose head would be next to roll. But I was back out there flying, and my passengers were the very people who had worked so hard to get rid of Maheu. Some Maheu loyalists criticized me for staying on, even after Maheu made a statement: "Bob has to do what he has to do." They thought I should have been loyal to Maheu, but I had to be loyal to the paycheck that supported my family. It all happened so fast, I really didn't have a choice.

And my supposed new "boss", John Seymour? Just as I suspected, that didn't pan out. A year later, he was gone.

Secrecy and the Fury of the Press

Meanwhile, under the cloak of darkness, Howard Hughes left the Desert Inn on Thanksgiving Day 1970. He was 64 years old and over six feet tall, and yet he weighed less than 100 pounds. So weak he was unable to walk under his own power, Hughes was taken to Nellis Air Force Base near Las Vegas, lifted onto a JetStar from the Lockheed corporate fleet based in Marietta, Georgia, and flown to the Bahamas, where he took up residence at the Britannia Hotel. He had finally managed to make his long-awaited escape from Vegas—only to return to the same reclusive life he had left behind.

Hank Greenspun, publisher of the *Las Vegas Sun,* plastered his front pages with news about Bob Maheu's expulsion and the vanishing of Howard Hughes from Las Vegas. Greenspun was a close friend of Maheu's, but he also had the ear of several Hughes aides, including senior aide Johnny Holmes and Roy Crawford, whose wife was widely known as having a loose tongue. Was it Crawford's wife who consistently leaked details about Hughes's condition to the press?

All the secrecy practiced within the organization and Hughes's personal life was only part paranoia. In part it was also to avoid the press, who were obsessed with Hughes's movement (or lack thereof). About a year before Howard left Las Vegas, I was called into the office of Jack Hooper, chief of security. He briefed me and Joe Williams on Hughes's move out of the Desert Inn, explaining that there would be a train standing by in Kingman, Arizona. He advised us that we would not be flying Hughes to the Bahamas, but we would be flying the entourage back and forth. Howard Hughes rarely did anything personally in a hurry, and certainly he took his time leaving Las Vegas, but not on that train.

For instance, one night my half sister, Eileen, and her husband, Ben, who were living in Ontario, California, were visiting us in Las Vegas. I took them to the Desert Inn to see a show, and suddenly my pager went off. I went to a phone, and Bob Maheu was on the line asking me how soon I could fly over to Burbank, California. I told Bob that I could probably have the airplane ready in a couple of hours, but it wasn't good enough. Maheu said he could only give us an hour. I said, "You got it."

I called Joe and my mechanic, Smitty, and told them to get the airplane ready—we had to leave right away. I said good-bye to Eileen and Ben, and just as I got to the airport, Smitty was positioning the airplane in front of the terminal. Joe, who had already filed the flight plan for Burbank, was running toward the plane. A limo drove up, and I shook our passenger's hand and helped him get on board. We fired up the plane and flew to Burbank.

Who was the passenger? To this day, I have no idea. But I know this flight, organized on an hour's notice, was generated directly by the authority of Howard Hughes.

Another time a passenger boarded our aircraft and Bob Maheu called—he didn't know the identity of this passenger, and he encouraged me to try and find out. I tried to make small talk with the guy, asking him questions that would help me find out his occupation. I could not get anything out of him. The gentleman just was not talking! Later, I found out he was a medical specialist from the Los Angeles area—whether to treat Hughes for something real or imagined, I'll never know.

We had a secretive passenger on board on at least one other occasion. Maheu had already been fired, so all our communications came straight from Romaine Street. The folks down there wanted me to stay in touch with them by phone throughout the flight, so if Mr. Hughes wanted us to turn around and bring the guy back to Las Vegas, we could. I stayed in touch on two frequencies with both the Las Vegas and the Santa Monica control towers, and with Romaine Street on another. I also gave Romaine Street the two control towers' numbers so they could call with instructions in case our flight plans changed. Unless we heard otherwise, though, we would just keep going. Eventually, I found out that the guy was yet another doctor—typical of Hughes. Just as typical was the indecision: Hughes probably thought he was ready to let the doctor go, but then again, he might just change his mind ...

Out of the Frying Pan ...

Though he may have "escaped" the brouhaha in Vegas, Hughes slipped back into reclusiveness in the Bahamas and continued to surround himself with some interesting people. Gordon Margulis, the physical fitness buff, acted as his bodyguard but also would carry the sickly Hughes when necessary. And then there was Mel Stewart, Hughes's personal barber and something of a male nurse. We flew Mel a lot —in fact, he was one of our favorite passengers. I especially remember the time he left the Bahamas without permission from Hughes and refused to come back.

Initially hired to cut Hughes's hair, Mel was later summoned regularly to act as much more. In the Bahamas, he was a permanent fixture at Hughes's beck and call. Hughes showed his typical indecision about when he needed Stewart's nursing services. Many times Stewart was summoned to give Hughes the dreaded enema but it didn't happen. Over Christmas one year, Mel got fed up with the wait-and-see routine and decided he wanted to spend the holidays with his family.

Hughes aide Howard Eckersley recalls that Stewart "was having trouble with his wife and family for not being [home] to take care of things," according to Donald Barlett in *Howard Hughes: His Life and Madness*. Stewart wanted to fly home to Utah, but Hughes wanted him in Freeport. When Stewart went anyway, Hughes was anything but pleased. When he told one of his aides to get Stewart back immediately, the aide handed him the following note:

Mel's wife recently has more or less given Mel an ultimatum that he must choose between his indefinite type of position [and] his family. As a result, Mel has practically suffered a mental breakdown and feels that after all these years, he should have been given relief by you. I would suggest that when he returns and assists next time, the two of you settle whatever it is you have in mind.

What followed was a bribe offered by Hughes to get Stewart back—as usual, money was expected to solve the problem. Stewart, however, had his own agenda. He agreed to go back to Freeport if within six hours of his arrival he'd be used by Hughes. If he wasn't used within the six-hour period, he'd receive $500 a day, and he agreed to stay only four days. The deadline came and went, and as usual Howard just could not make up his mind.

Before it was over, Hughes ended up owing Stewart thousands of dollars. From what I understand, his personal aides were not one bit happy with the fact that the barber-nurse was getting paid $500 a day to do nothing. After three weeks, Stewart gave up his wait and flew back home to his family without permission. He basically had to sneak out of Freeport, boarding a commercial flight to Utah. Once Hughes found out about it, he had Stewart paged at every airport along the way.

A short time after Stewart made it home, he finally was talked into coming back to the Bahamas. We were instructed to take the Cessna 421 and pick him up in Cedar City, Utah. We were not to tease him or razz him in any way, because he was rather angry—and understandably so. We took the Cessna to Utah, picked him up, took him back to Vegas, and put him on a commercial flight back to the Bahamas. Believe me, he was not a happy camper.

Bill Gay was another interesting man. He came into power by making himself "indispensable" to Hughes. I heard that Gay had a degree in philosophy or something of that nature—certainly not an MBA or a college degree that allowed him to function in his high-level position with the Hughes organization. Gay was Mormon, however, and thus wiggled his way into Hughes's favor. In the early days, whenever

Hughes was in a meeting, Gay positioned himself outside the door, and if Hughes needed something, he opened the door and told Gay to get it. One way Gay made himself useful was by positioning nondescript Chevys in and around Los Angeles, next to telephone booths in various key locations. He knew where a particular car was and the number of that pay phone, and if Hughes popped up someplace in Los Angeles, Burbank, Van Nuys, Santa Monica, or wherever, and needed a set of clean clothes, a white shirt, or some money, Bill Gay would make that phone call and it would be there. This sort of forethought and getting into the spirit of Hughes's everyday reality helped Gay become quite powerful even before Hughes became a recluse.

By the time Howard Hughes had set up living quarters in the Britannia Beach Hotel on Paradise Island in the Bahamas, I officially became the chief pilot of Summa Corporation, the umbrella organization under which all the other Hughes companies were controlled.

All About Bob?

So now I was be based in the Atlantic again—this time, in the Bahamas. Living in Las Vegas had been, thus far, a life-changing experience. Once our family was entrenched in that lifestyle, my relationship with my wife became totally bizarre. For many years, I didn't understand Dr. Juraski when he said that Ruth would never accept my "climbing the ladder". I guess in my own way, I was playing "the game", too.

The fact of the matter was, Ruth was a very good wife—and a great mother. She taught our daughters a lot, but things became quite different when they reached their teenage years. I guess Ruth felt that she'd done her job and she could now move on with her own life. She used to tell me how she had wasted her life by not getting a further education after high school. That made me sad, but I knew I had never held her back. On the contrary, I had encouraged her to follow her plan of becoming a flight attendant, but she decided not to, and we got married instead.

After some years in Vegas, Ruth was experiencing feelings of inadequacy. This became a serious problem. Basically, she felt she'd lost her identity. As an Air Force wife, she always knew where she stood. In the Air Force, wives were intentionally encouraged to be a part of their husband's life, to support him. Because in the service we often had to leave on TDY (temporary duty), our wives had to accept responsibility while we were gone. There were plenty of support groups on base for the wives, both organized and informal. Ruth's unspoken expectation was that the Hughes organization would be the same. But it wasn't. It was not a close-knit group. In Las Vegas, was all about the men—even worse, the corporate men. In Ruth's eyes, life in Vegas it was all about Bob Wearley.

Ruth did her best to make acquaintances with the other employees' wives—in particular, Pete Maheu's wife, Rosemary, and Dick Ellis's wife, Sue. Dick was Bob

Maheu's accountant, and we lived in the same neighborhood. Sue often invited Ruth to the Desert Inn to play tennis. As employees of the Howard Hughes organization we didn't have to be members to play at the tennis club. Ruth and the girls really got into the game, and soon our daughter Roxie was working for Pancho Gonzales, the resident tennis pro at the Caesar's Palace tennis shop. When Roxie went away to college, Ruth took over her job and thoroughly enjoyed it. So for a while, she had her own thing going on, and she was satisfied—to a degree.

That jealous streak just wouldn't go away, though. Wives of high-level Hughes employees often flew with me, and these wives also played tennis. It was another point of contention between Ruth and me: When these women told Ruth what a great pilot I was, she just cringed. Later she said to me, "You may be God's gift to aviation, but you are still just Bob Wearley from Woodburn, Indiana … even here in Las Vegas." To me, it seemed like emotional blackmail, and that's when things really began to sour.

Sometimes, especially when I was being playful and cracking corny jokes, Ruth said the same thing to me but with more fondness: "Boy, you can take Bob out of Woodburn, but you can't take Woodburn out of Bob." And I'd say, "Thank God!" You see, I never lost my small-town attitude. I've never been ashamed to tell people that I was born and raised in a farming community. It didn't matter if I was a pilot for the powerful Hughes organization. Even during those years I got caught up in the phoniness, I would brag about the small school I attended, and the fact that I knew everybody in our town … that I was the ping-pong champ … that I played first chair clarinet, played baseball, and was a cheerleader at Woodburn High School. Perhaps I was succumbing to the temptation of life in the fast lane by bragging about my humble beginnings. I was enjoying my own brand of notoriety.

As I said before, I'm the first to admit that my life at this point was full of phony motivations. I had no idea that what I was experiencing—throughout my frolicking days in the Air Force, my employment with the Hughes organization, and my later flying years, was indeed a midlife crisis. This crescendo of phoniness kept building up and finally erupted during the last 10 years of Ruth's life, when I began to study the Bible again and saturated myself with its teachings. Then, and only then, did I begin to see how wayward I had been.

That was the greatest turning point in my life. Now I feel very secure in sharing my faith with others, even strangers, and in sharing my "born again" trust in the Holy Spirit, who gives me the courage and the words to pray and to write this book. I firmly believe that if, through this book, I can reach other middle-aged men who are only living for materialism and status, they may wake up to the facts: They are not going to be billionaires, CEOs, and presidents of companies. They are not going to go down in history as great men. Believe me, it's easy to get caught up on that treadmill. It all happens so subtly, with that "live for today and the hell with tomorrow" attitude. Well, hell may be exactly where those men end up. It's so easy for that attitude to become a vicious circle of slovenliness and egotism.

I left all that far behind when I returned to a deep, deep faith and belief in God. While I never stopped going to church during those crisis years, I was only going through the motions. There was no depth or breadth to my beliefs. It was more out of habit than anything else.

I became a part of the St. Paul's Lutheran Church outreach team in Fort Wayne. We never went into a home unless we were invited, and I never present the Gospel without asking permission of the listener first. But I continually remind myself of one question: *Do you know what you don't know?* Spreading the word of God is a lot like flying. As a Christian, you may be a pilot, but when you become an instructor pilot—someone who presents the Gospel—your skills are really challenged. It takes a very experienced pilot to make a mature judgment or to analyze his or her own abilities. The safest pilots are those who know their limitations.

Trust me, the Holy Spirit must have worked overtime on me, because He opened my eyes and I realized that my life had to change. No one is perfect! Certainly not a sinner like me. But it's our imperfections that form our character. I'm sure many of you reading this have memorized John 3:16 early in your life: "For God so loved the world that he gave his only begotten Son, that whosoever believeth in him shall not perish but have eternal life." Even though I could quote it verbatim, it was not until I explained it to a nonbeliever that I really grasped the meaning. The key word in the verse is *believe*. Whoever believes will have eternal life, and therein is the key to salvation.

Think about it: Why do so many people go to church, sit righteously in a pew, and go through the creed, but walk out the door only to act like hypocrites? Either you believe in the Bible as the word of God … or not. God leaves us with that choice. For my part, I firmly believe that everything that has happened to me—all the doors that were opened for me—was God's plan.

To borrow from C. S. Lewis, if Jesus was not who he said he was, he was either a lunatic or a liar. In my book, he is who he says he is. You have to have more than intellectual faith to survive this life and enjoy eternal happiness—you have to *believe*. Surveys indicate that more than 80 percent of the population living on earth today believe in God, but they don't necessarily believe in the God of the Bible or that the Bible is God's literal word. If more people read the words of the Bible, though, I truly believe that they would better understand life and find their own path to follow, not just during times of crisis but everyday life.

I believe that if Howard Hughes and those who surrounded him had more than intellectual faith, they would have found it in their hearts to save this man's life.

FIRST STOP: THE BAHAMAS

FOLLOWING HIS DEPARTURE FROM the Desert Inn in Las Vegas, Howard Hughes lived for six years in a number of similar situations at different hotels abroad, leasing or renting and securing the top floor for him and his staff. The elusive billionaire escaped the public, the press, and the government, first at the Britannia Beach Hotel on Paradise Island in the Bahamas from late 1970 until early 1972. When Hughes relocated to the Bahamas, he left a trail of doubt back in Las Vegas. We at the airport were instructed to be constantly at the disposal of Mr. Hughes and his lieutenants should Mr. Hughes need anything or anybody to join him at his new tropical home. By this time Colonel Triola, John Seymour, and Bob Maheu were all long gone; our flying orders came directly from Bill Gay, through Kay Glenn.

During Mr. Hughes's stay in the Bahamas, we were instructed numerous times to fly his aides and supplies back and forth from the mainland. We had the Cessna 421 down there, and we made trips primarily to Miami International Airport. Mr. Hughes was especially particular about the brands of supplies he used. It was during his time in the Bahamas that, as I mentioned earlier, he ordered cartons of paper towels, Kleenex products, and bottled water from the States; the bottled water had to come from a particular East Coast state (New Hampshire), and the paper products had to have a certain ply count. Luckily we didn't have to shop for these items; they were procured and brought to the airport for us, of course, by other Hughes employees.

We pilots were living at the Emerald Beach Hotel, where Hughes had stayed years earlier and still kept rooms available. Eventually, I gained access to Mr. Hughes's penthouse—I'm not sure how it started—where I could procure us some entertainment. Remember, this was before the VCR, so for entertainment, we were allowed to view the movies, with a 16 MM projector borrowed from the hotel, after Mr. Hughes was finished with. At times there were 20 or more movies stacked outside of Mr. Hughes's door at the Britannia—those he had already screened off to one side and those he had not yet seen on the other. The aides let me go up and select a couple of movies, which I took back to the hotel, where we spent the evening watching the back to back movies and eating popcorn.

While I was there at the penthouse, Mr. Hughes's door remained closed. It occurred to me that if, by chance, Mr. Hughes had gotten out of bed and walked out to the duty area, he would have seen me there. Perhaps he would have asked who I was, and an aide would have told him. And later, the aviator in him might have gotten the better of his paranoia, and he might have said, "Get me that pilot to talk to." We might have had some great conversations about our flight experiences.

But I knew too well that Jack Real was Hughes's only window to the world as far as aviation goes. Real, after all, was an aeronautical engineer. The two of them supposedly talked for hours about airplanes.

Anyway, after a while my time in "company housing" came to a close. In 1971, upon Kay Glenn's approval (probably thanks to one of our pilots, Brent Neal, who was his cousin), we were allowed to move our families to the Bahamas. Ruth and I rented a house, and the kids loved it. Robin was just starting her freshman year in high school, and Roxie was still in elementary school. They absolutely adored life in the Bahamas—but unfortunately it was short-lived.

Fleeing the Bahamas

Howard Hughes was kicked out of the Bahamas in 1972. It all came down to politics: One member of the opposition party was trying to use to his advantage the fact that Hughes was in the Bahamas illegally.

So much publicity had swirled about Hughes and his alleged autobiography that the opposition political party in the Bahamas saw an opportunity to embarrass the government of Premier Lynden O. Pindling, the Bahamas' first black ruler. Not long after the press conference, Cecil Wallace Whitfield, leader of the Free National Movement, announced that he intended to submit a series of questions to the Pindling government concerning the immigration status of Hughes and his aides. Hughes's residency permit had long ago expired. His staff did not have work permits—all foreigners employed on the islands were required to have them—and they came and left the Bahamas as they pleased. Faced with an election in the coming year, Pindling moved to squelch any controversy by sending immigration officers to the Britannia Beach Hotel to make an inquiry. But when the officials arrived at the hotel on February 15 and asked permission to enter the penthouse, the request was denied. While Hughes's guards outside the ninth-floor suite stalled for time, aides carried Hughes down an outside fire escape to a floor below … When the immigration inspectors left, the remaining aides carried Hughes back up the fire escape, placed him again in his bed, and waited while arrangements were made for an escape from the Bahamas. (*Howard Hughes: His Life and Madness*, Barlett and Steele, page 473)

When the aides found out that the immigration people were on the way, Hughes was moved quickly. They took him from his suite at the Britannia down to the floor below. Hughes probably could still walk at the time, and many of us assumed that he had left the island mostly under his own power.

The Hughes organization had bought a house for Mr. Hughes in Miami Beach, which he was to use as a stopover. Chester Davis's yacht was in the Bahamas, but it was in dry dock and unavailable as a getaway vehicle. Instead they secured another boat, which I dubbed the *African Queen* (after the Humphrey Bogart/Katharine Hepburn film) because it was not at all fancy, to get him from the Bahamas to Miami Beach. Hughes was then flown out of Miami by a corporate Lockheed JetStar belonging to Eastern Airlines. His destination: Nicaragua.

During this "great escape", Warren, Charlie, and I were in New York attending flight safety school at the Marine Air Terminal at LaGuardia Airport, in preparation for our type rating in the JetStar. We had flown the DH-125 208H from 1969 through 1971; it was eventually transferred to the Hughes Tool Company, located in Texas. While we were living in the Bahamas, however, the Summa Corporation board decided that we pilots needed to get qualified to fly the JetStar. Mr. Hughes, who was partial to Lockheed, was collecting Lockheed JetStars the way some people might collect antique automobiles. He bought the last four JetStars off the assembly line, until eventually he owned or leased about nine JetStars. In order to depreciate the JetStars, the Summa Corporation made a deal with the IRS: We would fly each aircraft a minimum of 50 hours a year.

During our classroom course, once again I received a phone call, as I had two years earlier—this time from Jim Hilligardt, the Cessna 421 pilot in the Bahamas. He was frantic. "Bob! They're all gone!"

"Who's gone?" I asked.

He replied, "The penthouse ... it's empty! Everybody left! What are we supposed to do?"

I instructed Jim to stand by while I called Kay Glenn, who told me in no uncertain terms that we had to get our families out of the Bahamas immediately. I went back and told Jim that we had to follow instructions, so he went around to the homes of the pilots and their families, including our condo, telling everyone to pack up and get on the first flight out in the morning.

My wife and two girls—along with all the other families of my staff—had to leave with whatever they could take with them. Ruth, Roxie, and Robin made it to the airport at the crack of dawn with our little poodle, Okie (we got him while we were stationed in Oklahoma). They put Okie in a cardboard carry-on box, but he didn't want any part of it. He clawed his way out several times before they managed to get him on the airplane.

I can only imagine the case the immigration folks would have made with all of our families still in the Bahamas when Hughes, our employer, was no longer living there. As it was, we made the news. The account in a Nassau newspaper on Friday, February 18, 1972, read as follows:

BILLIONAIRE 'FELT STAFF EXPULSIONS WERE RIDICULOUS'
So, 2 Pilots, Families told to go in 4 hours.

The number of Howard Hughes' aides known to have been kicked out of the Bahamas this week rose from three to five when it was learned today that two pilots and their families were given four hours to get out on Wednesday.

The two—Robert F. Wearley and Jan Moore, both Americans—are employees of the Hughes Tool Company of Nevada. They had been staying at Delaporte Point Apartments for six months until on Wednesday they were confronted by Immigration officers and told they had four hours to leave the country.

Each of the men has a wife and two children.

St. Andrew's School lost four students when the Hughes party left Nassau hurriedly. Roxanne, 14, and Robin, 15, daughters of Mr. and Mrs. Wearley, did not return to school Wednesday morning. Also absent were Jamie, 13 and Millicent, 12, daughters of Mr. and Mrs. James H. Hilligardt... .

Three Hughes employees were escorted to the airport on Tuesday by Immigration officials who made sure they left the country.

Jan Moore actually was one of our mechanics, and he was the best. He could finetune that Cessna 421 to run like a Swiss watch. When Jan tried to go back to our hangar to get some things, the immigration people stopped him and were about to take him into custody. That's when a gentleman by the name of Cleveland intervened.

Cleveland was a big Bahamian and a former heavyweight boxing champion whose dad was the bailiff of the Supreme Court of Nassau. He was a sizable man hired by the aides as a driver for the penthouse—obviously, a good man to have in that position. I knew him well. I used to bring him pumpkin pies and custard rice pudding and cheesecake from the Sands hotel bakery in Las Vegas. The Sands had the world's best baked goods—and the best rice pudding you would ever want to eat. Walter Kopp was in charge of the bakery and a friend of mine. Every Christmas he baked gingerbread houses, and I always got one.

Well, the staff at the penthouse (Hughes's aides) loved the pudding and the cheesecake, too, whereas Cleveland was partial to the pumpkin pies. So when we flew from Las Vegas to the Bahamas, I brought along the baked goods, from the Sands Hotel Bakery, and give the pumpkin pie to Cleveland. He had a big appetite, naturally, and he'd pull off to the side of the road on his way to the Britannia and eat the entire pumpkin pie himself.

I don't know about his boxing career, but that day at the hangar Cleveland was worth his weight in gold. When he saw what was happening, he confronted the immigration people who were trying to nab Jan and told them to keep their hands off him—after all, Jan was following their orders and leaving the country. In the end, they didn't arrest Jan—I don't know if it was Cleveland's size, his family connections, or something else that stopped them—and he was eternally grateful to Cleveland for that maneuver.

For my part, I never saw Cleveland or the Bahamas again. The Hughes organization hired Jean Rich's Rich International Airline, out of Miami International Airport, to pick up all our household goods that were left behind in the Bahamas, and all our tools and paraphernalia left in the hangar, and fly everything back to the States. Jean started the airline in Miami with old C46 airplanes, flying hazardous cargo and fruits and vegetables around the Bahamas. We got to know Jean primarily because her office was at the FBO at Miami International where we always parked our planes. (As a matter of fact, it was Jean Rich who purchased a brand-new DC-6 that Mr. Hughes had in storage in Santa Monica. After Hughes died, Hughes Tool Company ordered it brought out, cleaned up, and put up for sale. It was cargo configured, and Jean bought it. We would see it flying around the Caribbean with Rich International printed on it.)

This was in the middle of winter, (tourist season), and when our families landed in Miami, there were limited hotel rooms available. Eventually everyone found just a few rooms into which they could all cluster. I was still in New York at Flight Safety International and trying to find my family; all I knew was, they were somewhere in Miami. When I finally located the motel and phoned the room Ruth and the girls were in, Robin answered the telephone.

"What are you doing?" I asked in exasperation.

Robin replied, "Daddy, we're playing refugee!"

As soon as we could make arrangements, Ruth and the girls flew back to Woodburn, Indiana.

Next Stop: Nicaragua

In spite of all the confusion in the Bahamas, it was still business as usual within the Hughes organization. We were still required to get our type rating on the Lockheed JetStar, so Warren, Charlie, and I flew from New York to Miami. There we met Bob Luther, the Lockheed pilot who would train us using JetStar number 1622 Delta, which a Lockheed crew had flown to Managua from its hangar in Burbank. Together we flew commercial out of Miami down to Nicaragua and proceeded to check in to the Intercontinental Hotel in Managua.

It was no secret when Hughes landed in Nicaragua—by then, the whole world knew about it. Several female reporters followed us up to our rooms, determined to find out exactly where Mr. Hughes was staying. Hughes and his aides were on the eighth floor. My room was actually right above Mr. Hughes's suite, and it intrigued me that I was sleeping just feet away from The Man. One of his aides even asked me if I could hear the speakers from Mr. Hughes's room, but I never did hear anything. His room must have been well insulated!

Hughes aide: Bahamas' loss is Nicaragua's gain.

State Department sources in Washington said they understood Mr. Hughes had business interests in Nicaragua.

Although the office of President Anastasio Somoza of Nicaragua announced yesterday that Mr. Hughes had accepted the president's invitation to visit his Central American country, and 17 rooms of the Intercontinental Hotel has been booked for Mr. Hughes, the eccentric recluse has managed once again to avoid having his picture being taken. And even the pilot of an Eastern Airlines Lockheed JetStar who flew a Hughes Tool Company party from Miami to Managua, capital of Nicaragua, was unable to confirm if Mr. Hughes was on board. (*The Miami Tribune*, February 18, 1972)

Although we tried very hard to mislead the reporters, eventually the newspaper managed to photograph the JetStar while we were in training. It made headline news, and although Hughes rarely read a newspaper anymore, he happened to see the picture and the story. One of the aides told us that when Hughes saw it, he "blew his stack."

So I purchased some rope and had stanchions built, roped off the JetStar in the hangar, hired a guard, and booked a Pan Am flight to Los Angeles.

Poor Bob Luther was sitting in the lobby at the Intercontinental Hotel and saw us leaving. "Where are you guys going?" he asked, alarmed.

"Home," I told him. I guess Bob finally got an introduction to the way things were done within this mysterious organization: Don't ask questions. I was reminded of the refrain from *The Charge of the Light Brigade*: "Ours not to reason why, ours but to do or die."

Simply put, we could not fly anymore in Nicaragua.

Bob Luther asked, "What am I supposed to do?" I had no answer for him. He got a flight back to Atlanta.

We boarded the Pan Am flight and flew into Los Angeles. Ruth and I no longer owned our home in Vegas; we had sold it when we moved into a condo in the Bahamas. The only logical thing for me to do was fly back to Fort Wayne and join my family in Woodburn.

Shrouded in Secrecy

Our living arrangement back in Woodburn was, to put it lightly, somewhat inconvenient. My mother had sold her house on Center Street (where I was born) some time previously. While it was my boyhood home and I was sad to see it go, it had been built in 1912 and was badly in need of repair and updates. It had become very costly for my mother to heat, so she sold it through a realtor, Virg Hoeppner, and moved to an apartment in downtown Woodburn, above what used to be a hatchery. For the time being, Robin and Roxie lived with Ruth's mother, and Ruth and I slept at my mother's just three blocks away. Small towns are notorious for gossip, and when the Wearleys landed back there from the Bahamas, I'm sure tongues wagged.

For instance, I made a ritual of running down the street each morning to Ruth's mother's so I escort the kids to school—Robin was a freshman at Woodland High School, previously Woodburn High School, where Ruth and I had graduated, and now it was a consolidation of two townships' schools. Roxie was in the eighth grade at the Lutheran Elementary School in Woodburn. At the end of the street there lived a lady by the name of Clairie Lampe, and I passed by her house on my way. Now, Clairie Lampe's best friend was the telephone, and when I ran by in the morning, she called Ruth's mother. My mother-in-law dreaded those lengthy calls from Clairie, because Claire did all the talking. She said, in her rather thick Dutch German accent, "I saw Bob running dis morning. Vas he yogging, or vas he late?" That became a standing family joke.

Whenever I was back in town, it was news. Small towns are like that, especially when you're a hometown kid who has "made it big" somewhere far away. I guess it was particularly true in my case, because some people saw me as an enigma. They could never figure out what I was doing. Rumors flew. One rumor started because I was gone for exactly one week, once a month. I had to return to Las Vegas to get my USAF reserve training; I flew out commercially on Monday and was back in church the following Sunday morning. To some people, however, this frequent, regular travel meant that I must be working for the CIA.

Even the truth was larger than life in little Woodburn. Whenever I returned to my hometown, there were some folks who wanted the skinny on what was happening within the organization. Howard Hughes was big news. He was constantly in the press: when he moved from country to country, when he was entrenched in the TWA debacle, and especially in 1972, when Clifford Irving's phony Hughes biography was all over the papers.

The book was completely false, nothing more than a big con job, which of course made it unbelievably intriguing. Irving made up yards of lies about Hughes and falsified interviews and conversations with the wealthy tycoon. In the February 21, 1972, issue of *Time* magazine, journalist Elmyr de Hory wrote:

As Irving's outrageous story collapsed in on itself, one principal element in the puzzle loomed ever larger and more baffling: Where had the material he spun into his summa of non-books come from? Several experienced publishers at McGraw-Hill and *LIFE* magazine had read Irving's work and found it convincing in its tone and above all its remarkable wealth of detail about Hughes' complex life ... It had an undeniable smack of authenticity.

On March 13, 1972, Clifford Irving, his wife, Edith, and an associate, Richard Suskind, entered guilty pleas to the criminal charges they faced in New York. Their scheme involved bilking McGraw-Hill out of $750,000 for the rights to publish the false biography. Irving was found guilty and sentenced to two and a half years in prison, and was ordered to pay McGraw-Hill $756,000 in damages.

Shortly after my arrival in Woodburn to join my family, Herb Roemer (Woodburn's mayor for more than 20 years) informed me that the *Fort Wayne Journal Gazette* had called—they wanted to do an interview. I told Herb that I'd do it, but not if it was just for tabloid fodder. And I had to have final editorial license on the story. I wasn't about to be labeled a gossipmonger—or another Clifford Irving.

The reporter called, and I reiterated that I wanted editorial control of the story. If he wanted to tell the story about a young boy who grew up in Woodburn, Indiana, and ended up flying for one of the richest men in the world, I was happy to do the story. If he wanted tabloid fodder, forget it.

"Hughes has an awful lot of lawyers and very deep pockets," I warned him.

All I got in response was a click on the other end of the line.

What can I say? That reporter would have gotten a great story. So much for investigative journalism.

Understandably, there were a lot of nervous employees on Hughes's payroll at this time. Getting caught in a press-leak scandal was the last thing I could afford right now. Also, no one, including me, had a contract with the organization. This prompted me to recall the advice of my Air Force friend Keith Garland, who had cautioned me not to go to work for such a large organization without a contract". I began to think that Keith may have been right.

Stuck in Limbo

I spent six months in Woodburn with my family after the Hughes organization was summarily kicked out of the Bahamas. Most of the men in the flight department did the same after the Bahamas fiasco, heading back to their homes and getting their kids back in school. The understanding was that once school was out for the summer, we would reunite in Vegas and pick up again—a plan I had suggested to Kay Glenn, who had OK'd it.

So when school was out for Roxie and Robin, we reassembled in Las Vegas and became an active flight department again. It seemed for a little while as though things would get back on track for the organization. I even made an effort to finish my helicopter training, in a Hughes 300 helicopter in North Las Vegas.

During that time, back home in Woodburn, I'd signed up for a helicopter rating at a little grass strip near Kendallville, where a laid-off Pan Am pilot had set up a training program under the G.I. Bill. I got my helicopter license in less than 25 hours and then decided to go all the way—to become a helicopter instructor.

In the meantime, I still had about four hours of flight time already paid for, so I took my brother-in-law Verne with me to get the aircraft. We flew it back to the Woodburn airport, where I had quite a few little nieces and nephews lined up and waiting for a ride. Then, on the way back to Kendallville, I took my brother-in-law

Fritz with me. Our plan was to make a quick stop at the home of my other brother-in-law, Harry Meyer, who lived on Lahmeyer Road, near Fort Wayne. Behind Harry's place, a new subdivision was under construction, and the cul-de-sac right behind his house created an ideal landing pad—or so I thought. I got a rude awakening. It was my inexperience in flying a "chopper" that got me. The helicopter whipped up a good deal of dust, restricting visibility and forcing me to put that chopper on the ground pretty darn quick.

Back in Vegas, I signed up to finish my training, but I only did a couple of flights. I never did become a helicopter instructor. In fact, I never flew a helicopter again after that. I guess I just didn't want to take the time, didn't have enough interest. Plus, that "dust storm" I'd created in Indiana had been enough to scare the daylights out of me.

Although we were back "home" in Vegas, it still wasn't completely back to what things were like prior to our leaving for the Bahamas. There were tons of rumors about Mr. Hughes—who presumably was still in Nicaragua—and his failing health. But it wasn't Mr. Hughes's health or his wealth that had everyone talking as Christmas neared that year.

While in Nicaragua, he almost met his fate—but not in the form of government officials or the spread of germs. On December 23, 1972, the first shock of a terrible earthquake shook his room at the Intercontinental. Once again, Hughes was whisked away from his hiding spot—this time with the building literally falling down around him. He was taken down flights of stairs, placed in the backseat of a waiting Mercedes, and driven to President Somoza's estate.

At home in Las Vegas early that morning, I received a call from Jack Real, requesting that I get the Cessna 421 ready and fly it out to Santa Monica, California. He told me that I might have to fly down and get Mr. Hughes in one of his JetStars.

Initially they had arranged for Barron Hilton's private Gulfstream II, based in Santa Monica, to go down and pick up Mr. Hughes. I spent the better part of that day in a phone booth (no cell phones back then), waiting on a call from Romaine Street, where Bill Gay and company were trying to decide what action to take. The Hilton pilot was also there, standing by, and he was getting very angry. He wanted to go home for Christmas, but they had him on the hook. Plus, there was rumored to be a large crevice in the runway at the Managua airport—another reason the Hilton pilot was out of sorts. He didn't want to land there! I tried to convince Kay Glenn that I could put enough fuel in the JetStar to make a pass at the runway, see whether a plane could be landed there, and if not, I argued, we could go on to Costa Rica and fly Hughes out from there.

As it turned out, the runway was perfectly safe. Mr. Hughes was taken from Somoza's estate to the Managua airport, where a Northrop Aviation Gulfstream II arranged by and piloted by Don Short (a retired USAF Special Air Mission pilot and now Director of Aviation for Northrop) sat waiting to transport him and his aides out of Nicaragua to escape the disaster. That flight took Hughes to Canada—Vancouver, British Columbia, where he sequestered himself for the next five months at the Bayshore Inn, which now has a plaque on the door that says *The Howard Hughes Suite*. Back in Vegas, it was business as usual. Or so we thought.

See Appendix B for Don Short's interesting Narrative on "Flying Hughes".

Close Calls

Howard's body was starting to implode. At one point on Sunday evening his vision became blurred and I heard him say to George Francom, who was standing a few feet away, "I can't see you." Dr. Larry Chaffin later explained to me that this was a sure sign of his kidneys beginning to fail.

By now, the drugs that had ruled Howard's life for so long had taken it over almost completely. In all of the years of Howard's drug addiction, the only doctor who had the nerve and the guts to try to get him off the codeine was Dr. Larry Chaffin, but he was never successful. He would forever blame Dr. Verne Mason, who had started Howard on the substance after the XF-11 crash in 1946. Dr. Chaffin always told me that if he were given a chance, and Howard had the desire, it would not have been difficult to clean him up, but Howard would tell him: "It's my only vice – so leave me alone."

Howard woke up before midnight and started to inject himself with codeine. There were four men with Howard in the room—Gordon Margulis, George Francom, Dr. Crane, and Dr. Chaffin. I was just outside the bedroom, where I could hear Howard crying, whimpering, and begging.

"Please help me," he gasped weakly. "Help me. Help me." I surmised that he probably didn't have the strength to complete the task of injecting himself ... I heard Howard cry out again, louder this time. His pleas were becoming more urgent. He had apparently stuck the syringe in his arm, but was too weak to push the plunger to complete the injection ... The syringe just hung from his arm for a moment and then it dropped on his bed. I don't know what happened next. I just turned my head. His pathetic sounds were growing softer as, apparently, someone completed the job for him. (*The Asylum of Howard Hughes*, Jack Real, pages 237–238)

When we pilots got to know and work with the people surrounding Mr. Hughes, and we heard some of the comments they made about him, we understood how some of his aides had managed to finagle their way into a position of authority. These aides continued to refer to his drug collection, which went with him when they moved him from place to place, as his "goody bag." I couldn't help but wonder if they'd discovered that Hughes, with all his difficulties and requirements, was more manageable when he was high on drugs and sleeping all of the time.

We heard a lot of tidbits like this during conversations with the aides. The aides were very, very guarded, but naturally some factual information about Hughes came out from time to time. They made it a habit of coming into the cockpit while we were flying, or approaching us while we were on the ground waiting for something to happen. Bill Gay was always notoriously late, so if some of his guys were coming along on a flight, it could mean hours of waiting before Bill finally showed up—and that meant time to kill, often with conversation.

Some of the aides liked to use their so-called authority to detain us for unreasonable lengths of time in preparation for departures. For example, we'd sit in the Lockheed JetStar on the ramp for hours at a time while Bill Gay was trying to decide what color of pillows would go best with the aircraft's interior decor. This didn't come entirely as a surprise—Bill Gay had spent agonizing hours over every minor detail in redesigning his gem, the Desert Inn. I remember Jack Real and others saying that this was absolutely the dumbest thing in the world to do. Bill Gay wanted a small, luxurious, state-of-the-art hotel, something that—as anybody in the hotel business (especially on the Las Vegas Strip) would tell you—could not recoup the costs of redesign. There simply were not enough rooms. It was common knowledge, however, that Bill Gay was overseeing the renovations and spending a lot of money on this losing proposition.

So we knew that Bill Gay took his designing to the nth degree. For the JetStar, he even arranged for the famous designer Mario Zamparelli to come up with our flight crew attire. After Zamparelli was done with us, though, we were wearing nothing more than the "typical" corporate pilot uniform: dark, navy blue blazer, gray slacks, and light blue shirt with striped tie. We hardly needed a designer to dress us like every other corporate pilot in the industry! Actually, I have to admit, the attire was sharp-looking. But that's not the point. Gay continued to be wrapped up in the little stuff—at one point even telling me what kind of gum to put on board the JetStar.

I was called into Bill Gay's office one day, where I waited an extremely long time before I finally got to talk to him. Hughes was living in London at the time, and Gay wanted to plan a trip there, but he was trying to justify the cost of the trip.

"Bob," he said, "tell me how much it'll cost to fly the JetStar to London."

Of course, I gave him only the direct operating costs—the fuel and engine overhaul time, the crew expenses—which I knew offhand. The indirect costs, such as the depreciation of the airplane, the crew's salary, insurance, and hangar fees, were already paid for and would be covered whether or not we flew the airplane. With flying time to London, the figure equated to about $5,000.

He then calculated in his head what nine first-class seats to London on a commercial flight would cost, and finally said, "Oh! Well, that's a no-brainer. Let's take the JetStar."

We planned the trip for nine people, and that's quite a load across the Atlantic. We flew from Los Angeles to Milwaukee to Goose Bay, Labrador, to Iceland, then down to London. We were there a week; the crew and I stayed at the Hilton while

Gay and his people stayed at the Inn on the Park, where Mr. Hughes was living. After a day or two, Bill Gay decided to fly back with some of his staff, on a commercial flight. He instructed me to stay there with nine of his remaining staff(including his son, who was among the passengers) and to fly them anywhere they wanted to go. It turns out they wanted to take a sight-seeing trip around Europe. Remember, this excursion was all on Howard Hughes's expense account.

Once again, Charlie, Warren, and I were crewing the airplane. Every one of the nine people wanted to go to different places and see different parts of Europe. We flew over to Amsterdam, landed, piled into taxis, and drove into the city for lunch.

We flew down to Spain, and when I had to go in for clearance, they wanted to see the insurance papers. Of course, I had to fake it, because I didn't have anything like that on the airplane. (You have to really plan ahead to fly into these countries, which our passengers hadn't.)

"Oh, I'm sorry," I said, "the papers are out in the aircraft." I then went out to the plane and told the guys that we needed some insurance papers—or something that *looked like* insurance papers. We found some documents written in English, and because I knew those officials in the terminal building could not read them, I just presented them and was on my way. Back then, you could bluff your way through the protocol and get away with it.

One evening while we were in Amsterdam, the entourage wanted to fly over Venice—very low, so they could see the canals. By this time I was pretty tired of their unplanned trips, and I told them so. I said I'd fly them anywhere, since I'd been instructed to do so, but did they know that flying from Amsterdam to Venice was like taking off from Los Angeles and flying one and a half hours away, circling, climbing back up to altitude, and then finally landing?

"Do you really want to waste a whole afternoon doing that?" I asked.

They decided to fly to Copenhagen instead.

It was late in the afternoon, and as we took off from Madrid, again I reminded myself of what a waste of time this was—and what an extravagant expense, all without Mr. Hughes's knowledge. We took off from Madrid and were up to altitude. We had retrieved the forecast for Copenhagen (and London as the alternate), which was fine. But at approximately 8:00 in the evening, the continental weather was starting to close in. What we really needed on that plane was new Collins Flight Directors. Instead, we had the dubious, older TWA Bendix Flight Directors, which were giving us fits!

So there we were, basically over Hamburg, Germany, and the good old Bendixes were not working properly. I was frantically trying to get the weather for our destination, and now the weather was closing in fast. It was getting down to minimums —that is, below the minimum requirements for landing, and we had to make a decision. The best weather I could find was Hamburg, and we were right on top of it.

I immediately told Charlie to call in and change our destination to Hamburg, and I started my descent.

"Well, Bob," said Charlie, "aren't you going to ask the guys in the back if they want to land in Hamburg?"

I said, "Charlie, if you go back there and ask them that, you're going to get nine different answers. I'm the captain of this ship, and we are putting it down here. They will just have to deal with it!"

Once we were sitting on the ground in Hamburg, our bewildered, unhappy passengers had difficulty finding a room. Some of them were questioning why we couldn't just go back to Amsterdam. I explained once again, as I had when we landed, that the weather was below minimums all over the continent and that Hamburg was the best weather we could find. We weren't going anywhere.

Luckily, here again, because of my networking I was able to help. I had discovered how to make a deal with Pan American some time earlier, while on reserve duty at Nellis AFB and assigned as assistant base operations officer. Pan Am had a special division that assisted corporate pilots and planed our flights whenever we had to go anywhere overseas. Like the time I was on reserve duty in the Air Force for two weeks and I got a call, asking how soon I could get over to Bangkok, Thailand, pick up the Archbishop of Cypress en route from China, and take him back to Cypress. (This was a payback trip for Lockheed, which had flown Hughes out of Las Vegas to the Bahamas—itself a payback trip after Hughes bought the last four Jet-Stars off the assembly line from Lockheed. Lockheed wanted to sell the Archbishop some L1011s for his Cypress airline but didn't have an airplane available to pick him up.)

That week, rather than call the necessary embassies in Washington in order to get flight clearance in all the various countries, I had planned our flights through Pan Am. When we arrived at whatever country, we got in touch with Pan Am operations and the flight officer took care of the red tape. All I had to do was talk to Pan American and pay as I went, and they took care of me.

Since I already had a relationship with Pan American, I made one telephone call to the Intercontinental Hotel, which Pan Am owned, and said, "This is Captain Wearley with Pan American Airlines. I have a crew of twelve people and will need twelve rooms for the night."

The answer came back immediately: "Yes, sir, Captain Wearley."

And that was it. Within minutes I had procured our rooms for the night in Hamburg at the Intercontinental Hotel.

When we got to the hotel, Charlie, Warren, and I went to the bar, had a drink, and then moved into the dining room for dinner while our passengers went out on the town. The next morning I met with them for breakfast. My goal was to plan the rest of the itinerary for this European tour. I'd finally gotten fed up with our passengers' indecisiveness. They had split in the end—some were the type to visit museums and libraries, and others ... well, others just wanted to visit the party scene. It eventually came out why they wanted to go to Copenhagen in the first place when they approached Charlie, who was single, and said they wanted to see the live sex shows that the city was famous for.

"All we're doing is burning up jet fuel by jumping from country to country with no plan," I said. I suggested flying to each new city at night, so the next morning they could tour that city, then in the evening fly to yet another city, where they could then tour that city the following day ... and so on. That way they could visit five different countries and spend a day in each one. And that's what we did.

On our return flight to the States we refueled at Keflavik, Iceland, a small island just off the coast that had experienced a devastating volcano earlier that year. The volcano was still somewhat active, so I asked the passengers if they'd like to see it, and they all agreed.

As we were approaching Keflavik, we descended to about 2,000 feet and circled the island. We saw the devastation that the volcano had brought to the island's main town. After circling the island, I flew directly over the volcano and banked the aircraft so our passengers could actually look down into the volcano. It was not erupting and no smoke was coming out but we could feel the heat as the aircraft burbled. It was fascinating, and our passengers got some good photographs. The devastation that volcanoes could cause an aircraft was not yet known, but in retrospect it was a very stupid thing to do.

The Demise of Howard Hughes

On February 10, 1976, Hughes was flown from Freeport to Acapulco and moved into a bedroom of the Acapulco Princess—his fifth foreign hotel room in five years, his 1,892nd day in exile. A fresh supply of codeine was waiting for him. With its sparse furnishings, movie screen, and drawn drapes, the penthouse looked like all the other penthouses of the last ten years. Nevertheless, there were subtle differences. The food tasted strange. There were breakdowns in the electrical and air-conditioning systems. Hughes was a creature of habit. The surprise alterations in his routine unnerved him, intensified his already overactive anxieties, and hastened his decline. He stopped eating and drinking. Day by day, he wasted away. When he was finally loaded onto the plane for the flight to Houston, a ninety-three-pound skeleton clinging to life, it was too late. Fifty-five days after his move to Mexico, Howard Robard Hughes, Jr., was dead. (*Howard Hughes: His Life and Madness*, Barlett and Steele, page 579)

The months passed. The location of Howard Hughes at any given moment had become, especially in these last years of his strange life, a matter of public contemplation, if not public record. After leaving London in December 1974, he went back to the Bahamas, where he made his home for two years at the Xanadu Princess in Freeport, and finally to the last hotel he would live in before his death: the Acapulco Princess in Acapulco, Mexico, in February 1976.

Two months later I was once again in ground school with the other pilots when panic swept through the Hughes organization. This time we were in Savannah, Georgia, at the FlightSafety International Training Center, receiving ground school and simulator training in a Gulfstream I refresher course. Charlie, Warren, Jim Hogan, and I had initially gone through the ground school training, and when we returned to Las Vegas we had an instructor train us for the FAA check ride, after which we'd get our type ratings. Our plans were to leave Vegas on a Sunday in order to be in Savannah on Monday. On Saturday, however, my beeper went off.

It was Romaine Street calling.

When I returned the call, the powers that be at Romaine Street informed me that I was to call a particular number down in Acapulco. Jack Real was on the other end of that line, and he had some very interesting questions. He wanted to know the distance and flying time from Acapulco to several locations, including Quito, Ecuador, and Port-au-Prince, Haiti. He instructed me to not say anything to anybody about this. I went out to the airport and researched our maps before giving him my estimates.

After I told him that we were heading to Gulfstream I refresher training, the last thing he said was this: "Oh, good. When you get to Savannah, go out to the manufacturing plant where they build the Gulfstream IIs, and measure the doorways—both the entrance and the cabin doorway—and tell me how wide they are." And then he hung up.

Of course, I knew what this was all about: Real was making plans to move Hughes out of Mexico and to another location. I knew exactly what they were going to do: use a Gulfstream II to move Hughes. Real wanted the measurements to see if they could get a wheelchair or a stretcher through the doorways.

As soon as I got to class on Monday morning, April 5, 1976, I told the instructor that I would be right back: I had to go to the hangar. When I got there, everyone was busy building the airplanes. I borrowed a tape measure from someone, measured the doorways, and phoned Jack in Acapulco. What he told me blew my mind!

He said, "Thanks, Bob. Actually, the situation has taken care of itself. I will call you from Los Angeles tonight."

I went back to the classroom and said to the other Hughes pilots, "Something is up." I told them that Jack was leaving Acapulco and he no longer needed the measurements for the Gulfstream II.

Brent immediately called his cousin, Kay Glenn, who we thought would be able to tell us what was going on. But Brent couldn't find anything out—or if he did, he didn't tell us. As soon as classes ended, though, we went to my room and turned on the television, looking for national news relating to Howard Hughes. We flipped back and forth between all three national news channels, and we finally got the news: Mr. Hughes had left Acapulco and had died en route to a hospital in Houston, Texas.

According to those who were present, Howard Hughes was loaded onboard a Learjet in an attempt to fly him to Methodist Hospital in Houston. But it was too little, too late. The Learjet touched down in Houston at approximately 1:50 p.m. that day, but Mr. Hughes—the pioneering aviator—had already died in midair.

The news didn't completely surprise me. From what Jack Real had said, I'd surmised that Hughes was very ill. Usually Kay Glenn, not Real, was the one who made the arrangements for Mr. Hughes's flights. I'd become especially suspicious when Real said that the problem had "taken care of itself" and that he'd call me from Los Angeles—I knew for certain that Hughes wouldn't have gone to L. A. That was pretty typical of Jack. It was always *I can't tell you this—you have to read between the lines.* I knew enough not to ask Jack specifically what was going on.

Still, it was a bit of a shock. The Man was dead—my employer these last six years, whom I'd never met—and now would never meet. But what could we do? Life went on for the rest of us, as it does. After we heard the big news, we went to the hotel bar and ordered ourselves a drink. Then we went out to eat.

A Death Wish?

Regardless of which hotel's top floor Howard Hughes occupied from November 27, 1966, when he set up housekeeping on the top floor of the Desert Inn, until his 1976 death purportedly in midair, flying from Acapulco to Houston, Hughes's goody bag and syringes were always close at hand. Did Howard Hughes have a death wish, or was he a victim of his own paralyzing fears?

Perhaps the downward spiral into severe illness could have been prevented had Hughes been more cooperative with his staff, his doctors, and Jack Real. But he seemed unable to help himself. His peculiar behavior has been attributed partly to his overprotective mother, who herself was paranoid about germs, addicted to avoiding them at all costs. But Hughes's addictions went beyond germ phobia and even beyond the drug-induced stupor that characterized much of the last two decades of his life; he was addicted to being the richest man in the world. He still had a lot of traveling to do, and when lucid, he still had big plans to capture the attention of the entire world.

The real question is not whether he had a death wish but why, with so many influential people around him, didn't someone (especially his physicians or personal aides) try to help him?

While Hughes's addiction to a various assembly of narcotics began after his fateful XF-11 accident, when his injuries were so severe that he needed the drugs to wipe out the pain, long after his injuries were healed Hughes continued to abuse prescription drugs. He slept for days at a time and, when he was awake, rebounded into a stupor. Those drugs, it is well documented, were stationed at Hughes's bedside. A handful of his closest aides continued to purchase them using their own identities and, up to the end, may have assisted Hughes in administering them.

Those who claim to be closest to Hughes knew exactly what he was doing. Why, then, did no one *insist* on helping him get clean and sober? That question will always bother me.

One might surmise that the entire gang really didn't want Hughes in his right state of mind. One could even suppose that perhaps greed played a role—especially considering what came to pass after his demise.

The Scramble for the Millions

Did Mr. Hughes's inner circle allow him to languish in a drug-induced state for the primary purpose of gaining control of his huge empire? It's a question that will probably never be answered satisfactorily, but one thing is certain: What followed Hughes's death was complete mayhem. There were some very frightened and confused people, both in his inner sanctuary and at the airport. Word of Hughes's death struck terror in the hearts of those who were convinced the Hughes empire would never tumble, whether Mr. Hughes was dead or alive. Some felt there was enough money there to sustain them in their position with the Hughes organization, whether they were actually working or not.

In the summer of 1975, with Hughes drugged and slowly dying, the Summa Corporation high command and the aides mounted a campaign designed to gain two objectives—corporate employment contracts and a favorable will. Without one or the other, all jobs in the Hughes hierarchy were in jeopardy. (*Howard Hughes: His Life and Madness*, Barlett and Steele, page 569)

On the Friday that followed Howard's death, there was a high-level meeting; it appeared they were scurrying about, looking for his last will and testament. All the aides gathered and held a strategic brainstorming session to try and figure it out: Had Mr. Hughes left any hints about where they could find a will?

That meeting broke up late in the afternoon. Some of the aides got on the JetStar, and we flew them up to various airports near their homes in Provo, Pocatello, and Logan, Utah. One of the newer aides, Jim Rickard, jumped into the cockpit with us. Rickard had been a pilot in World War II and had some experience with the early jets that required, as he recalled, eight hours of maintenance for every hour of flight. He enjoyed riding in the cockpit with us whenever he flew with us. This particular time, Rickard made the strangest remark: "Well, the aspirins got to him. The old man just took too many aspirins."

I was reminded of the line from Shakespeare's *Hamlet*: "The lady doth protest too much!" Was this a rumor the aides were supposed to put out after Hughes's death—a common story to tell people? If they had allowed Hughes to take the drugs, it could place some of the blame on them. Was the aspirin story supposed to exonerate them? After the autopsy, the truth would be known. Hughes was malnourished, of course, but he also died with a huge amount of narcotics in his system. The aides may have convinced themselves that they were just doing their job. But to me it was pretty pathetic.

We had finished our ground school training, and Kay Glenn (via Nadine Henley, John Holmes, and Bill Gay) then instructed me to go to Redbird Airport in Dallas, Texas. They were sending a mechanic there to preflight the brand-new JetStar that had been in storage in an air-conditioned and dehumidified hangar. The plane had only five hours of flight time on it. The interior and avionics were in mint condition. That beautiful JetStar had come right off the assembly line back in the early 1960s and had been sitting in storage all this time, unused.

I had mixed feelings about this move. It was obvious to me what was going on: Bill Gay and company wanted desperately to get their hands on that nice, new JetStar in order to fly it as their executive airplane. After all, Mr. Hughes was dead, so what would it matter? That didn't seem entirely right. But there was a certain renewed freedom among those who worked closest to Mr. Hughes. Perhaps they were doing the right thing in getting that beautiful JetStar out of storage and making it the corporate plane. They were simply putting a perfectly good JetStar back into use—something that should have been done all along.

In any case, the JetStar was pulled out of the hangar at Redbird, and the mechanic gave it a preflight check. I had sent the other pilots back to Vegas, but Brent Neal and Smitty were still with me. We took it up on a test flight—everything on that plane worked perfectly. The only "squawk" we found was a minor problem with the avionics. We landed it and had the line boys fuel it up; then we headed for Van Nuys to pick up Nadine Henley, Kay Glenn, and whoever else needed to fly up to Boeing in Seattle, where Air West had bought a 200 Series 727 that was about to make its inaugural flight.

Within a few hours of landing at Van Nuys, we were flying Bill Gay and some of the board's directors in the JetStar up to Boeing Field, where they met with officials, attended a cocktail reception, and watched the brand-new 727 take off. Tex Parsons flew the Gulfstream I with the rest of the directors, the Summa officials, Hughes's male secretaries, and so forth.

During our return flight, on the descent into Van Nuys, I suddenly felt something odd. I slowed down and checked everything, but could not find anything on the instruments. Smitty went to the back of the airplane to listen for anything unusual. When he returned to the cockpit, he said he had not detected anything out of the ordinary.

As soon as we landed in Van Nuys and the passengers deplaned, Smitty laid the gear pins out for the line boys to put in, then made a quick walk around the aircraft. He still didn't see anything unusual.

As the passengers left the hangar in limos, we started doing our paperwork and cleaning up the cabin. Smitty hurried came back in.

"I want to show you something," he said. He took me around to the back of the plane, and there was a two-foot-by-one-foot inspection panel missing from the strut that holds the number three and number four engine pods to the fuselage. It had been ripped off and probably hit the tail! That's what I had felt on our descent. Fortunately it had not done any real damage.

Some of the key players in the Hughes empire had been on board that flight—Hughes's aides—including John Holmes and Levar Myler—whom Bill Gay had been shrewd enough to make board directors for the Summa Corporation.

ON A COLLISION COURSE

OVER THE COURSE OF the next seven years, between the ages of 45 and 52, I found my life once again taking twists and turns that no one could possibly have anticipated. My mother had passed away. My marriage was breaking up. I was dealing with financial difficulties (self-induced, of course). And then I was facing a new job and a new culture, all rolled into one. The combination of these life stressors meant that, all in all, it was a pretty lonely and frustrating time.

After our hurried flight from the Bahamas, the time spent hopping back and forth between Woodburn and Las Vegas, and the death of Howard Hughes, things just never seemed to get back on track with Ruth and me. Our marriage and our faith was deteriorating. Finally, I applied for a captain's position with Singapore Airlines, and pending a few obligatory tests, I got the job.

Ruth and I decided on a trial separation.

I had never felt so thoroughly alone in my entire life as when I arrived in Singapore. It seemed as though I was experiencing all the critical changes that can happen in a person's life, all at the same time. And yet even in the depths of despair there was a flicker of hope that God would once again intervene—and of course, He did.

The airline put me up in a hotel in Singapore—not the best of hotels either, I might add. I stayed there for a week, studying to pass the Singapore Airline Transport Pilot exam. The test material was stiff and difficult—heavily influenced by the British, like most everything in this former colony. I hated the hotel food. I was not familiar with the city. And anyway, I was virtually locked in that hotel room, studying day and night, getting very little help from anyone. To make matters worse I had a horrible cold. It seems almost comical now, but at the time I was absolutely miserable.

I already had a 707 rating, because the U.S. Air Force's C-135 was essentially a Boeing 707/720B. It soon became clear, however, that the 707s I was going to be flying for Singapore Airlines were the 300 series—quite a different aircraft from the one I was used to flying in the military. Not only that, but Singapore Airlines' nine 707s had slightly different systems: Three of them were purchased directly from Boeing, three were purchased from Australia's Qantas Airlines, and three were from Continental Airlines. And I was expected to jump in and fly them all as though I were completely familiar with each one.

There were a limited number of operating manuals available, though none that I was familiar with from my military days. There definitely was no refresher ground school course. Essentially I had to teach myself. Fortunately the airline had a 707 flight simulator, which jump-started me in the process of re-familiarizing myself with the aircraft. It had been 15 years since I'd flown a 707. I knew I had my work cut out for me.

Not only was the loneliness eating me up, not only was I fighting an uphill battle to prepare myself for a new job in a new country, but I also was absolutely strapped for cash. Our elder daughter Robin was in the Hughes Air West flight attendant school, and I was trying to scrape together as much money as I could to support her financially. Roxie, our younger girl, was going to college, which also required my financial support.

And Ruth, back in Las Vegas and working at Poncho Gonzales's tennis shop, was hardly making any money at all. The job paid very little, and I knew she was capable of making far more at another job—but Ruth wasn't sure what other job she might be willing to do. I had to confront her: If she was going to make some real money, then she'd have to get a real job—not just a fun job where you wear tennis clothes and bask in a false sense of security. The payment on the condominium we owned in Vegas was $330 a month—a lot of money back then. I kept paying it so Ruth had a place to live while we were separated. What she was making would not have been enough to sustain her without my financial support. Later, long after her death, I found out that she was also receiving funds regularly from her father. But I didn't know that then, and I was worried that—if we should split up for good—we'd be facing serious financial problems.

Despite all my concerns, I passed both the written Airline Transport Pilot exam and the flight check in the 707, and soon I was flying regularly for Singapore Airlines.

The temptations were everywhere in Singapore. Some of the young female flight attendants would have been more than happy to capture the heart of an American captain, marry him, and eventually get to live in the United States. And there were quite a few to choose from: Singapore Airlines was hiring expatriate captains to appeal to the majority of its passengers, who came from countries other than Singapore. It was such a small country that only a fraction of the people flying with the airline actually came from Singapore. For a passenger, having a captain in the cockpit who originated from your own country—South Africa, The Netherlands, Britain, Taiwan, China, Australia, France, Belgium—was somehow comforting. It gave a favorable impression, a "hometown" feel. And these expatriate captains were a prime catch for a beautiful, young Asian flight attendant.

I observed various captains from different countries, who had left their wives back home and were living with young Singaporean flight attendants. These aging men looked foolish to me. But then it occurred to me that I wasn't all that different from them. Singapore was a place that tested my morality. There were many opportunities to spend time with some of the lovely flight attendants who worked for the airline. I took advantage of those opportunities, even though I knew deep down inside that it was wrong. Ruth and I were separated, but we were still legally married. I still had feelings for her. Morally and ethically, it wasn't right. But at the time, it was as if my conscience was dead. Ruth had started dating, and she was getting a little taste of what it was like to be single again. Why shouldn't I enjoy being on my own, too?

In fact, during my Singapore Airlines tenure I became involved with several women. One relationship went on for a couple of years, to the point where I actually considered marrying her. This Singaporean woman was older, more mature, and very special. She was a senior chief flight attendant, very Chinese in her nature. She had no inhibitions about the obvious differences between us, nor did she care what other people might think about us. She had a quality about her that would not be compromised when it came to race or anything else.

This came to light one day when she and I were walking down a street in Frankfurt, Germany, and a little boy in front of us kept turning around and staring at her. "He probably has never seen an Oriental before," she remarked (using the term everyone used at the time). She was very accepting of her culture and mine, and of our relationship.

She and I did get into discussions about marriage, and that's when things began to cool a bit. I was scared. The environment in Singapore was a melting pot, with all different cultures running wild and interracial marriages in vogue. I contributed to that scene by introducing a beautiful Sri Lankan lady to a bachelor Australian ship captain—my next-door neighbor. They ended up getting married, but she would not live with him beforehand, out of respect for her parents. No matter how open things were, there were always vast differences between our Western and Eastern cultures.

These cultural differences were significant enough for me to think carefully about divorcing Ruth and marrying the Singaporean woman I had been seeing. My hometown values and lifestyle took over. While it could have been very comfortable for us to live in that melting-pot environment in Singapore, I knew I could not live there indefinitely. I was a hometown boy, and I had to go home eventually. If I took her home with me, she'd be totally removed from her culture and her family and friends. It would be the other side of the world (in more ways than one), and that would not be fair to her. In Singapore, I was the foreigner, but in Indiana *she* would be the one with the accent, and it might be hard for her to be accepted.

We probably could have worked it out, but it didn't end up that way. Shortly after I arrived in Singapore, Ruth started hinting that she'd like to join me.

Ruth's Ventures

Perhaps she discovered that the dating scene wasn't what it was cracked up to be, and perhaps she was realizing how difficult things would be for her financially—maybe her reasons included a little of both. I wasn't ready for us to get back together, and I flatly told her not to come, but she begged me, saying that she was determined to purchase a ticket. It was obvious to me that she had made up her mind, so I told her not to spend the money—I could send her a free ticket because legally we were still husband and wife.

In the beginning, things appeared to be working out fine, but the situation soon turned sour. We had not sought counseling or established any guidelines for our marriage—ground rules for how to move forward. We both continued seeing other people. I was very discreet about my liaisons with other women, but I also knew that Ruth had some liaisons going on with other men at the same time—and she was not all that discreet about it. In fact, she rather flaunted it, while attempting to keep me on the defensive by accusing me of things that were absolutely not true.

This indiscretion was all around me—both at home and among the Singapore Airline crews. Some of my coworkers, when they found out who was fooling around with whom, would capitalize on this, feeling free to tell the wives about their husbands' shenanigans. By telling the wives about their husbands' infidelities, some were hoping these women would feel free to do the same—and hop into bed with them. Some were just being malicious. And some were Singaporeans who didn't like the fact that the flight attendants were enamored with expatriate captains.

Some of the Singaporeans I met had a particular trait: They were mean gossips. Sometime there were even anonymous telephone calls to my house while I was gone on a flight. When I got home, Ruth was livid and justifiable so. But what could she say? The reality was, she was also fooling around.

Ruth was not satisfied living in a meager two-bedroom apartment for very long. She wanted to be more independence. She got a full-time job with the IRS, as a secretary in the U.S. office. In fact, she wanted to start her own business. With her knowledge of tennis wear from her tenure at Gonzales's pro shop in Vegas, she felt she could make a go of it in Singapore.

It was a clever idea. What Ruth wanted to do was export tennis clothing made from, a special cotton material called Batik. She would design it in Singapore and send it to the U.S. to sell. Unfortunately, this business venture was not successful. It never got off of the ground because batik needed ironing, and nobody in the U.S. wanted clothes made from a fabric that was high maintenance. There wasn't much call for it there; American retailers weren't even willing to stock it on their shelves.

What did catch on, however, was merchandise going in the opposite direction: the clothing Ruth brought to Singapore from the United States. She put American tennis clothing in Singapore's golf and tennis shops on consignment. Her connection in the U.S. was with a couple of ladies she'd met while purchasing tennis clothes from the Caesar's Palace tennis shop; they lived in Los Angeles and sold Ruth tennis clothes at wholesale prices. Whenever I had a flight into Los Angeles I rented a car and went over to their factory. I picked up cases of this clothing and took it back on board with me as crew luggage, courtesy of Singapore Airlines. Occasionally I even went right through customs without paying duty on it, which was not the right thing to do, but at the time it didn't bother me.

When I got back to our Singapore apartment, if I had several days between flights with nothing to do. I unpacked the boxes myself, hung the clothes on racks in the spare bedroom, and offered to price the items. Ruth said, "No. I'll take care of it," but she usually just let them sit there.

"If we go ahead and price the clothes," I said, thinking about cash flow, "we can distribute them tomorrow."

But her typical response was "No, I don't feel like it. Let's go to the club."

Many evenings we went to the popular Tanglin Club to play tennis, then swim and have dinner. But we seemed to end up quarreling. I became exasperated about the clothing. *Here is this great product sitting in our apartment,* I thought, *and I made the effort to get it here, and nothing is being done with it!*

That clothing sat there for weeks. It drove me nuts. Bit by bit, Ruth got it into the Singapore shops and collected her money—but only when she felt like it. She wasn't motivated, and she was not an entrepreneur. She was a dreamer. It was so frustrating for me! I could see all this money tied up in inventory, and she didn't seem to care.

In the end, Ruth didn't make a dime on her clothing venture, but it did provide me with a tax write-off. Singapore has a 30 percent income tax, and I was able to write off 10 percent on Ruth's venture. We broke even.

Ruth and I continued with the same social pattern to which we'd grown accustomed during our military days. After her workday at the IRS she met me at the club. I had her tennis gear ready, and we participated in club tennis—a social time when anyone could just walk onto the four courts and either play singles or, when others joined us, doubles. The camaraderie was unbelievable. It was fun because we met so many people from different countries and different backgrounds. Some days it was a mini United Nations. I was playing tennis with guys from Belgium, Germany, Australia, and Singapore—including a few doctors. So we already knew the best doctors to rely on, and they soon became invaluable to us.

When Ruth started getting sick, they ensured she was getting the very best care possible.

Moving Home

While we lived in Singapore, Ruth was diagnosed with polycythemia. It's a rare disease, with no known cause, that affects the red blood cells, allowing one's bone marrow to make too much blood. The diagnosis didn't seem to faze her that much at first. In fact, there is a traditional marathon in Singapore organized by the Ladies Hash House Harriers, an international organization of men and women runners. Just before her initial diagnosis, Ruth was determined to sign up for it, but I cautioned her against it. She was 50 years old and certainly in no condition to compete against women in their 20s, in 80-degree heat. She had already started living in denial. But I knew she would have to address her unique situation if she wanted any quality of life in the years to come.

In 1984, just as we were starting to deal with Ruth's illness, a former Singapore Airlines colleague from Australia, Peter Ivanhoff, who was now flying for Royal Jordian, told me they were looking for another 747 captain. I left Singapore Airlines and joined Royal Jordanian Airlines (referred to at that time as Alia). During my one-year tenure as a captain at Jordanian, Ruth and I moved from Singapore back to the States—to Fort Wayne. Ruth's polycythemia diagnosis was confirmed. The Dr. treating her was an Oncologist as well and discovered a serious Melanoma mole that needed to be removed. The surgeon that removed, the mole on her chest made a one-and-a-half-inch excision. When she was checked by her oncologist, he said that she really needed a three-inch-deep excision. So once again, Ruth was admitted into the hospital for surgery.

It was then that Ruth told me she thought she could live in Fort Wayne. She started looking for a new home for us in earnest. She contacted a high school friend, Gail Persyn, who was in real estate. Together, they shopped the market and looked at quite a few homes. That's how we found the house we finally bought, in Kekionga Shores in the western part of Fort Wayne. It was in a lovely setting on a small lake, with a master bedroom that had a large window facing the water. Ruth's illness was progressing, and I thought it would be a great place for her to enjoy the scenery from her bedroom window. We made the offer and bought the house.

When I returned home after a flight with the airline, Ruth had a surprise for me: All the furniture that we'd purchased in Singapore had been delivered, and Ruth, my sister Doris, and Ruth's Woodburn friends had set it up in the new Kekionga Shores house.

Our daughter Robin, now a flight attendant with Northwest Airlines, was transferred from her base in Phoenix to Detroit, and she moved in with us and commuted to Detroit for a year. That situation turned out to be totally unmanageable. When Ruth and Robin were home alone, they got along just fine. But when I was home and Robin was there, Ruth's and my relationship deteriorated. Being exposed to our bickering made it very uncomfortable for Robin to live there, and the inclement weather sometimes made commuting difficult, so she moved to Ann Arbor, near Detroit Metropolitan Airport. What should have been a win-win situation—financial benefits for Robin and quality family time for all of us—just didn't materialize.

At this point Ruth's condition was in a steady decline.

After a year, Alia sold one of its three Boeing 747s and no longer required the employment of all three captains—Ivanhoff, a pilot from Iceland, and me. The other two were offered captain's positions to fly 727s, and I was offered a Boeing 707 that I would be flying exclusively in the Middle East. That part of the world was heating up in the mid-1980s. While I didn't think that any of these radical Arab organizations could manage to hijack an American captain of a 707, I did not want to take the chance. I decided that it would be prudent for me to return to my roots.

Back in Fort Wayne, my good friend Ernie Bohren from Woodburn—owner of Bohren Trucking—introduced me to Jim Kelley, a well-known Fort Wayne businessman (now deceased). Jim owned a charter service called Consolidated Airways, located at the Fort Wayne International Airport. I soon went to work for the Kelley organization as chief pilot.

The copilots were enamored of me because of my background as a military pilot and an airline captain and my experience as chief pilot for Howard Hughes's personnel fleet of aircraft. My background and experience did not bode well with the other captains flying the various Kelley aircraft, however. Nor did my efforts to standardize the emergency procedures and checklists for operating four or five different types of aircraft. I met stiff resistance from these captains, who were used to doing things their way, not a standardized way.

As chief pilot, I felt it was my responsibility to implement the safety procedures that I felt were absolutely acceptable in any professional flight operation. I wasn't given the authority necessary to make this a reality, however, and it became extremely frustrating for me. In the end, Kelley and I basically agreed to disagree. I took three months' severance pay and left the organization.

I looked at other opportunities for about six months before realizing that there was something I had overlooked: Maybe it was time to pursue my dream of starting my own business. My entrepreneurial instincts had been tugging at me. And in October 1986, on a wing and a prayer, I founded Commercial Filter Service.

THE TURNING POINT

BY THE TIME I'D reached my early 50s, I had experienced so much in my life already. I'd spent 17 years in active duty with the United States Air Force and an additional four years in the Air Force Reserves (eventually retiring at age 60 as a Lieutenant Colonel). I'd flown for nine years with the Howard Hughes organization and six more years as a 747 captain for two major airlines, Singapore and Alia. I had been thrust into an unintentional role in the Watergate hearings, and I knew powerful people. The glamour of being an important pilot, especially as chief of Howard Hughes' personal fleet of aircraft, included invitations to exclusive parties and connection in a social network I would never have encountered back in Indiana.

By no means do I consider all these life experiences to be man-made. That is, I don't think I could have orchestrated them on my own. No way. However, it took me 50-plus years to realize that I was not the one controlling my life, but God.

I won't lie: It was easy for me to become prideful of what I accomplished—well, what I considered to be "my" accomplishments. I believe this stems from my childhood. My dad died when I was very young, and I grew up without a father and never felt as sure of myself as some of the other kids seemed to be. I was insecure, so I found a sense of worth in the prominent company I was keeping and the illustrious experiences I enjoyed as a young adult. It is not my intention to brag or boast. What masquerades as arrogance is in fact the insecurity that followed me through the first part of my life.

Now I see that God is the one who put me in this position, and I am convinced that only He could have directed me. My early experiences are what led to the transformation that came when I stopped to take stock of my life and to make a major change. You see, God's grace is a free gift that comes with having faith. The nature of man is to think that we can take credit for our accomplishments, and we like to think that we deserve all the credit. But that self-righteousness, that pride, is without any basis. Only God can guide us through life.

Titus 1:6-9 tells us that a man "must not be arrogant or quick-tempered. He must live wisely and be fair. He must live a devout and disciplined life." Yet I'd never made this an important goal for my life, and throughout all my experiences, even when I was at the "top of the mountain" in this or that coveted job, my life had felt so … empty. I'd chased my dreams and even achieved some of them, but in the process I lost that sense of my internal identity. I was plagued with nagging questions: *Why am I here? What is my purpose?*

As Ruth's illness began to take hold, I began to realize what a phony I had become. As I thought about the real me, and as I looked at my life, I didn't like what

I saw—all that hypocrisy, all those missed opportunities to make a positive impact. I felt pulled, in my spirit, to deal with my fraud. I had to return to my Christian foundation, my Christian values. In essence I had always been a believer, but I needed to get back to walking the walk, not just talking the talk.

What do I mean by this? Well, I *knew* the faith, but I wasn't *living* the faith. Most of us are intellectual about our faith, not that's not *spiritual* faith. In other words, we talk about what the Scripture teaches, but it sticks in our throat and doesn't get into our heart. We haven't truly absorbed it. Only when intellectual faith works its way from our brain and into our bloodstream, where it feeds all the cells of our body, are we *living* the faith.

At this time in my life I felt a powerful urge to explore and witness what the Bible says about Christ, about His death, His resurrection, and His plan for salvation— and for my redemption. And it had to be more than just Sunday school stories and a feel-good moral code. It had to be on God's terms, not mine.

I know now that this was the Holy Spirit awakening my long-dormant consciousness and sparking my faith. When Ruth was diagnosed with polycythemia, it was God shaking me into realizing just how short life is. Scripture began to challenge me. As I read the Bible, its message jumped out at me. This is how the Holy Spirit works once you commit your life to Christ, and that's what was finally happening in my life when I returned to Fort Wayne. I got back into studying the Bible. As pilots say, I took a 180-degree turn. The Master was changing my flight plan.

Confronting the Truth

Back in Indiana, I had to face the facts: Ruth was going to get very sick. Going back to our roots, where we were surrounded and supported by family and friends, had been the wise thing to do. In Fort Wayne, we sought out the advice of Ruth's cousin Dr. Steve Meyer, one of the best oncologist/hematologists in the area. Ruth underwent several operations. For many years she suffered setbacks both minor and major. The illness was slow-moving, but it was terminal.

Ruth didn't exactly embrace the diagnosis. She was in denial. She had been raised as the apple of her daddy's eye, and her two older brothers treated her that way, too. She couldn't believe that anything bad was going to happen to her, because she'd had so many things go her way. But this time, the prognosis was against her. The doctors gave Ruth 10 years. And life during those 10 years would not be at all like it had been in Las Vegas and Bermuda.

Our marriage had been volatile, and there were faults on both sides. We had lied, cheated, and deceived each other. We both did our share of drinking, partying, and fighting. We sat in front of more marriage counselors, psychiatrists, and pastors than I can count. Emotions ran high—one minute everything was fine, and the next minute Ruth was accusing me of being the devil himself. There were days when Ruth was absolutely irrational, and deep down inside, I knew something wasn't right. Now I think there may have been other conditions that weren't correctly diagnosed or treated. Why didn't her doctors recommend medication?

For my part, I became defensive which sometimes escalate the fighting. Too many times I packed up and split, only to come back in hopes that things would change. When things were at their worst, Ruth would threaten to divorce me, even meet with a lawyer, but when I finally agreed that I didn't want to stay in the marriage any longer, it called her bluff. We never went through with it.

I didn't want a divorce—I wanted a happy marriage. So instead of a lawyer, I went to counselors and pastors. Counseling taught me that Ruth harbored some animosity toward my climbing the ladder of success. When people found out about my job as a pilot, I often became the center of attention, and Ruth resented this. This understanding was a first step toward a more harmonious relationship.

Oh, the stories I could tell … But that's between God and me. If Ruth were alive today, I'm sure she'd would her share of stories, too. I've prayed for guidance since her death, but I may never figure out why we went through what we did. No, things weren't perfect in our marriage. But when death is imminent, there is a newfound sense of urgency. People soften and change.

Becoming an Entrepreneur

I had moved on from my short stint with Jim Kelley's Consolidated Airways because my heart was not in it. I'd always wanted to own my own business, and being an entrepreneur at heart, I felt certain that I could be a success. But I did not have a lot of capital.

When, quite by accident, I came upon an ad in the newspaper offering a business opportunity with a guaranteed net of $50,000 the first year, my immediate response was, "Boy this sounds like a come-on." But a number was printed below the heading *Putting a Fort Wayne Family into Business*. I took a chance and called it.

On the other end of the line was a man in Dallas by the name of George. He was selling distributorships in other areas—a service business to change heating and air-conditioning filters on a regularly scheduled basis. I looked at the projections and the cash-flow analysis, and it intrigued me. I realized that once a person landed enough accounts, it was just a matter of time before the distributorship could start seeing a profit.

George happened to be in the Fort Wayne area the next week, and he stopped in to see me. When I told him a little bit about myself—in particular, that I was a former airline captain and former chief pilot for Howard Hughes—he immediately perked up. Perhaps he saw how it would be beneficial to him in future marketing.

I took the idea to my lawyer and my banker, who thought it had merit. They agreed that there were great margins in this business. So I handed George $2,000 to hold the district distributorship for me.

Getting this distributorship actually ended up costing me a total of $12,000. Ruth and I traveled to Dallas to attend George's first "family reunion" of sorts, for those who had bought distributorships across the country. Although Ruth was not enamored with the business at first, I explained that we didn't have a choice. I had to have a job, and I could see the potential of this endeavor—and that's what entrepreneurship is all about.

We put our home in Kekionga Shores up for sale to help raise the capital we needed to get up and running, and once it sold we moved downtown to the Three Rives Apartments complex. Commercial Filter Service started out in October 1986 in the Fort Wayne Enterprise Center, a business incubator built by Graham Richard, who later became mayor of Fort Wayne. I put together a makeshift sales presentation booklet and went from business to business in the Time Corners area of southwest Fort Wayne, trying to sign up clients for our service agreement. Once I started selling accounts, Ruth warmed up to the idea. In fact, she wanted to continue as president under the name of her former business, Ruth Enterprises, Inc., Singapore. As a minority-owned business, we might be able to land more accounts, but eventually we formed a 50/50 ownership.

Money was tight when we first started the company. I received an offer to fly co-captain for Lincoln National Corporation in Fort Wayne, one day a week to fill in on the company's Lear jets. They were going to pay me handsomely, but Ruth was adamantly against it. And even though it was slow at the start, we managed to grow the business every year. We worked nicely together: Ruth had the talent for office management, whereas I had the operations and sales skills.

As we were growing Commercial Filter Service, however, her illness worsened. And as her illness progressed, it took its toll on the company. For about 10 years, we barely survived. Ruth was having her good days and her bad days, but she very much wanted to be part of that business. There came a point, however, when Ruth was simply too sick to go in to work. She didn't want me to go in either. Her rationale was that if she didn't show up for work, everyone would know she was in declining health. But if I stayed home with her, they might think we just took a day off to be together.

If only that were true.

Ruth Meyer Wearley with Joe DiMaggio (left) and Joe Louis Taken in the Caesars Palace indoor tennis courts during the "Night of the Heavyweights". Ruth was Manager of the Pancho Gonzales Tennis Shop at Caesars Palace Hotel Tennis Compound

Living with a Difficult Illness

Ruth's health concerns were ongoing. Other problems just seemed to be compounded by the polycythemia. While living downtown, in 1991 or 1992, Ruth became sick over the weekend, but Dr. Meyer wasn't able to admit her without a specific reason. We had to wait until Monday to be seen. When her condition worsened, and she became lethargic and could hardly move, finally the doctor was able to send her to the hospital immediately.

At first, Ruth was treated for pneumonia, but she wasn't getting any better. The doctor called for a CAT scan and determined that the pneumonia was actually disguising a blockage in the portal veins that drain the liver. The clotting had caused cirrhosis, and she was immediately put on medication to dissolve the clot.

But after several months of the clotting blood being forced to flow into the lower esophagus (the medical term is "esophageal varices"), it caused a rupture. Late one night, Ruth woke up vomiting blood. I thought it was a lot of blood, but she said she felt fine. So rather than calling 911, we just got into the company pickup truck. We thought we could drive the five minutes to the hospital quicker than the ambulance would arrive.

As it turned out, I should have called the EMS. Her esophagus had ruptured and filled her stomach with blood. The next morning she was in intensive care being prepped for an emergency helicopter flight to University Hospital in Indianapolis. The surgeons at University Hospital ultimately put rubber bands around the ruptured veins to stop the bleeding and put Ruth on medication that, from that point on, she had to inject every 12 hours until the day she died.

In 1993, Ruth became very sick again and was being treated at a local hospital. Robin, a physician's assistant at Kaiser Permanente, in San Francisco, got the diagnosis and decided to check in with a surgeon and an oncologist she knew there. Both told her that every minute counted. Immediately we got Ruth on an ambulance to Indianapolis, where she underwent surgery that evening. Her surgeon said we got her there in the nick of time—gangrene was about to set in. Ruth had to have a portion of her lower bowel removed and remained in Indianapolis for about a month. I drove home to Fort Wayne to do payroll each Fridays and returned that same evening. We were still using the company pickup truck and didn't have a decent car at the time, so I rented a car for those trips back and forth.

In the summer of 1994 we drove to San Antonio to attend the 40th reunion of my USAF Pilot Training Class 54-G. By this time we'd bought a brand-new1993 Bonneville Pontiac, but the trip made it obvious that traveling long distances by car—something we had done countless times and took for granted—was now very difficult, at best, for Ruth. We couldn't get off the highway fast enough for urgent stops, and even in intense heat, she was freezing cold. We had to keep the windows up and the air-conditioning off, even in the 90-degree heat. It was miserable for me, but you do what you have to under those circumstances.

Our friends Ebb and June Harris were at the reunion. We'd spent the previous New Year's with Robin in San Francisco, and Ebb and June had driven up from Southern California to join us. Now, six months later, at the 40th reunion, June was stunned at how drastically Ruth's health had deteriorated. I was happy to see the Harrises, and at the same time the situation was filled with sadness. It forced me to accept that Ruth probably didn't have much time left.

On the Road ... One Last Time

We all knew Ruth was reaching the end of her life, even though she was still in complete denial. As sick as she was, one of the things she desperately wanted to do was travel. I could not reason with her, and I had a hard time saying no. We began planning trips to the Southwest and California, then across to Florida and up to Washington, D.C. One of her doctors chastised me for even considering such an expedition without skilled personnel to accompany us along the way. But the trips meant the world to Ruth, and I wasn't about to tell her she was too sick to go. Dr. Meyer had authorized it and was confident that, with Robin's help, I would do whatever we had to do. I knew Ruth's time was short, and staying put would not change that. I told myself she had a right to die the way she wanted to. If she wanted to travel, we'd travel.

I knew traveling for Ruth would be awkward because of her deteriorating condition. A journey by plane or car, as we'd discovered, would have been virtually impossible. So we bought a small, older motor home from my old neighbor and childhood buddy John Moser, who owned a used car lot downtown. Ruth didn't want to spend another winter in Fort Wayne. She hated the cold and the gray, dreary weather. The RV helped us get to warmer climates comfortably. But we'd made only a few short trips with it, one down to Branson, Missouri to visit our dear friends Tommy and Shirley Butler, from our stint in Bermuda.

I sold the used model and bought a brand-new Pace Arrow from Jim Kelley's Chevrolet dealership. This unit was much larger and cost much more, but with it we were able to plan an extensive trip that would last a few months and take us down several thousand miles of road. After a stops in southern Indiana and Mississippi, we were going to visit our Air Force friends Al and Arlene Johnson in Houston; then head to West Texas and then to Phoenix to meet with Bob and Candy Jones, tennis friends from our days in Las Vegas; then move on to San Francisco to spend time with our daughter Robin; before traveling back down through California and Arizona, around the Gulf of Mexico, and into Florida, where we'd stay for a while. Then we would swing back north to Washington, DC, in time for the cherry blossoms in spring.

On December 31, 1994, we loaded up the motor home and pulled out of Fort Wayne, heading south. We just missed an arctic winter blast that hit the Midwest right after our departure.

Our ambitious itinerary was cut short in Phoenix. In the middle of the night, Ruth became very sick, suffering tremendous abdominal pain. At first we thought it was food poisoning, but I soon realized it was simply that her illness had progressed. I ran from our motor home, parked outside the Joneses' house, into the house, waking up Bob and Candy to ask about the nearest hospital. Once we got to the emergency room, it became a fiasco.

The ER doctor thought it was a routine emergency and was attempting to treat Ruth like any other patient I had to phone our doctors back in Indiana and ask them to provide guidance and instructions to this young physician. The ER doctor didn't appreciate my involvement, to say the least. He looked at me as if to say, *Who do you think you are talking to?*

I thought to myself, *You might be a doctor, but I have a better handle on what's going on with my wife's illness.*

Ruth was in a bad way. We were thousands of miles from home. In the hospital in Phoenix, she prayed that she would not need surgery. But when she asked the surgeon about the alternatives, he told her if she didn't have the operation, she would die. She had no choice.

I sought a Lutheran pastor to come in for Ruth before she went into surgery. He didn't make it in time, but he sure was there for her afterward. I remember him well —a former Indiana highway patrolman who, while listening to the Lutheran Hour on the radio had decided to become a Lutheran pastor after his retirement. Though he had also since retired from the ministry, he was helping out at a local church. I was grateful for his presence.

I parked the motor home in the corner of the hospital parking lot, and set up camp, awaiting her release. Ruth was in the hospital for a week. Robin and Roxie flew to Phoenix and stayed in the motor home with me. When Ruth was released, she didn't want to go home to cold Fort Wayne, but she didn't want to travel any farther either. So we set down in an RV park and waited until April to return. During our stay Ruth was hospitalized once more, this time for a bacterial infection in her abdomen.

When it was time to finally return to Fort Wayne, we did so very gingerly.

Headstrong to the End

After the ill-fated RV trip, business began picking up at Commercial Filter, and we needed to expand to meet demand. Ultimately we sold the motor home—at a $10,000 loss.

The doctors and I agreed that there was little left to do for Ruth. Home would be the best place for her to spend her final days, and we tried to make things as comfortable as possible.

One Saturday evening, the weekend before Ruth died, Robin was visiting from San Francisco and Roxanne, who lived in Fort Wayne, was with us. We ordered pizza and, thinking Ruth was asleep in the bedroom, the girls and I were sitting around the dining room table. Roxie heard something, and we scrambled to the bedroom to find Ruth on the floor of the bathroom.

Blood was everywhere. Robin cleaned her mother up, examined her injuries, and got her back into bed for the night. Or so we thought.

Later that night Ruth suddenly got up, determined to walk around. I tried desperately to get her back into bed, but she resisted. True to her nature, she continued to be headstrong right up to the end.

That night she slipped into a deep coma. In the morning I spoke with Dr. Meyer, who said he'd stop by, but there really was very little he could do. He gave us morphine in case Ruth appeared to be in any pain, but we were thankful that she did not frown or seem to be uncomfortable.

Sunday evening I slept by my dying wife, holding her hand through the night. At one point she emerged from her slumber to say very clearly that she did not want to die. Around 4:00 in the morning I got up and started busying myself around the apartment. For some reason, it was not clear to me that Ruth was on the brink of death. I was convinced she would live a few more days. Perhaps I was not ready to let her go. I stood beside her bed and read the Psalm 23 to her.

The Lord is my shepherd. I shall not want.
He maketh me to lie down in green pastures.
He leadeth me beside the still waters.
He restoreth my soul.
He leadeth me in the paths of righteousness for His name's sake.
Yea, though I walk through the valley of the shadow of death, I will fear no evil:
for thou art with me, thy rod and thy staff, they comfort me.
Thou preparest a table before me in the
presence of mine enemies:
thou anointest my head with oil—my cup runneth over.
Surely goodness and mercy shall follow me all the days of my life:
and I will dwell in the house of the Lord for ever.

Then I took our springer spaniel, Wendell, for a walk. It was 5:00AM. When I came back to the apartment, I woke Robin. There were sure signs that Ruth's death was imminent. Robin and I propped her up in the bed and called Roxanne and the hospice nurse to come over.

Two hours later, I took the dog for another walk. When I came back, Robin was kneeling alongside her mother's bed, crying. She hugged me and told me that Ruth was gone. We cried together. I was numb to all that was happening, but I will always remember the look of peace on Ruth's face after she had passed.

There was so much to do. Nothing had been prepared in advance. I planned a small, simple funeral and burial.

Ruth had died on Monday, August 21, 1995. She was 62 years old. She is buried in the Woodburn Lutheran Cemetery, next to our baby son, Scott Allan. We had been married for 41 years, but because Ruth was always determined to make her own way in life and to have her own identity, I made sure her headstone included her maiden name. The epitaph also includes the verse she chose for her confirmation. It reads:

Ruth E. Meyer Wearley
January 9, 1933–August 21, 1995
Be thou faithful unto death, and I will give thee a crown of life.
Revelations 2:10

May she rest in eternal peace.

A New Chapter Begins

When Ruth died, another chapter in my life closed. I was suddenly confronted with the fact that I was really alone. Before Ruth's death, I never took the opportunity to consider what I'd do after she was gone. I had not allowed myself to contemplate what I was going to do with my own life, knowing I'd feel guilty thinking in those terms. Other widowers have told me they felt the same way. During the extremes of her illness, I just kept thinking, *I am going to do whatever it takes* right now *and not think about the future.*

Now that daunting moment—the future—had arrived. I rested in knowing that Ruth's faith put her squarely in Heaven. Something I heard a Catholic priest say on the radio comforted me: "Life on earth is not the ultimate goal of our existence." Ruth had achieved her ultimate goal, although sooner rather than later. As for Roxanne and Robin, they had their own lives to live. Sometimes I felt quite lonely. There were days that really tested the strength of my faith. Yet I knew God's hand had been guiding and directing my life from the very beginning, so why should I question His reasoning now?

When I reached out to friends in Las Vegas to share the news of Ruth's passing, one of the pilots I had hired for the Hughes organization offered me a special chance. Warren Bachelor was flying a reengineered Lockheed 731 JetStar on a contract basis and asked if I'd like to fly with him. Although I hadn't flown a JetStar in 17 years, or any plane in more than 10, I had been the one to train Warren for his FAA JetStar type rating so he could fly as captain. I knew that Warren was an exceptional pilot, and if he wanted an old codger for a co-pilot, it might be a good distraction from the loneliness I was feeling after Ruth's death. So I said to myself, *Why not?*

I got an FAA physical from Dr. Bill Kammeyer, a pilot and the son of a farmer from my hometown of Woodburn, and told Warren I was ready. Within a week I was flying again.

We made a trip to Michigan and then to Fort Lauderdale. While Warren's employer went out on his yacht, Warren and I enjoyed some time in the Florida sun. I reconnected with Ginny and "Van" Van Kesteren, friends from my days at Charleston Air Force Base. Van flew over from St. Petersburg in his turbo-prop modified Malibu to pick me up, and after several days he flew me to Port St. Lucie to spend some time with more friends from Charleston, Fred and Lois Koepke. Fred was a retired Eastern Airlines Captain. I then went on to Fort Pierce to meet my nephew David Cox and his wife, Girlie, who drove me back to meet Warren in Fort Lauderdale.

My excursions with Warren went on several months before the JetStar was sold. It was fun while it lasted, but I was ready to return to Fort Wayne and my business.

Alone once more, I continued to pursue the growth of Commercial Filter Service. Growing a business is not a bad goal, but the way I was going about it wasn't healthy for the long term. I was grateful for the good people working for me, especially Terry Braton and my son-in-law, Chris DeAngelis, whom I knew I could trust. But still, I buried myself in my work from sunup to sundown. Little did I know that my life was about to change dramatically once again …

AN OUTSIDER LOOKING IN

IT WAS TIME I made a clean break. The apartment I shared with Ruth in downtown Fort Wayne was one among many at the Three Rivers Apartments complex, so there was always a vacant apartment available. It wasn't difficult to find the one for my new home. Roxanne and Robin helped me clean out all of their mother's things. I gave most of the furniture we owned to Roxanne and Chris, and after spending two weeks with Robin in San Francisco, I moved to a one-bedroom apartment just a few floors down.

I was doing my best to find my way during this lonely period in my life. I engaged myself in my work at Commercial Filter Service, and I was very involved in my church. I also served as committee chairperson for the Boy Scouts of America's Explorer program, on the board of directors for the Fort Wayne–Allen County Airport Authority, and as a board member of the Washington House Treatment Center. On top of all this, I was flying the Jet Star with Warren Bachelor on occasion. But I had been married for 41 years, and it was a habit I was finding hard to break. I desperately missed female companionship.

A block away from the apartment building, there was a nice restaurant. Now that I was on my own, I frequently walked over there for dinner. Sitting at that restaurant one evening, I realized the single life wasn't all it was cracked up to be. I would generally sat in the bar area, where I could dine alone but take in the atmosphere and observe the people around me. I felt like an outsider looking in. There were patrons from all walks of life, and plenty of widows, widowers, and singles romancing the bar area, striking up conversations with perhaps an intent to get more than friendly with each other.

There were occasions when divorced women from my apartment complex approached me with hints of companionship. One especially embarrassing occasion was when I befriended a neighbor, and we had dinner together at the restaurant, then I invited her to join me for breakfast the next morning. When my daughter Roxanne walked into my apartment – without knocking – the lady was sitting in my dining area. Roxie was shocked, to say the least, to see a woman in my apartment at 9:00 in the morning. When I explained the situation, she finally relaxed. Her husband, Chris, later pointed out that my privacy is important and that she couldn't just walk in on me without knocking. I was her father, but I had my own life too. Roxanne had to understand that her mother was gone and my life had to go on.

Even so, it was another turning point in my life. I didn't want the sort of fleeting relationship that seemed acceptable for some lonely widowers. If I was going to find companionship, it would have to be the real thing. I began praying for a mate who could share my faith. Every day I said a prayer I had found in the Lutheran quarterly publication *Portals of Prayer*. And I just tried to carry on with hope in my heart, keeping busy with work and my other responsibilities.

Through my position on the board of the, Fort Wayne Allen County Airport Authority I was invited to a Christmas party where I had a couple of beers with friends and colleagues. I drove home afterward, but I couldn't stand going back to a vacant apartment with no one to talk to. Plus, I was hungry. So instead of making myself some breakfast, I decided to go out to an all-night restaurant.

What a mistake!

I was no more than a few blocks from my apartment when one of "Fort Wayne's finest" pulled me over. The officer had just stopped me randomly, because the streets were pretty empty at that time of the morning, but he decided to give me a sobriety test. Unfortunately, those few drinks and no food in my belly meant that I didn't pass. I had to call my attorney from the lockup. When my case came to court, it was determined to be reckless driving (as opposed to a DWI), but I still lost my driving privileges for a few months. That was a blow!

But it was also a blessing in disguise, because it was a turn of events that lead to my meeting the love of my life.

Love at First Sight

Roxanne and Chris owned a four-bedroom bungalow home on the city's north side but had decided to put it on the market so they could purchase a new home. One day, a woman came to look at the house. She had five children of various ages, two of whom were still living at home, and her mother often stayed with her on extended visits during the winter months. The woman really needed a four-bed-room house, and her daughter Sherese encouraged her to buy Roxie's because it suited the family's needs at the time.

That woman was Sharon "Sherry" Daenens.

The day of the closing, Sherry and Roxie finally met. They immediately liked each other, and Roxie thought Sherry was a very nice and attractive lady. She had an idea: Since I was starting to date, perhaps I should meet Sherry.

One evening after dinner at Chris and Roxie's new home, Chris asked me if I'd like to go over to the "old" house and help him clean out the garage. He needed to give the new owner her keys, too. While Chris and Sherry were busy discussing the details of her new home, I was busy sizing Sherry up. She was attractive, just as Roxie had described her, but my initial assessment was that she was entirely too young—to me, she looked about 35 years old. I'd decided it would be best, since I was 62, if I didn't date anyone under age 50. But the three kids with her that evening were her youngest; she had two more, and the oldest, Dawn, was 30! I did the math —Sherry just made it "under the wire". It was official: I was interested.

Still, I felt I had to wait until I got my license back, so it took me three months to finally ask Sherry out. She'd said she was working in the gift shop at the Marriott Hotel, and one day I stopped in on the premise that I was looking for a men's jogging suit. The shop had a number of them available, and before long I was choosing out a new athletic outfit – and more important, meeting the women I would soon ask to marry me.

I left my phone number, and she gave me hers, and eventually we arranged to go out on a date. Later, I learned that during the three-month delay while I waited to get my license back, Sherry had thought I just wasn't interested in asking her out.

Before we met, Sherry says now, "I threw myself into that job. I'd get there at 7:30 in the morning and still be there at 9 at night. Then I'd meet friends at the bar adjacent to the gift shop, and I wouldn't get home until it was very late. Then it was back up and in to work, and the whole routine started all over again. One of my daughters would get very upset with me, because this wasn't the Mom she remembered." Yet after a difficult divorce, Sherry was living with a struggle similar to mine: "I'd go home, she says, and there wouldn't be anyone there."

"I could see that my behavior was not going in a very good direction," she adds. "Had my life been filled with more Christ-like activities, maybe I wouldn't have felt that void so deeply." Also like me, in her loneliness Sherry turned to prayer: "I started praying that I would find some comfort in my life and that God would help me find a better direction."

Together, our prayers worked.

For our first date, I picked Sherry up on a Saturday morning and we drove to Wright Patterson Air Force Base, a two-hour drive, near Dayton, Ohio. First we went to the Air Force Museum, and that evening I took her to the Officer's Club for dinner. By the time we headed home, our date had lasted a total of 16 hours.

That night after we drove back, I stopped off at my apartment on the pretense that I had to let out my dog, Wendell, a Springer Spaniel. In truth, it was kind of a test: I needed to know if Wendell would like Sherry. He fell in love with her immediately, which confirmed my own thoughts: I had something really good here, and I wasn't going to let it slip away by dragging my feet.

So I seized the moment. Since we had spent the last 16 hours together, I figured that was the equivalent of four dates already. A grown man doesn't ask his date to go steady, but I told Sherry that from then on, if she had no objections, I intended to occupy a lot of her time. Thankfully, she didn't object.

Sherry confessed that she had her own test: Her dog, Ginger, had to like me as well. Now, I wanted to cover all the bases, because I really wanted this woman to like me. The next time I went to her house to pick her up, I made sure I had a dog biscuit in my pocket.

I felt I had to share some of my past so there would be no surprises. One thing I confessed to Sherry was the situation with a senior flight attendant in Singapore – the woman I considered marrying. At the time, the woman thought she was pregnant. It had scared me, because I was still legally married to Ruth (although separated), and the obligation of a child was profound to me. But I'd been on the verge of divorcing Ruth because of our tenuous situation, and I would have done the right thing and married this lady rather than consider an abortion – a possibility that did come up. As it turned out, she was not pregnant, but the issue had stuck with me. Now I found myself sharing this story with Sherry.

At that time I did not have an opinion on abortion one way or another. That's not true today, particularly after the premature birth of my twin grandchildren, Ben and Anna. Once I realized that those two beautiful babies could have been terminated by choice, it convinced me that abortion is absolutely, totally wrong. I firmly believe that life begins at conception, that God creates babies for a reason. No baby should ever be aborted.

All of this and more I revealed to Sherry. I don't think I could have found a woman who'd be more understanding and accepting of my past.

Shortly after we met Sherry went to a wedding in Detroit with her daughter Sherese and remarked that although she'd been dating me only about four weeks, she "just knew" it was right. She knew I was the person she wanted to spend the rest of her life with.

"The thing that really made me feel comfortable with Bob," she explains, "was that we shared the same goals and the same moral feelings. We could be open and honest with each other and accept each other for who we were without feeling like we had to put on a false face." Together, our spirituality became stronger: "Knowing that he shared the same faith brought me back to my faith and beliefs," Sherry says. "It just worked."

I told Sherry that I'd been praying for God to send me a mate. She admitted that she'd been offering up the same prayer. To me, it was obvious that God had answered our prayers, and I was not going to argue with Him. And at my age (I was now 63), I didn't have time to procrastinate.

When I asked her to marry me, she immediately said yes, and on October 26, 1996 – about six months after our first, 16-hour-long date – we were joined in holy matrimony.

Bob & Sharon Wearley while on a June, 2005 cruise to Bermuda with three other couples with whom he was stationed there in the late 1950s

---

I have a beautiful life. There isn't a day that goes by that I fail to notice this and give thanks for it. I always enjoyed going to the office at Commercial Filter Service, especially working with Sherry. I had always possessed an entrepreneurial spirit, and it helped me even when times were tough. I hocked everything I owned to get the business going, back in October 1986, when I was 53 years old. And today, our company is thriving due to the hard work of my wife and our employees. As a result, and also thanks to Sherry's son Jason Daenens, who is now our CEO, Commercial Filter Service is financially secure. Sherry continues to tolerate my "extracurricular activities": my interest in aviation has not waned. I still would love to have my own airplane, but it will have to wait. At the time I was president of Indiana Strategic Air Transportation Services (INSATS), I concerned myself with aviation and how it affects the economy. And then I'd go home, happy to be with Sherry. After all these years, I no longer had to walk on eggshells … not anymore. Now I could do what I enjoy with the woman I love.

The author with his family & extended family (or "Bonus Family" as he likes to say). Taken in Fort Wayne, IN, in 2003. Bob is in the middle of the back row, his wife Sharon directly in front of him and Sharon's mother "Mamie" is to the right of her.

A New Chapter

I don't visit Ruth's grave much. That chapter in my life is over. I guess I believe that what's in the past is in the past. Ruth lived her life to the fullest up to those last 10 years of declining health. I watched her suffer the consequences of a terminal illness that was slowly eating away her vitality and health. I'm sorry she left this earthly life in that manner. But life goes on for the rest of us, and following Ruth's death, I didn't reminisce on the past as much as seriously contemplating my future and the changes I was determined to make.

I make no excuses for our tumultuous marriage. I believe we were two people looking for the same thing, but in different places. There was nothing I wanted more than a strong, supportive marriage. But, the truth is that our marriage only appeared to be strong. We did not support each other. A spouse is supposed to be the soft spot where one lands when having a difficult time. Too often, Ruth and I failed to be that soft spot for each other.

There is no underestimating the pain that infidelity can cause. Trust is the foundation of any marriage, and for me and my first wife, that trust was destroyed years before she died and continued to crumble as we moved from base to base, and it eroded even further when we moved to Las Vegas and were exposed to a lifestyle that fed temptation.

Maybe it started after I cheated death in the Connie accident – that movement away from the modest life and toward recklessness. In later years, I walked on the edge of envy and celebrity while working for Howard Hughes. While a captain for Singapore Airlines and Jordanian Airlines, I continued down the same path I learned so well while dancing with the devil in Sin City. I was conditioned to blend in with the circumstances that surrounded me. *Boys will be boys* was the motto so prevalent within my circle of acquaintances.

If anything truly wonderful came out of my marriage to Ruth, it was our daughters Robin and Roxanne, both grown now. Roxanne lives in Florida and teaches art in grade school. She has given me three grandchildren, 22-year-old twins Ben and Anna and 14-year-old Sammy. Robin lives in San Francisco.

My extended family, consists of 2 "bonus" daughters and 3 "bonus "sons,(I prefer to call them "bonus" vs step- children), all grown with families of their own. They certainly keep Sherry and I busy with birthdays, school and sport activities of the grandchildren. Dawn (Al) the oldest has Matt, Justin and Amanda. Matt gave her two grandchildren, our great-grandchildren of course. Kirt has 4 children, Aleena, Kirisa, Keenan and Rylan. Sherese, (Kevin) who I have mentioned before has 2 children, Sara and Connor. Dean has 3 boys, Racee, Logan and Luke. That leaves Jason (Jeremy) our CEO at Commercial Filter. They are all very successful in their own right. Sherry (and I) are extremely proud of each one and their accomplishments and justifiable so. She did a great job raising them and instilling values and a work ethic that has served them well in their lives.

Giving Thanks

My path back to righteousness was a gradual process, but it began when Ruth and I returned to Fort Wayne and started attending church regularly. I got reacquainted with the Word of God and the concept that "faith comes by hearing". I had to listen and truly hear the Word of God to be reminded of what is important in life. And today, Sherry and I together make this a priority in our life.

If I am thankful for one thing above all, amid the many blessings God has granted me, it is a wonderful extended family and true friends. Whenever I am asked to speak to a group of young people, I offer them this advice: When you make friends, good friends, stay in touch. Over the years, it will be beneficial to you in more ways than one. The true friends I made as a youngster in Woodburn, during my Air Force career, in Las Vegas, and during my stint in Singapore and with Royal Jordanian Airlines – they are still my friends today. There's no substitute for surrounding yourself with good people whom you can count on.

We must learn to lead by example and true respect has to be earned. Throughout my 81 years on this earth, I have not always been the best example to my family, my friends, and my business acquaintances. I certainly am not one to say that I'd always accepted and welcomed God into my life and "walked the talk". There are numerous moments that, given a second chance, I would love to relive. I would love the chance to do it the right way. If only we could undo the harm that has been done! But unfortunately, we can't. We can only pray and repent.

I know a lot of people who don't go to church after they get married. Some people don't see the need for it. But once they start a family, many decide they better start going again. I went to church as a youngster, but as time wore on I sometimes strayed. Now I find it comforting to attend church services as a family. It brings the entire week full circle. It reminds me to be thankful for all the wonderful things in my life. *"Train up a child in the way he should go: and when he is old, he will not depart from it."* Proverbs 22:6 KJV

As I look back upon the many experiences, both good and the bad, that I endured and enjoyed throughout my lifetime, I am continually amazed at how God watched over me these many years. On too many occasions, while my body was strong, my soul was weak. I knew full well the meaning between right and wrong. It was instilled in me as a small child in Woodburn, Indiana, attending church services with my mother and sisters. While I never lost total sight of the goodness of the Lord, I did stray … in some instances further then I care to remember.

I am so grateful now to have the chance to share my story in hopes that it may help others, including, my family, friends, work, and volunteer activities. These blessings are a part of my life, and that they have helped me return to the light of the Lord.

I now devote much of my time as a Volunteer Chaplain in the Allen County Jail (Fort Wayne) working with the substance abuse classes that are attended by 30 inmates and taking a book cart into the blocks to help inmates pass the time in a positive way. This gives me an opportunity to get some "one-on-one" time that I can use to encourage them to make positive changes in their lives. Over a period of several months, I've gotten to know some of them who asked me to be their mentor after they pay their debt to society. Some call me; others drift back into the environment that precipitated their downfall, mostly due to a lack of support and a society is ambivalent to their needs. It is gratifying to see the Holy Spirit at work in their effort to "stay clean'.

We all should support their commitment to be productive members of society, remembering what Christ said, *"Continue to remember those in prison as if you were together with them in person…"* Hebrews 13:3 and *"You came to visit me… Whenever you did for one of the least of these brothers and sisters of mine, you did it for me."* Matthew 25:36, and 40.

After returning to my "roots" in Indiana, I settled in Fort Wayne, just 20 miles west of my home town of Woodburn. I quickly integrated back into the comfortable lifestyle of my youth, attending church, starting two Aviation Explorer Posts (Part of the Boy Scouts of America Young Adults), joining the Fort Wayne Downtown Rotary International service organization, etc. I was appointed to the Fort Wayne-Allen County Airport Authority Board of Directors by the mayor Paul Helmke which led me to resign from the BOD and assumed the position of the first Director For Marketing for the Fort Wayne International Airport (FWA). The company I started in the fall of 1986 was growing and had a great deal of potential but was "suffering" financially due to Ruth's declining health and our lack of daily involvement. The company needed a "jump start" which was provided by my new job of marketing at the Airport, and Sherry accepting the position of General Manager of Commercial Filter Service.

The Fort Wayne-Allen County Airport Authority was only a few years old when I was appointed. During my seven years on the board, I was part of the growth from Fort Wayne Municipal Airport, Baer Field, to Fort Wayne International with a huge cargo complex then operated by Kitty Hawk Cargo, an airline providing international service to freight forwarders with Boeing 747's (the aircraft I had flown for Singapore and Royal Jordanian airlines).

My challenge as FWA Marketing Director was to "put Fort Wayne on the map" internationally. For this reason, I attended trade shows in Singapore, Canada, Europe and South America, and I was able to take Sherry along (at our expense).

As I approached 70 years of age, the younger generation was eager to "get their hands on" and take over the airport marketing under a new city-county joint venture "umbrella" organization.

So it was time for me to move back to Commercial Filter where we were able to build our present building which allowed for future growth and expansion. "Bonus Son" Jason and his Mother Sherry, who handles the HR part of the company, are doing quite well in growing; www.Commercialfilter.net; into a mature business that is providing jobs and making a difference in the community. In the meantime I plan to continue busing myself as a volunteer Chaplain in the Allen County/ Fort Wayne Jail. Sherry and I are free to travel and "dig into" our bucket list, enjoy the grand kids, cottage on Lake Huron, and winter in Florida or Hawaii, wherever our time share has vacancies. Our lives are fulfilled, we enjoy good health, family and friends and most of all comfort in knowing we have eternal life through the Grace of God and the Faith he has instilled in our Hearts that as John 3:16 (NIV) ensures us "…. that whoever BELIEVES in him shall not perish but have eternal life."

Epilogue: Bob's Post Flight Debriefing

The Prodigal Son

This is not the type of a book I thought I'd write.

Those of you who knew me in the past may be shocked that I wrote a book at all, and even more shocked that in this book I opened up my life. To be sure, this isn't the Bob Wearley Story I would have liked to tell. Much of what lies within these pages, I am not proud of. Nor is it a new story: Some people will read this book and say, "Ah, just another conversion story." How can I blame them? I, too, have heard more than one guy-sows-wild-oats-then-parades-as-white-knight-later-in-life tale. Others will read this book and say, "I knew Bob when he was just one of the guys. Who does he think he is, trying to sell his version of the same old God-saved-me story?"

To all those people, I can only answer the truth: I was selfish. I was stubborn. I sought my own gratification, and many times I used others to attain it. And then I found God. I became a born-again Christian, and despite what others believe about this conversion, nothing could be more real or more important. My life has been transformed, and I owe it all to God.

Living in Vegas, Bermuda, and all around the world, I'd known I wasn't "walking the walk." Inwardly, I wasn't proud of my choices. But I wanted to keep it all hidden from family and friends back home in Indiana, so I tried to hide it from myself first. I survived on ignoring reality or filling my life with other things. I attempted to justify my behavior, my attitude, and my actions on the circumstances, on the lifestyles of those around me. I chalked it all up to the "everybody does it" philosophy: the good ol' boy, wink-and-a-nod syndrome that is prevalent in some circles. When you attain a certain "status" in your social life, those sorts of attitudes and behaviors come with the territory. I was encouraged by doing my own thing, and on the surface, it seemed to be working. But the longer I did it, the more silent my conscience grew.

After being hit with the reality of the world and the consequences of shifting moral standards—the pain and suffering of a tumultuous marriage followed by a difficult death—I had to come back home to do what was right. I was the epitome of the modern-day prodigal son, straight out of the Gospel of Luke.

Our prideful, sinful nature allows us to see ourselves as more prominent and more significant than we are. If there is anything good in life, though, it comes from conforming to God's will and turning over my life to Him. It's only by His power and grace that I can claim anything of value in this life. God has given me a saving faith in him. Make no mistake about this; it's nothing that *I* have done. Grace is a free and undeserving gift from God. Scripture states it very clearly in Ephesians 2:8: "For it is by grace you have been saved, through faith—and this is not from yourselves, it is a gift of God—not by works, so that no one can boast." And again in Romans 10:17: "Faith comes from hearing the message, and hearing by the word of God."

It's very clear to me where my slide into immorality and unfaithfulness to God began: with my unfaithfulness to my first wife, Ruth. Those trysts of mine were a response to my denial, an outward expression of my unwillingness to do what was right. It was not my lack of knowledge that kept me living that false life, but my lack of obedience. I received a bit of advice once from Hank Greenspun, a Las Vegas newspaper publisher whom I had flown to Orange County from Las Vegas. Hank invited me and the other pilot to lunch with him and his colleague, and when we made light of "fooling around" during typical back-and-forth banter, he chastised us. "Boys," he said, "the only legacy you can leave your family is to be faithful in your marriage vows." That hurt, and although I didn't follow his advice right away, clearly it stuck with me. Hank was right. All the while, it was like eating a gourmet meal, with all the experiences and pleasures—and yet with no nutritional value. Instead of being satisfied, I found myself still hungry. Cheating created an empty emotional vacuum, and I kept hearing my conscience say, "You'll never be content."

I tried to justify my sin by saying, "It's not so bad. No one is getting hurt." I told myself that after all, I had a lot to deal with, so I was entitled some liberty, some permission, some leeway. Yes, I had plenty of excuses in my pocket, and many of them revolved around how I was being wronged by Ruth and her attitudes. But as my friend Guice Tinley pointed out when I confided that I didn't attend church regularly, "One excuse is just as good as another." It was never entirely Ruth's fault; it takes two to tango, as they say. And in her case, the trouble could have been rooted in a true illness that was never diagnosed. As I look back with the benefit of hindsight, considering the progression of medicine in the past 35 years, today she might have been diagnosed with borderline personality disorder (BPD). Her bewildering mood shifts and unpredictable behavior, if they were influenced by neurotransmitter disturbances, might have been treatable with medication and therapy.

But Ruth wasn't diagnosed with BPD—she was diagnosed with a terminal illness. Prior to her illness, our constant battling had led me to develop a defensive mindset. I became bitter, and I hardened my heart. I wasn't open to being helpful to her, and instead I started to make a laundry list of her faults—while conveniently overlooking mine. I wrote it off as her own selfishness or even as a woman having PMS. I really didn't care to think beyond that.

After returning to our roots—in Indiana, in the Scripture—things changed. With a rekindled faith in God, I was able to change my attitude and behavior. I accepted things that I had been conditioned to reject based on "secular" advice. I opened myself up to, as Paul Harvey used to say, "The rest of the story."

The Rest of the Story

Remember, too, that the prodigal son had a brother—the one who didn't leave home and cried out in anger when his returning brother was honored. The prodigal son's brother was a sinner, too; he was arrogant, envious, and bitter. He just kept it hidden and tried to justify himself.

Some of you may be prodigals like me, and you know the joy of finally returning to the light of faith after of years living in the shadows. Others might look at me and respond judgmentally, as did the son who stayed home. Now that you have read this book, I ask you to keep your heart open, rather than respond in bitterness. Remember that you have to answer for your own life, not for the actions of others. It's a lesson that took me a long time to learn.

What turned me around? It all comes down to the words of Psalm 51, sung during the Offertory in Lutheran Church services. This song was the prayer of King David after he had committed a great sin. The prophet Nathan rebuked David after he'd committed adultery with Bathsheba, got her pregnant, and orchestrated her husband Uriah's death in battle. David recognized his guilt at last and confessed his sin, asking God's forgiveness:

Create in me a clean heart, O God,
and renew a steadfast spirit within me.
Do not cast me from your presence
or take your Holy Spirit from me.
Restore to me the joy of your salvation
and grant me a willing spirit, to sustain me.

And the Holy Spirit did indeed forgive and sustain King David.

I sang that Offertory for years, only going through the motions. It took a while for this to sink in—too long for a church-going person like me! It didn't take on any real meaning for me until I finally put myself in David's shoes. And then it became crystal clear: Anyone could be forgiven. All someone had to do was sincerely ask God for forgiveness, and the burden would be lifted. That is what Christ died on the cross for—our sins and the sins of the world.

Wow, talk about grace! *Would God do that for me?* I wondered. And suddenly I knew He would. I knew that even after all I had done, God's voice was still speaking and pleading with me, and my spirit wanted what God offered. It's truly amazing.

My point is this: We are all sinners. It doesn't have to be adultery; it can be just lying, giving in to mean-spiritedness, or acting like the son who stayed home and was envious of his "sinful brother." Whatever your crime, when you disobey God's word, you are a sinner.

Mark 7:20 gives us Christ's own words in explanation:

What comes out of a man is what makes him unclean.
For it is from within, out of man's hearts, come evil thoughts, sexual immorality, theft, murder,
    adultery, greed, malice, *deceit, lewdness, envy, slander, arrogance, and folly.*
All these insights come from inside and make a man unclean.

You have to understand a few things about the God of the universe: God is the antithesis of sin, He wants your heart to be filled with love, and He's willing to forgive you. It's not that God wants to punish you; no, He just wants to bring you into His family, to give you a purpose, to offer you joy.

When I offered my life up to God, I finally got the message. I finally heard the rest of the story. God took my sins and "created in me a clean heart"—and He can do the same for you. If anyone asks God for forgiveness and help in turning over a new page, who knows what good could come of it?

A Public Affair

Much of this book is centered on the Watergate crisis, Richard Nixon, and the Howard Hughes connection. When you think about it, Nixon's situation, which caused his political demise, was largely the same as mine; like me, he knew right from wrong but chose not to follow his conscience. He had grown up surrounded by Quakers, yet he ignored their teachings on nonviolence, revenge, and *malice.* To me —and in the opinion of others, such as former White House chief of staff H. R. Haldeman—that's what was at the heart of the Watergate break-in: Nixon's malice.

Haldeman contends that it was Nixon's desire, thanks to the politics of personal destruction, to bring down national Democratic Party chairman Larry O'Brien, who (Nixon was convinced) had contributed to his election losses in California, against Kennedy in the 1960 presidential election and then in the 1962 gubernatorial election. Even with polls clearly showing a huge victory imminent this time around, Nixon was determined to find dirt on O'Brien, particularly regarding his connection to Howard Hughes. The whole affair can be traced to a motive of pure revenge; Nixon allowed his malice to rule his judgment. Plain and simple, he wanted to cause pain.

History shows that Nixon was a brilliant man and could have been one of the best presidents the United States ever had. Instead, he went down as a scorned man, disgraced and laughed out of any future in public life—all because he had "vendetta", "a score to settle". The resignation of Nixon still ranks as one of the most shameful moments in U.S. history. It will always remain as such, but Nixon won't be the last political figure to succumb to this trap unless, in my opinion, we as a people and nation return to biblical values and precepts.

See Appendix C - James L. Etsler's relevant comments

Whereas the Scripture (Colossians 3:8) instructs us to get rid of rage and malice, Nixon only built on it. Harry Truman, a man known for staying true to his Missouri sensibility, called it "Potomac fever": a malady that causes leaders to become big-headed and forget what is right when they get to Washington. As 19th-century English historian and politician Lord Acton wrote, "Power tends to corrupt, and absolute power corrupts absolutely." I don't have to cite examples of power leading good men astray; sadly, they are plentiful.

Alexis de Tocqueville, a 19th-century French political scholar who toured the United States, was positively overwhelmed by the New World and its potential. In the midst of his praise, though, he offered a warning: "America is great because she is good. If America ceases to be good, America will cease to be great." The Scripture is clear on this: "Righteousness exalts a nation, but sin is a reproach to any people". (Proverbs 14:34).

Perhaps it is time for this great nation to stand up and be righteous once more.

An Unwilling Conversion

All the time I was going about my life selfishly, attending church but failing to truly live the Gospel, I had many chances to make that most important change in my life. Through the flow of current events, I often found myself experiencing history firsthand in the midst of my own wanderings. Thinking back on it now, I know that God was using key historical figures to make

me question my life's path, and to deal with my soul. It just took me longer than expected to learn those lessons.

One of these spiritual milestones came while I was flying for Royal Jordanian Airlines, when I had the opportunity to befriend Lucille "Sis" Levin, the wife of Jerry Levin, the CNN bureau chief who was kidnapped in Beirut in 1984. She was a passenger on one of my flights while on a personal mission to the Amman, Jordan, to expedite her husband's release. After going off duty at our Amsterdam layover, I sat in the vacant seat next to Sis. We talked about her husband and her faith, and she said something (paraphrasing legendary British author C. S. Lewis) that struck me: "Jesus was one of three things: a liar, a lunatic, or Christ the Messiah." He couldn't have been anything else. The things He promised and spoke about made Him more than just a guru or a good man. Jesus was who He said He was.

Christianity has always been challenged by atheists and skeptics who endeavor to prove it false, to find or build cases for disbelief. And yet brilliant men and women, far greater thinkers then me, have responded and justified the Christian faith. When intelligent people come face to face with irrefutable proof again and again, they find only one possible answer: The Scripture is true. The claims of Jesus were true, and we must believe.

Simon Greenleaf, a Harvard law professor in the 1800s, was a prideful man who authored a three-volume work on the use of evidence in court and always encouraged his students to examine the evidence in even the best-laid legal plan. Greenleaf, an atheist, tended to blast the beliefs of his Christian students, until one day he was personally challenged by a student to investigate the evidence. The student had used the Bible as a source in one of his classroom cases, setting off a tirade from Greenleaf, who railed on the student for minutes without end. Finally, when the great legal mind was finished, the student humbly asked, "Have you examined the evidence?" Greenleaf had to admit he hadn't done so.

Now he embarked on a mission to contradict the faith, to find enough ammunition to crush even the best claims of those silly Christians. And yet after making his investigation, using his own legal standards of evidence, Greenleaf eventually embraced Christianity intellectually and in his lifestyle.

Lee Strobel is a modern-day example of a critic who, after seeking proof, conformed to the Christian faith. Strobel had solid intellectual credentials as a Yale Law student and a former investigative reporter for the *Chicago Tribune*. He set out to prove that his wife's spiritual conversion to Christianity was just silly emotionalism, and in the process he wanted to expose the hypocrisy in a suburban Chicago church that was growing beyond anyone's expectations. Quietly, Strobel attended services at this church, paying meticulous attention to the details of the church members' lives. Not only couldn't he find anything corrupt, but furthermore, as he began to listen to the lessons of Bible teachers, he was convinced. In fact, he became a Christian pastor.

During empty hours of reflection in a dark cell, with only a Bible given him by his captors, Jerry Levin made a conscience decision to follow Christ. Even though he was an atheist Jew, he read the word of God, and the Holy Spirit worked the miracle of faith in his heart. Levin remembered the claims of his Christian wife and explored the words of Jesus himself in Scripture, and eventually, Levin broke away from the hostage takers and scurried to freedom and a new life. He couldn't wait to tell his beloved Sis about his conversion, his experience of grace, his faith.

Today, Sis and Jerry divide their time between Israel and their home in Alabama. In Jerusalem, Sis is teaching how to foster nonviolence in children, and Jerry is a member of the Christian Peacemaker Teams in Hebron. Talk about the Holy Spirit working in people's lives! The Levins are the epitome of living the Christian faith, of "walking the walk". They are an example for us all to follow in whatever way we can. I am reminded of a favorite Lutheran hymn:

If you cannot speak like angels,
If you cannot preach like Paul,
You can tell the love of Jesus,
You can say He died for all.

My own conversion was not dramatic. I am certainly not an intellectual. I just know I was running from belief and using arguments that couldn't be justified. Like Nixon, I knew what was right, but I didn't do it. Sis Levin challenged me to recognize that Jesus was more than just a man with good intentions. Now I know His claims were true.

Afterword: Postscript

In December 1980, various sources including *The Wall Street Journal* and *Newsweek* magazine estimated that at the time of Howard Hughes's death, his wealth was valued at over $2 billion. Hughes had employed 67,400 people. His holdings included:

- Hughes Tool Company
- Aircraft Division
- Oil Tool Division
- Hughes-Hawthorne Division
- Hugh B. Williams Manufacturing Divison
- Hughes Sports Network, Inc.
- Hughes Executive Air Service
- KLAS-TV Station
- Hughes Air Corporation
- Seven Las Vegas Hotels and Casinos
- Land ownership (including Paradise Valley Golf Course and Country Club)
- Culver City real estate
- Real estate in the Bahamas
- The Howard Hughes Medical Institute
- Hughes Aircraft Company
- Teleprompter Corporation
- Atlas Corporation

About the Author: Biography by Grandson Sammy

My Grandpa

My Grandpa, Robert Franklin Wearley was born on February 25th 1933, Woodburn, Indiana. He has two older sisters named Lois and Jean Wearley. He also has an older half brother named Homer and two older half sisters named Eileen and Hillis. My grandpa had an extremely fun childhood with his parents and playing sports like table tennis, basketball, and soft ball. My grandpa also liked working and had many jobs through out his life. When he was little he wanted to be a pilot. Every time he heard a plane take off he would rush over on his bike to the airport and beg to get a ride. When he was 12 he got his first job as a newspaper boy. When he was in high school he played the clarinet and was the drum major for his marching band. In 1950 he got his first car which was a 1937 two door Chevrolet. When he was 18 he graduated high school and joined the U.S. Airforce. In the Airforce he was a pilot. When he was in the military he also went to college. He went to the University of Maryland, University of Oklahoma and Purdue University. In 1954 he got married to Ruth Emma Meyer. 2 years later he got in a horrible plane crash in Saudia Arabia breaking most of the bones in his back. He was only one out of ten who survived the crash. 7 months later his first daughter was born on March 17th 1957. Her name was Robin Renee Wearley. 1 year later his second daughter was born on June 17th 1958. Her name was Roxanne Ruth Wearley. My grandpa finished the Airforce as a lieutenant colonel in 1968. That year he started flying for Howard Hughes personal fleet. He did that for 7 years. At time Howard Hughes was one of the riches man in the world. In 1970 my grandpa flew John Wayne a famous actor and met Joe Dimaggio, a New York Yankee baseball star. He met a lot more actors but one of his favorite was Bob Hope a comedian actor. In 1977 my grandpa flew 747's for singapore airlines til 1974. During that time he played tennis with Lord Emma the vice president for Richard Nixon. In 1984 he started flying for Jordanian Airlines and did that for one year. In 1986 he started a business called Commercial Filter service and still owns it today. In 1995 Ruth Emma Weary died of a extended illness. In 1996 he got married to Sherry Daenams on October 26th. That year he got a job as a Marketing Director for Fort Wayne International Airport. He did that for 5 years. Now he lives in Fort Wayne, Indiana with his wife sherry, and his dog Molly, a mutt. He has 28 people in his family, Including himself. Today some of his favrite things to do is volinteer work, organise county projects, and vist his grandchildren in florida. This keeps him busy!

Name:	Organization	Support	Conventions
Sammy	6	6	6
	100%	100%	100%

Sammy was 9 years old in the 4th grade when he wrote this biography.

About the Author

Bob Wearley attended Purdue University, the University of Maryland and the University of Oklahoma. He retired from the U. S. Air Force as a Lt. Colonel after 17 years on active duty and 3 years in the reserves. He served as Chief Pilot for Howard Hughes' personal aircraft fleet for 9 years, as a Singapore Airlines Boeing 747 Captain for 5 years and as a Royal Jordan Airlines Boeing 747 Captain for 1 year.

He also served for 7 years on the Ft. Wayne Int'l Airport (FWA) Board of Directors, for 5 years as Marketing Director for FWA and as Chairman of the Voters Assembly at St. Paul's Lutheran Church, President of the Congregation of Promise Lutheran Ministries LCMS, Board member of the Washington House Treatment Center, President of the Allen County Jail Chaplaincy, Volunteer Jail Chaplain, Board member of the Faith Based Mentoring Ministries and Founder and President of Indiana Strategic Air Transportation Services (a part of NASA's SATS Program) from 2000-2005.

Bob created and owns Commercial Filter Service which employs 15 and serves customers in four states.

Appendix A: El Paso & Beyond

" El Paso And Beyond"

By William E. Meyer

I was assigned to a B-I 7 crew as Co-Pilot and my orders said to report to the "94th" Bomb Group, 331st Squadron at Biggs field, El Paso Texas. I was at Salt Lake City Utah in transition training on the B24 "Liberator. "When I was called into the office to be handed my orders, I was told that I was picked because of my low flying time, " so they said." Was anxious to be on my way to see what lies ahead. The orders were written 25th Nov.1942 and was to report not earlier then Dec. 1st 1942,this gave me three days delay in route with not much to do although I did make good use of the time. Upon reporting was assigned to crew # 10.by Captain Buck Steele and the crew had been waiting for a Co-Pilot to get on with the phase training.

It was a dark winter evening when the Jeep took me to the B.O.Q. and I met Willard Roemke, crew 10s Command Pilot. We liked each other right away. Roemke dug out a fifth of "Old Granddad" and we cemented an already favorable friendship, then went to the mess hall and found a cup of coffee and talked late into the night and developed a strong bond of love and respect. Learned that we were both raised in Northern Indiana Perhaps fifty miles apart. I had only seen a B-17 from a distance and now up close I could see why it was called a " flying fortress" I was short nearly 5'- 7"and at first it seemed that everything about the fortress was taller then me Wow! Four 1200 H P Engines and so far I had only flown twin engine A.T.9. Which had two 185 hp Lycoming engines, was light, fast and tricky to land, its glide speed was 120 mph. I was soon to learn that the B-17 was stable, dependable and a love affair developed that was to last a life time. We were like ducks in water, a home away from home.

We flew night and day, practice formation and navigational flights and it wasn't so unusual for us to call the base Nurses quarters and ask if anyone wanted to go for a ride. We carried extra parachutes and the enlisted men of the crew were to help the nurses with their "chutes" and Hamilton who was flight engineer and gunner came to the cockpit and spoke into my ear "How does the chest strap go, is it under or over" I laughed and said "It sounds like a problem for an Officer alright" "you

just let them handle it". We were serious airmen but we never lost our
sense of humor.

Soon we finished our phase training and had orders to go to Salinas
Kansas and pick up our very own brand new B-17 and to proceed to
Gulfport Mississippi. To join our Group the 94th and to fly a practice over
water flight across the gulf to Morrison field Florida and then over water
to Natal Africa to help in the Desert campaign. We were airborne and on
the first leg of our trip when I noticed the oil pressure drop on an
outboard engine, we shut down the engine and feathered the prop but it
came unfeathered and we had a run away prop. Looking at the map we
were on course to Jackson Mississippi so I tuned the radio to the correct
frequency for radio beam and we followed it to the air base and saw the
oil pressure drop on another engine which we shut down right away. We
called Jackson air base and told them we were coming in for an emergency
landing and asked the length of their runways and the east west runway
was 2200 ft with a 10 mph headwind. We decided to touch down in the
first few feet of the runway and when we got to the end I would unlock
the tail wheel and we would ground loop to the left. Coming in on low
approach we lost the third engine but landed according to plan and there
was a circle at the end of the runway and we ground looped on it and
taxied up on one engine. It was a repair depot and when Roemke called the
Group Commander at Gulfport he said nearly every one in the group had
made an emergency landing and one crew had bailed out. We were to go
ahead and have all four engines changed—seems studebaker had
assembled the engines for Wright cyclone and had used the wrong oil
rings on pistons causing loss of oil pressure and since it took so much
pressure to feather a propellar some props had unfeathered and became
runaway props thus causing some to break loose and come through the
Pilot compartment----Ho Hum, what a dull job!

It took four days to change out the engines and seventeen days to get
the instruments working . We partied until we got the call that our air
craft was ready but we were not allowed to fly it until I was sober and I
swear I only had two beers "ha ha" and we once more left friends behind.
By this time the African campaign was well in hand so we were informed to
proceed to Bangor Maine and we would open the Northern route to
England via Greenland.

We had a delay in route so since Roemke and I lived in Indiana close
to Ft Wayne we landed at Baer field and took a short leave. We did

everything according to our orders and when we got to Bangor Maine it was cold and the glycol heater wasn't working so there was another today stay. We were "Gung Ho" to get to the war. We went to the office and were briefed on the flight over and given maps with routes marked and with a stearn warning that there was a German submarine off the coast of Greenland and all at once our radio compass would swing to the left and the sub was trying to lure us over its lair and we would be shot down. Some pilots had fallen into the trap and sure enough when we approached the area our compass drifted to the left and we ignored it. Our first stop was Goose Bay Labrador, we spent one night and proceeded to Tuly Air Force base Greenland, and spent one more night and headed for Iceland. We landed in what seemed to be a tunnel as the runway had the snow piled so high on either side and it was a rough landing, I ought to know, I was at the controls on this one.

While at Iceland I walked down to a pier where the natives were fishing and saw my first flounder. I didn't know what the strange fish was but I found a line and a hook, borrowed some bait and helped the natives catch a mess of fish. It was fun and I was off by myself, no other crew was around.

Our next stop was Prestwick Scotland, which was south of Iceland. Early morning takeoff and we had 800 Miles or so before we would see land again. We had an uneventful flight but when we got to Prestwick we had gray skies again and it seemed to me at this writing the sky was darkening a mist hung in the air. When we made our approach a tall column, at the tower, suddenly turned red and we poured the coal to the B-17 and went around and on this approach the lights were green and we touched down in Scotland. "Whew" was the right expression and you can say it again—we had flown The Atlantic. A year ago we still had barn yard manure on our shoes and in a few days we would be in combat. As we sat and relaxed I thought of our flight remembering that as we approached Scotland we looked down on the most beautiful landscape I had ever seen. We also learned that a B-17 piloted by Lt. "La-Coste" would lead us to our Base in England. The reason being A lot of Navigators' were mistaking Free Ireland for
England and were interned for the duration. Our destination was Bassingbourne-Home of the 91st Bomb Group and the famous "Memphis Belle" .and we were to be given indoctrination. They were to host two

squadrons of the 94th Group. Upon landing we were met by a U.S. Major. And I ask him about getting in touch with my twin Brother who was a crew chief with the 303rd Bomb Group—360th Squadron. He said "come with me I have a safe phone direct to Molesworth and you feel free to say what you want" Of course Willie knew that eventually I would be heading over seas. We had a hurried visit and I told him about a nice looking Italian Pilot who lead us over from Scotland by the name of "La Costa". Willie said "he was my Pilot when I was on a crew and I knew him well and he is a very good pilot." Willie promised he would look me up when he got a pass.

We were billited in Neesworth Hall a majestic large estate. The Butler met us at the bottom of the stairs each morning with a "demitasse" cup of coffee that was half strong coffee and half cream. My first "half and half" ever. We learned that German airman were called " Jerries" and we needed V.H.F. Radio training

"Heino Gals" first mission would be an air field at ST. Omer France and we would be placed with experienced crews . There were four missions from Bassingbourne and my only call to fame was the day we taxied out in back of the "Memphis-Belle" who finished her 25th mission and would be heading back to the States to be honored in Memphis Tenn. I did not know until I got back to The "States" that Andy Rooney wrote for the "Stars and Stripes" and was there with the 91st at Bassingbourne and I always had the pleasure of watching him on C.B.S. News.

Willie and a couple of his buddies come for a visit and brought a bottle of Scotch We had a good visit and took some pictures that I still have We had an emotional good By and realized it could be a very long time be fore we would do this again. His hand shake seemed to say "why in hell are you in combat, don't you know I will worry each Day" but when we laid our hands on the shoulders it said "Take care, remember Ma is praying for us" She had three other sons besides Willie and me in this war and she just knew we would all be home when it was over "over there" Could have fooled me. After the first raid in to Emdem Germany I didn't see how it would be possible but then if any one could, why not us!

Willie didn't have long to wait for his worries to start. On our first mission from our second Air base at Earlscolne we were flying our own B17 "Hell No gal". She had been sluggish on previous missions from Bassingbourne. A crew had flown her the day before and it was redlined and was to be inspected before it flew again but same how

It fell through the cracks of the system and here we were at 26000 ft. unaware of this except we could tell the plane was sluggish and hard to fly in formation and we were the leader of the three planes on top, called "C" flight. Our orders for today were--as soon as bombs are dropped lose 1000 ft. altitude and we kept on descending and we were out over the coast at 12000 ft .I had just taken off my oxygen mask to light a cigarette when I noticed all the gages for #2 engine were going to zero and smoke was in the cockpit. An M.E. 109 [German Fighter] had come up in a loop and while on his back he shot up our #2 engine and then split on out to safety leaving us with a burning engine. As co-pilot it was my job to spot trouble. First the engine was isolated, fuel and switch off. Then feathered the prop. Fire still burning so hit the fire extinguisher and prayed that I would do the right thing, its so easy to screw up. We were post the coast line and noticed that the landing gear on the right side was hanging down and left gear was up, tucked into #2 engine nacelle where it belonged and the life raft on

The left side had ejected leaving the one on the right side intact.

The engine started burning again and the flames rolled over the wing as we headed down for a water landing. A 96th bomb group B-17 passed to the front and underneath us with their #2 engine on fire which engulfed the wing and they started bailing out their crew and their parachute canopies would burn off before they hit the water.

Ma taught us to pray while we worked on a problem and all at once the light bulb lit in my mind and automatically I opened the mike and ask the engineer to crank down the left wheel . Lo and behold , the burning tire rolled off and the fire was out.

"Crank them both up, the fire is out and we are going home" I yelled the words then I thought of the 96th Bomb Group and ask the Pilot if we could circle and drop our remaining life raft to them. He nodded his head and made the circle and dropped the raft and headed west to England

As we flew it was with confidence that we would see land again and it never entered our mind that we might need the life raft we had given away. One thing for sure, when we hit terra firma , it would be a wheels up landing. As we neared the coast the gas gages for the three engines was on red indicating a low level in the tanks.

Passing over the coast line at the British wash I notified the Pilot of our situation. We spotted a level grass field in the distance and made the decision to land. We were perfectly aligned with the runway and as we came in we could see it was a grass runway for fighters, so we fired a flare showing the colors of the day which was white and red . Suddenly a man appeared on the runway signaling with a code lamp, and "Lord we were in no shape to read code! "We went around and fired a red flare as we approached and landed on grass alongside the runway, so as not to spoil the runway for the Fighters After we were safely on the ground, I approached the man with the code lamp and asked "what were you trying to tell us"? He replied, "I was telling you your under carriage was not down! If you had held the plane off much longer I could have put pillows under it"

A belly landing is quite simple if its on smooth ground. Engineering estimated two weeks to repair the plane. We had wing tip tanks called Tokyo tanks, which were supposedly blocked off but gas had leaked by block valve and both wing tip tanks were full and that's why she was sluggish to fly. All this we did not know until after Our return. We had always complained about this plane and made a side of the mouth remark "If she's sluggish again today we will bring her in wheels up". And that's exactly what we did! "And this was the end of a very long day"

Appendix B: Flying for Fun and Profit

FLYING FOR FUN AND PROFIT

After discharge from the Marines and counseling by my older brother serving as a Captain in the Air Force, I undertook a competitive examination for entrance into the Air Force Aviation Cadet Program and was "accepted for pilot training." The announcement of that fact following two days of intensive testing of all types, written, oral, practical, psychomotor and physical ranks up there as one of the greatest high's for me of all times. When I entered cadets I had four years enlisted time in the Marines and had been wounded in the Korean War. I was a couple years older than most of my classmates, consequently, I found myself in a position of leadership throughout my training. My experiences during two years of Aviation Cadet training exceeded my own fantasies and I completed all phases with honors. After primary training at Bainbridge, GA I went to multi-engines at Reese AFB, TX. As an upperclassman at Reese I served as Cadet Colonel and graduated as "Distinguished Graduate of the Pilot Training Program" with a regular commission. The door to opportunities was truly open.

Elected to remain at Reese after graduation as an IP in the B-25, where I put four classes through Undergraduate Pilot Training before getting "tapped" to be 'School Secretary'. As bad as it sounds, and I hated leaving the flight line, I wound up working for the Pilot Training Group Commander, a Colonel named Travis Hoover. Hoover had been on Doolittle's Tokyo Raid and was the second plane off the carrier. I learned a lot in that year and a half under his 'wing'.

January of 1958 I was transferred, McGuire AFB, NJ to the 30th ATS, 1611 ATW, MATS as a pilot flying C-118's worldwide, but mostly to Europe and the frozen environs of Canada, Greenland and Iceland. I moved up fast in the cockpit as I arrived there with over 2000 hours of multi-engine time and most of the three years in C-118's I was a pilot flight examiner.

I was one of four pilots in MATS selected January 1961 to be in the initial cadre for transition into the Boeing C-135. After completion of training on return to McGuire we started MATS' first jet transport squadron, as the 18th ATS and commenced training MATS pilots from both McGuire and Travis Air Force bases. Two years of running that program as Squadron Assistant Chief Pilot got me an invitation to the 1254th Special Air Mission Wing at Andrews AFB MD as a pilot flying VIP'S in a Boeing 707. Great job, good equipment and hand picked personnel, couldn't get better than this... or could it?

My Air Force assignments were always interesting, each one through the years more challenging than the last, and each new one more rewarding. Measured in different ways, sometime by opportunity to travel more or develop a new model plane into service or selection to a prestigious position kept my appetite constantly whet for the challenge. Nothing more graphically characterizes this progression than the events following the assassination of President Kennedy. Although I never aspired to be a Presidential Pilot, indirectly I had prepared myself for just such an opportunity. I was technically skilled and experienced in the latest model aircraft used in that mission. I had progressed and excelled to the point I had recently been assigned to the Special Air Mission unit from which the President's pilots are selected and then the tragic unexpected opportunity by chance completed the criteria.

We all remember November 22, 1963 and Kennedy's assassination which eventually would trickle down to the flight operations. After Johnson beat Goldwater in '64', and took office in January 1965 I was selected to be co-pilot on Air Force One along with Paul Thornhill working with the President's Military Aide and Aircraft Commander, Jim Cross. I was privileged to fly hundreds of sorties throughout the President's term. But the single most significant trip was the legendary and record-setting around-the-world flight in December 1967 during which President Johnson circled the globe in four days meeting with foreign leaders and furthering our country's interests. In January 1969 when Johnson left office I started a 75 day terminal leave and took a position with the Northrop Corporation, which lasted 21 years, in Los Angeles flying their new Gulfstream and directing their worldwide aviation activities. Never looked back and retired from the Air Force as an absentee April 1, 1969.

DON SHORT
JUNE 7, 2009
AUBURN, CA 95602
pilotelite@usamedia.tv

RECOLLECTIONS OF THE
HOWARD HUGHES CHARTER

BACKGROUND:

During the fall of 1971 I was Director of Flight Operations for the Northrop Corporation, a Los Angeles, CA. based aerospace contractor. They were expecting to receive a follow-on order for the F-5E fighter aircraft momentarily from the U.S. Air Force. The elusive contract kept slipping, by weeks, then months as rumors grew that the new Gulfstream executive jet was going up for sale. Northrop had purchased this jet to market and support anticipated worldwide sales of the F5E. I felt a responsibility, as a department director to come up with a business plan which would allow us to retain ownership and earn revenue to defray cost of ownership until the contract came to fruition. Not to mention, secure my own position, plus others in the department and continue to meet the corporate travel needs. Accordingly, I approached my superior, the C.E.O. of Northrop, Thomas V. Jones for permission to hire a consultant and acquire a Commercial Air Taxi Operator's permit from the Civil Aeronautic Board thereby allowing Northrop to charter the Gulfstream on demand. Nearby Hollywood was a potential fertile marketplace for this new asset. By February 29, 1972 I had in my hand the first Air Taxi permit issued by the C.A.B. for a Gulfstream 2 aircraft. We never looked back.

Mr. Marvin Keogh had performed the consulting service and acquired the certificate on Northrop's behalf. Keogh was a "can do" man and I offered him the position of Charter Sales; our first customer was about to call.

PART ONE: LOS ANGELES, MANAGUA, LOS ANGELES

Hughes Aircraft flight operations was based at the Hughes Airport, Culver City, CA. The man in charge of the operation was Robert M. Dehaven. Sometime before noon on March 13, 1972 Mr. Keogh received an inquiry from Dehaven at Hughes about the availability of the Northrop plane and the proposed itinerary. Subsequently, I acquired clearance to undertake the charter flight and terminated routine on-going preventative maintenance on the plane currently at Rockwell Aviation's FBO serving Los Angeles airport.

BACKGROUND

Typically catering is an important detail on most charter flights. Our plane had a larger than average galley, well designed with refrigeration and a variety of beverages on board. As crew meal requirements were being attended to the catering request for today's trip arrived from Dehaven. "CHEESE AND CRACKERS FOR SIX!"

Following the completion of the two flights described below I debriefed the crewmembers on March 15, 1972. This was the source of information that I was personally able to verify. This narrative is the information from those debriefing.

Co-Captains Tom Brougham and Jack Miller, assisted by Bob Cupery as flight engineer steward, lifted off LAX approximately 1430 hours March 13, 1972 for a six hour flight to Managua, Nicaragua with two passengers; both armed, according to Cupery. He stated "no threats were made or implied by either man throughout the flight."

On arrival at Managua's airport the plane was marshaled to a remote area where a fuel truck was standing by, as well as armed members of Nicaragua's military. Following a routine through-flight walk-around inspection and refueling, the crew was escorted some fifty yards away, under the eyes of eight armed guards until the expected departing passengers arrived. According to Robert Cupery, he was ordered to enter the plane through the external baggage door and assist with the loading of passenger baggage. He said he remembers well the leather suitcases and gold initials HH, stamped on them. Other items included linens in sealed plastic bags and a quantity of water in individual bottles. Following the loading process he was returned to the crew holding area. According to the debriefing, all the crewmen shared a major concern as they were being held, about the security of the G 2 sitting there with a full fuel load, the APU running for air conditioning, and vehicles arriving with un-identified personnel entering and leaving the plane. Under the wrong scenario they could have been witness to a plane-jacking capable of delivering it to Havana in less than two hours.

BACKGROUND

During the debriefing a disparity developed among the crewmen when it came to the person who was escorting Mr. Hughes at plane side for departure. Keep in mind they were detained fifty yards away from the plane. The two pilots thought Hughes was escorted on board by the U.S. Ambassador to Nicaragua, who entered the plane and visited with Hughes a few minutes. The steward was of the impression Hughes was escorted by the President of Nicaragua. None of the three crewmen were introduced or otherwise had passengers identified to them at any time. I am unsure how they came to their conclusions at the time.

Following departure of the escorting VIP, the crew was instructed, as they returned to the forward entry way, from that point on they were not allowed to enter the cabin area. If it became necessary for anyone of them to use the toilet facilities in the aft cabin area, to give ten minutes notice. At which time the cabin to cockpit door would be unlocked for their entry.

Following departure from Managua. Aeronautical Radio, Inc. (ARINC) notified Northrop of N8000J's expected 0400 hours arrival at LAX. Accordingly, Northrop notified U.S. Customs for routine port of entry clearance at the Rockwell FBO. During the course of the homeward flight the cockpit crew requested some beverages to drink. In a total roll reversal, due to enforced security on board, the cabin passengers served the crew drinks in "Irish Crystal Glasses." Normally, the crew would have used disposable plastic cups, with crystal reserved for the passengers.

Cabin steward Cupery stated he became bored, having been denied his usual cabin duties and this stimulated his curiosity during the long flight home. While restricted to the cockpit-vestibule area, he had access to the forward closet, which he entered and by removing a cabin temperature sensor was afforded a peep hole into the restricted cabin. "I did get a peek at Mr. Hughes, nothing exciting, just a skinny old man in a bath robe. Long neck, but his hair was not as long as I heard," Cupery said.

A single U.S. Customs agent entered the plane, accepted the pre-prepared documents and departed. None of the passengers left the plane, or opened the closed cabin window shades while it was being refueled and crew changed.

BACKGROUND

CO-CAPTAINS DON SHORT AND ED HAHN WEARING AIRLINE STYLE UNIFORMS WERE PREPARING A FLIGHT PLAN TO AN UNKNOWN DESTINATION AN HOUR BEFORE THE INBOUND FLIGHT WAS TO ARRIVE. FLIGHT ENGINEER-STEWARD, JIM HUNZIKER WAS ORGANIZING THE BREAKFAST DRIVEN CATERING SUPPLIES, UNAWARE HE WOULD NOT BE THE ONE SERVING HIS CABIN PASSENGERS ON THE NEXT LEG OF THIS JOURNEY.

PART TWO: LOS ANGELES – VANCOUVER – LOS ANGELES

About 0330 hours a tall, slender gentleman with executive bearing and demeanor entered the flight planning area of the FBO and asked for Captain Short. I introduced myself and he suggested we step outside where we approached the black Lincoln sedan he had driven to the airport. He motioned for me to get in, sit down as he introduced himself as "Jack Real, a vice president at Lockheed Corporation." His first question to me was, "do you know where you are going?" I responded, "I have no idea. I was hoping you could tell me". "Vancouver", said Jack, "but file your flight plan to a decoy destination and change to Vancouver after you enter Canadian airspace." I chose Edmonton, because the previous week I had returned from Europe. Had over-flown Edmonton, recalling the routing clearly to LAX. Time was becoming a factor as we talked and I wanted to stick to familiar values if we were to make this planned thirty minute turn around through LAX. The increasing noise of the Rolls Royce engines was nearing as I excused myself and returned to the task at hand in the flight planning room. I had my orders and nothing else. The same level of guidance we had received since the moment we accepted the charter.

With the same basic ground rules in effect for the crew, I taxied quickly the short distance to 25L. Traffic volume was low and the tower cleared us for a rolling takeoff before we had reached the runway threshold. At 0430 hours it was well before sunrise and with the night sky over LAX, departure control vectored us directly to our first airways fix at Gorman VOR. While checking in with L.A. center they responded with a clearance direct to Lakeview Oregon. The forecasted en-route weather was clear and unlimited visibility. We had not yet reached our cruising altitude when we were joined in the cockpit by one of the passengers wanting to know which city was this to our left, and to the right. "How about that one out there?" With answers in hand he returned to the cabin. It did not take long to figure out the curiosity factor. Mr. Hughes was getting an overdue glimpse of the great state of California and in particular all the cities up the San Joaquin Valley. Like most aviators, once he got his orientation established, he still had keen instincts and obviously took pride in basic air navigation. Sadly, if only "things" had been different, I would have eagerly invited him forward for a view from the cockpit, and occupy the "jump seat" between the pilots. I entertained myself with thoughts about how impressed he would have been with our state of the art technology, such as dual inertial navigators, color weather radar and dozens of items he never dreamed would be in an airplane since last flying one himself. That pipedream was lost on myself, for that was not to be.

Arrival at Vancouver was well organized and we had fooled no one by filing for a decoy airport. At ground level too; it was apparent the well oiled Hughes Organization had discreetly coordinated what they needed to have happen. I say that based on the specific instructions provided by the ground controllers. All handled very professionally, with no unidentified transmissions, like "who's the VIP? Or similar inquiries often bantered about to charter operators. We quickly arrived at a seldom used area of the airport which allowed parking between two rows of low, single story buildings. No other aircraft or activity was visible in any direction. The buildings appeared to be vacant; later we determined they were unlocked. I taxied between the rows of buildings; did a complete 180 degree turn which had the plane headed out the same way we had come in. My right wingtip was about twenty feet from the closest building and exactly opposite the only visible door in the low structures that I could see from the cockpit. This placed the air stair door, located on the forward portion, left side of the plane completely out of view from anyone in the adjacent building. When we opened the air stair door exactly two hours and thirty-five minutes had elapsed since leaving Rockwell's facility at LAX. The air stair had not yet fully extended when a passenger from within the cabin ordered the three of us to relocate ourselves to the first available door in the low building. To my surprise the door was unlocked and I immediately took up a position by one of the two windows that viewed onto the ramp where our plane was parked. I noticed in rapid procession two cars, one a black town car or limo arrived at plane side in front of the stairway. In a flash the back car door was opened by a man who had been riding in the passenger seat. I could see two pairs of legs, one pair in a business suit escorting the other pair in blue pajama's, slowly descending the steps with their backs toward the building where I was. The escort quickly seated the man in pajamas to the backseat, closed the door, proceeded behind the car, entered the left rear door and as quickly as they had arrived, they left. The second car, less conspicuous than the first, stopped behind the limo and three men who had remained on the plane, out of sight, descended the steps, entered the car and left without luggage. Before the two cars were out of sight a panel truck arrived for the baggage. This was not your typical "taxi" service. This was a smoothly functioning, well rehearsed, team of professionals. The man, who had ordered us into the building earlier, motioned for us to come back to the plane where we assisted with the download of baggage. Jim Hunziker was handing the bags and boxes out through the planes' baggage compartment door. I was standing below the door and passed the baggage onward to a man standing inside the van. Ed Hahn, my copilot was on the ramp, opposite me and we alternated handling of the bags coming out of the plane. I thought to myself, as I was processing the luggage, here we are transporting one of the world's wealthiest men and I haven't seen one decent suitcase so far. Contrary to what other crewmembers remembered seeing, I saw more cardboard moving cartons, held together with twine and tape than handsome monogrammed luggage. More than one of those boxes full of 16MM motion picture film canisters. In particular, I remember one box labeled, with black magic marker, "Outlaw". Several smaller boxes contained very old and often read, pulp fiction magazines, like detective stories of old, and motion picture magazines I recall seeing on newsstands when I was much younger.

After the entourage had departed, the crew turned to policing the cabin, primarily to ensure customer belongings were reunited with their owners as quickly as possible. A black, collapsible umbrella which could have belonged to anyone of them was tucked between a seat and the bulkhead. A molded earpiece used with hearing aids, was left in a seat I suspect was occupied by our VIP passenger. As we worked our way through the cabin, to our surprise every magazine, newspaper or other periodicals usually carried onboard, had been removed by our passengers. Typically, Time, Newsweek, New York Magazine, Redbook, Yachting, Readers Digest, Esquire, Aerospace & Technology and Architectural Design magazines were among the subscriptions and changed at issue intervals. Daily, the Wall Street Journal, L. A. Times and if available, the New York Times newspapers were supplied as a passenger staple. My guess, those magazines weren't necessarily their favorites, but they were so starved for current news that was otherwise not available in Managua. I did overhear our remaining passenger speaking to the van driver, mention the Bayshore Hotel, which I know to be one of Vancouver's finest. However, we had not a single name of any of the passengers, or a point of contact, other than Mr. Dehaven. On return to Los Angeles we did contact Mr. Dehaven. His advice; "do what you may; I have no way of returning them." I was told Jim Hunziker retained the umbrella as a souvenir. I have no knowledge as to what became of the molded earpiece.

FOOTNOTE:

A noteworthy start to a Charter Business of Integrity which would very quickly serve many "iconic personalities" not only of Aviation and Motion Picture Industries but the entire spectrum of modern day businesses, largely through the contacts and efforts of Marvin Keogh. I proudly say, "Not one word of those activities involving personalities of every genre ever appeared in any publication."

Don Short
May 20, 2009
Auburn, CA 95602
pilotelite@usamedia.tv

Appendix C: Richard Nixon and Quaker Doctrine

Quakers differentiate themselves from the rest of the Christian world by their learned ability to constantly pray. Quakers do not accumulate personal possessions nor do they follow any type of sports nor participate in extra-curricular activities, due to the fact, that if they did, it would have the appearance of not spending sufficient time praying. As one can imagine, as a Quaker ages, his ability to pray becomes more seasoned and mature. A child being reared in a Quaker environment immediately witnesses these prayer-warriors and their ability to pray. Resulting in each child being intimidated by the way prayers are spoken, leaving the child to assume that, since they can not pray that way, they simply can not pray. Consequently, a child that is brought up in a Quaker church will sit and be totally amazed at how well the older members of the church can pray. It takes a personal experience with God for a young Quaker to overcome this intimidation. Usually, this experience happens late in childhood as the child begins to pray more and more.

Regarding President Nixon, it is possible that although being reared in a Quaker environment, he never overcame this intimidation. Consequently, it is easy to believe that Mr. Nixon, assuming he could not pray, entered his young adult life never speaking of a personal experience with God. Further, Mr. Nixon rejected the Quaker doctrine of pacifism by enlisting in the Navy during World War II. And he also ignored the Quaker ban of swearing oaths when he accepted the offices of Vice-President and President. It appears that Nixon resorted to ignore God by failing to seek God at any level throughout his life. Therefore, as President of the United States, Mr. Nixon had no faith to rely on except only a title, and that he was born a Quaker resulting in failing both God and country.

James L. Etsler was born and dedicated as an associate member in the
Central Yearly Meeting of Friends in Alexandria, Indiana.

CPSIA information can be obtained at www.ICGtesting.com
Printed in the USA
LVOW04s1614080115

422027LV00019B/1097/P